few have either inspiration
or instinct for justice.

Mama

6 March 2001

SLAVERY IN A LAND OF LIBERTY

SLAVERY IN A LAND OF LIBERTY

English civil liberty and wage slavery in Britain

Malcolm Hill

OTHILA PRESS
2000

To those who have struggled to realise
a democratic State in Britain

First published in Great Britain by
OTHILA PRESS LIMITED
58a Abingdon Road
London W8

Typeset by Typesetting, Plymouth, Devon
Printed by Bookcraft (Bath) Ltd, Midsomer Norton Somerset

ISBN 1 901647 22 6

Contents

Preface

The intention of the book is to highlight liberties present and absent in Britain, as in democracies throughout the world, and to suggest that mankind needs one example of a nation which has achieved civil and economic justice in order for democracy to achieve its full potential.

It has been beyond the knowledge and experience of the author to include Scots law, Welsh or Northern Irish history, and the concentration on England is not to assume that it is more than one element of British life or that it is superior. Indeed, in law Scotland would claim pre-eminence in several aspects, but it is beyond the limits of the author's experience. In using the word British, therefore, there is no implication intended to suggest that Scotland and Wales are bound to follow the English example. When liberty and justice are being discussed any sense of nationalism dissolves.

Malcolm Hill

List of illustrations

These illustrations are reproduced by courtesy of the National Portrait Gallery, London.

SOVEREIGNTY IN BRITAIN

1

Sovereignty of Monarchy

The British people may claim to have been pioneers in parliamentary government which has been an outstanding feature of their history. Yet, at the end of the twentieth century, Britain is patently not a democracy. There are, it is true, regular, secret elections and each adult is possessed of a vote. Parliament holds legal sovereignty, the people enjoy certain freedoms. But large areas of life lie beyond democratic control. In these respects Britain is a *democracie imaginaire*.

For millions in Britain are unable to earn a livelihood sufficient to maintain an independent existence and look after their family, they are undermined periodically by inflation and unemployment, and oppressed by the increasing burden of taxation. So much is required to enable the state to discharge expenditure naturally belonging to the individual, who appears not to be able to fulfil themselves. The British people are deluged with media information, but it seems they cannot alter the causes of their situation. So immutable does this order appear, that it is believed to be an unalterable fact of life, for it is similar to what prevails throughout the globe. The free independent individual, however, is a reasonable ideal for a democratic society. In short, it will be argued in the third part of this book they exist in an unnecessary condition of wage slavery. This form of slavery is of an insidious nature and when people have grown accustomed to it over centuries, it is not readily apparent or believed.

The examination of the reasons that Britain is not a democracy, will be a theme of the whole book. As a first step it is important to locate where sovereign power lies in the nation. For there is little use in highlighting injustices if there is not a means of changing such an undesirable state of things. In this search a beginning is made with the British monarchy.

The throne is one of the oldest surviving in Europe. The throne itself is not, however, of unbroken antiquity; it was set aside in the middle of the seventeenth century by Oliver Cromwell. In 1680 Sir Robert Filmer published his claim of divine right of kings: the quaint notion that the Creator required the assistance of monarchs to conduct the Universe. But by then the temper of the British people had changed. The Bill, or Claim, of Rights, in 1689 contained articles to restrict the prerogative power of the monarch. Henceforth, tenure of the throne rested on the assent of the people and the acquiescence of the monarch to their will. The theory about the divine origin of monarchy was demolished by John Locke, the English philosopher, in 1690 in his *First Treatise of Government*. Despite the development of history and the advance of reason upon the expanse of superstition, three centuries later the divinity of the monarchy is sometimes proclaimed.

The Convention Parliament was summoned in 1689 by Prince William of Orange. It declared the throne vacated by James VII & II and invited William and Mary to jointly accept the throne. The present title of the monarchy derives from the Act of Settlement 1701. The remaining limitation imposed by the Act is that no Catholic can either marry a monarch or ascend the throne. In 1714 the House of Hanover succeeded and has continued to the present day with only one unnatural break in 1936 when Edward VIII abdicated in favour of his brother, George VI.

The British nation has evolved gradually as power has been take out of the hands of the monarch and bestowed in those of the people. So momentous a constitutional change has been wrought bloodlessly, apart from the casualties of a few civil wars and the neck of Charles I.

The monarchy, at the apex of the British social hierarchy, is the guardian of the status quo of society. The monarchy, however, should not be blamed for injustice in society. Rather, that is due to the acquiescence of the people themselves to live in a society that is unjust. Perhaps this readiness to accept things as they are is due to the fact that the British love tradition. They imagine that their history is filled with goodness and that their ancestors had amassed a great fund of wisdom, so that every institution of historical foundation becomes an object of veneration.

The function of monarchy has been confused by constitutional fictions. Several constitutional jurists over the last 150 years – Walter Bagehot, Sir William Anson, A.V. Dicey and Sir Ivor Jennings – have represented the monarchy as a mysterious phenomenon. They have clothed the monarchy in a mystique that defies rational enquiry. Though Scripture proclaims that each individual on earth is equally precious to the Creator, the British people wish to believe that, even in heaven, there will be a royal enclosure.

These jurists have made the monarchy a central component in the constitution by attributing to it a constitutional role which derives more from their imagination than present reality. It is time to penetrate the veneer of their handiwork and consider the monarchy as it is. That is to examine an institution, rather than any royal individuals.

The principal role of monarchy is often said to be its parliamentary role. The monarch, it was suggested, participated with lords temporal and spiritual and commoners to constitute Parliament. The monarch opens Parliament each year by reading a speech written by Government. This ceremonial occasion involves a character of medieval intempestivity, Black Rod, summons the commoners to their monarch's presence; an aristocratic swordsman walks backwards, ostensibly to defend the monarch but, in reality, he strains his utmost not to embarrass by falling over; and the Lord Chancellor, having retrieved the speech from an ancient sack, retreats precariously backwards down the steps to the throne.

The more substantial aspect of the monarch's parliamentary role is thought to derive from its duty to consent to the enactment of statutes. The power to withhold royal approval of a statute was last exercised in 1707, when Queen Anne refused to settle the militia in Scotland. Bagehot believed in the 1860s that a royal veto of a statute would amount then to notice of abdication. Thus the royal consent has become a constitutional convention that it follows automatically; the monarch is saved the tedium of stamping the prolific output of Parliament. The actual assent is given to a Bill by Commissioners on behalf on the monarch. It was argued that, in relation to Irish Home Rule legislation in 1913 and 1914, royal assent should be withheld. Yet such refusal would have had to accord with ministerial advice, which could not be imagined. For to defy her ministers' advice and Parliament's enactment would have been without constitutional legality.

The monarch dissolves Parliament on a request of the Prime Minister. It is difficult to imagine it could be refused, without upsetting the convention that the monarch governs through through Ministers However, there is no absolute reason why the monarch should automatically grant a request from the Prime Minister for a dissolution of Parliament.[1] Such a situation may arise when to do so would be inappropriate.

Having found no substantial sovereignty in the parliamentary role of the monarch, one must consider the monarch's control of Government. The monarch has the duty to appoint a Prime Minister. However, when the Conservative Party, like their opponents, adopted a mechanism to elect their leader in 1965, the monarch's power was removed where any party commanded a clear majority at a General Election. When, however, an election produced no clear majority party, or when no party held a majority in the House of Commons, then the monarch upon the resignation of the Prime Minister would exercise a discretion to bring about discussions which would produce a leader. Given media so attentive to political life, such a situation would be shared between the monarch and several million subjects, who would be familiar with such a situation.The idea that only the monarchy is possessed of sufficient genius is redolent of the sixteenth century, when the monarch forbade public political discussion.

Is a monarch bound to accept the advice of a Prime Minister? There is one precedent in which the monarch did not. In 1910 George V refused Herbert Asquith's request that he should undertake to create sufficient peers to prevail over the Conservative majority, who were minded to preserve the right of the House of Lords to reject a Budget. Instead, the king insisted that issue be put to a second General Election within that year before he would consider that request. Asquith was a cautious and courteous character and he accepted the king's insistence without demur. He also felt that the king had inherited the constitutional problem on his recent accession. and needed time to become fully acquainted with its peculiar circumstances. A few years later the

---

[1] *Constitutional and Administrative Law*, A. Bradley & K. Ewing ed 1998, p. 267

Conservatives called the alliance between the Liberal Governments and the Irish Nationalists a 'corrupt bargain'. They urged George V to call an election before the Irish Home Rule Bill became law. Asquith again advised him of his constitutional position and the king concluded that he could not withhold his assent to the Bill. He commented somewhat wistfully:

> unless there is some convincing evidence that it would avert a national disaster, or at least have a tranquillising effect on the distracting conditions of the time.[2]

In 1965 the Prime Minister of Rhodesia could have been dismissed after the Declaration of Independence. Instead his Government were outlawed as rebels. The Governor-General in Australia, Sir John Kerr, did dismiss Gough Whitlam for intransigence by refusing to resolve a parliamentary dispute by calling a General Election. His rival, Malcolm Fraser, succeeded and won an immediate contest.

The monarch retains full possession of 'the right to be consulted, the right to encourage, the right to warn.'[3] and enjoys a weekly confidential meeting with the Prime Minister. The monarch has long experience of successive Prime Ministers. The monarch is required to sign and read many state documents each day. Many public appointments require the monarch's formal consent. The people also enjoy rights to encourage, communicate with and warn, they retain memories and possess three more considerable powers : disapproval, remuneration and dismissal. The people also have a right to see Cabinet minutes and State papers, which become available to the public, in expurgated form, after thirty years.

The control of the monarch over its Government is no more effective than over Parliament. Ministers express their pride in serving their monarch. Being mindful of this relationship, they are induced to put service before arrogance. The example of service imparted by the present monarch is powerful. In saying the monarch lacks constitutional control over Government and Parliament, it is not to infer that the personal example of service of the present monarch is not a powerful influence in many institutions of the nation.

Several miscellaneous attributes ascribed to the Crown are ceremonial. The monarch is, for example, reputed to be the fount of justice. 'The King of England is, therefore, not only the chief, but properly the sole magistrate of the nation; all others by commission from and in subordination to him,' wrote William Blackstone, the legal commentator, in the middle of the eighteenth century. Some such notion has lingered despite the observation by Dicey this century that, 'It [Blackstone's assertion] has but one fault; the statement is the direct opposite of the truth.The executive of England is in fact placed in the hands of a Committee called the Cabinet.If there be any one person in whose single hand the power of the State is placed, that person is not the

---

[2] *Constitutional Government*, I. Jennings, Ch 13.
[3] *The English Constitution*, W. Bagehot ed 1963, p. iii.

King, but the chairman of the committee, known as the Prime Minister.'[4] The fount of civil justice is to be found in the breast of the reasonable individual, once described by a judge as the person on the Clapham omnibus. The Royal Pardon is extended occasionally to quash an unjust conviction. But its deployment follows a recommendation by the Home Secretary.

The royal prerogative powers have been described by Blackstone as:

> that special pre-eminence which the King hath, over and above all other persons, and out of the ordinary course of the common law, in right of his royal dignity.[5]

These powers were hotly contested during the seventeenth century and many were declared illegal in the Bill of Rights 1689. But as part of the development of a constitutional government important powers remained for use by government, rather than by the monarch. The prerogative powers – of declaring war, making dispositions of a military nature, making peace, dissolving Parliament before the expiry of its statutory term of five years, ratifying and signing treaties, recognising foreign governments, appointing bishops, judges, peers, Ministers, European Union [EU] Commissioners, ambassadors or chairs of public bodies, declaring a state of emergency, making Orders in Council other than under statute [which need the approval of the House of Commons], inter alia – constitute serious political powers. The Crown disguises the fact that the person exercising these powers is the Prime Minister, who is saved the problem of being accountable for their use to Parliament. Tony Benn, a veteran Member of Parliament, proposed a cross-bench Bill, entitled Crown Prerogatives (Parliamentary Control) Bill in the spring of 1999, under which these powers are not exercisable unless assented to by the House of Commons. It is highly undesirable in a democracy to vest that much power in any individual, for the reason that it adds to the already-excessive powers of the Prime Minister.

Prerogative powers are given the force of law by Orders in Council, that is orders of the Privy Council. Its meetings are formal and without discussion. Although the number of Councillors is about four hundred normally meetings are transacted by about four members. A Royal Proclamation is issued to publicise an Order, as,for example, an order dissolving or summoning Parliament. The Tudor Privy Council was described as the nerve of government, which after the civil wars, which followed the break down of feudalism, became an important instrument of central control. It taught 'not only Parliament to legislate but justices to govern.'[6] The Privy Council survived the demise of other royal bodies in the seventeenth century.

The monarch is Head of the Commonwealth. The position was created to allow India to remain within the Commonwealth, while declaring itself a republic. It is a

---

[4] *The Law of the Constitution*, A. Dicey, p. 8.
[5] *Commentaries on the Laws of England*, W. Blackstone, vol i, 10th edn, p. 239.
[6] *History of England*, G. Trevelyan, p. ?.

position with influence, if not power. 'The Crown has become the mysterious link, indeed I might say the magic link, which unites our loosely bound but strongly interwoven Commonwealth of Nations', wrote Winston Churchill.[7] That was a felicitous statement for an aged statesman to make about the throne, recently ascended by the youthful queen. There are fifty-five members of the Commonwealth and sixteen recognise the British monarch as Head of State.[8] Having entered the EU, Britain has severed those free trading links which provided cohesion to the Commonwealth. Loyalty to Britain becomes gradually weaker, as those who traded with her die out. In a referendum in 1999 the Australian people came close to severing their ties with the British monarchy. Just as children who stop playing with each other tend to make new friends, so traders find new markets. Their desire to be independent is due to a British political decision to abandon free trade with Australia.

The monarch is by the Royal Titles Act 1953 proclaimed the monarch to be, inter alia, Defender of the Faith, which is a title is of ancient usage. This is sufficient basis for the Prince of Wales to claim as the monarch's role to be Defender of Faith of the different religions at present practiced sincerely in Britain. The Church of England, however, owes its creation, not to some spiritual inspiration, but from the usurpation of the position by Henry VIII, when he needed a divorce from an obdurate pope. In law there is no statute to the effect that the monarch is head of the Church of England. Only canon law proclaims the monarch as head of the Church of England.[9] The Act of 1701 provides that the monarch shall join in communion with the Church of England.

The monarch is the nominal commander-in-chief of the armed forces. At the beginning of war, declared by the Prime Minister, the Crown invites the people to defend the land. Recruits enlist in Her Majesty's colours, often motivated by a desire to escape hopeless poverty. They risk their lives. When the fighting is over, however the living return with their injuries and memories to pay, not Her Majesty's, but the National Debt

The monarch is said to be the fount of honours. A constitutional jurist wrote: 'The advantage of the British system is that the Queen is associated with the award, so that person who receive an OBE is shown to the world to be a person who has been honoured by his Queen for his service to the community. One of the Queen's most important functions is to help to maintain the high level of attainment among the peoples of the United Kingdom.'[10] The monarch can award certain Orders without advice: the Order of the Garter, Order of the Thistle, Order of Merit and award the Royal Victorian Order for personal services and she can make appointments without advice, for example a Private Secretary or Master of the Horse. [The Latin for this personage was comes stabuli, from which the word constable derived]. Though the

---

[7] *Listener*, Feb 7 1952.
[8] *Political Facts*, R. Wooding.
[9] *Civil Liberties*, S. Bailey, D. Harris, p. 534.
[10] *The Queen's Government*, I. Jennings, Ch 2.

bulk of the honours are bestowed by the monarch on advice of the Prime Minister. Indeed the offer of a knighthood or peerage is often the price of 'political correctness'. He or she can reward party back-benchers, who have toed the party line, or their financial paymasters. It is an unfettered discretion and, thus, a considerable power.

David Lloyd George, the Liberal Prime Minister, sold honours for payments to his political fund. That was considered sharp practice. But to link the honour to the cheque book was more open than the present cashless traffic in preferment. But to honour men and women objectively, as is employed, for example, in choosing a sporting team on merit, is impossible in a world of appearances distorted by command of power and wealth. The honours system serve the monarchy as buttresses serve a cathedral. They may soar elegantly to a viscountcy, but they rest on the foundations of lesser honours, the names of whose recipients can only be picked out among columns of small print with the aid of a magnifying glass. In a democracy a more straight-forward system would be ex officio honours for public non-political offices and no others.

Britain suffers a condition which nature positively outlaws: a state of injustice. In ancient Rome the peace of the masses was secured by the provision of bread and circuses. Spectators, carried away with the spectacle of fatal combat, did not think much about society. In modern Britain the similar diversion is more varied and the deception more subtle. Bread is, in many forms, secured by the welfare state. Medicine, education, social security are available as of right and they appear free.Through such devices of graduated direct taxes, however, people believe the necessities of the poor are paid for by the rich. The raising of taxation to fund the welfare state is rarely considered.. Entertainment abounds in bingo sessions, football grounds, horse racing and television. The end is the same: to keep the people from thinking seriously about the state of society.

The monarchy is the symbol of national unity – a focal point of national loyalty, transcending partisan rivalry and strengthening social cohesion. It exist on a pedestal above the run of communal life. It embodies tradition, pageantry and unify palace, mansion, suburb and slum. They serve in the twentieth century the mystical purpose that the stained glass window served in medieval times, before the invention of printing. Then men and women had to gaze high in a church and listen to a learned prelate discourse on a biblical tale, which was depicted in coloured glass lightened by sunlight, far above daily experience. The Royal Family draw the nation, riven by class, together. Rich coexist happily with poor, powerful individuals with powerless masses, landed with landless, luxury with poverty. The Royal Family are accepted by the former and cheered by the latter. The monarchy is deprived of power but used to hide the exercise of its prerogative powers.

The monarchy occupies a curious position in the British Constitution. At the beginning of the millennium they were feared rulers but at the end they are sustained not by rational need but by the British fondness for tradition. Their role is to represent the nation at certain moments and in daily activities. The constitutional character of the previous millennium was a move from absolute monarchy to constitutional monarchy and the character of the next might be the completion of democracy.

The greatest threat to the monarch and the peace of the realm was considered to be treason. The common law offence was succeeded by the Treason Act 1351. The offence includes to compass or imagine the death of the monarch or their family, to levy war against the nation, to adhere to aid or give comfort to the monarch's enemies. Treason was a grave offence and punishment was accordingly severe. A convicted offender was dragged to the scaffold, hanged, disembowelled while alive, the head removed from the corpse, which was cut into quarters. The remains of the traitor were at the disposal of the monarch. Women were drawn and burned. Such a fate might seem appropriate to a common scoundrel or leader of a rebellion

The evidence of 'adhering, aiding giving comfort to the enemies of the nation' during the Second War in several ways seems to bring the Duke of Windsor, formerly Edward VIII, within the terms of the 1351 Act on several counts. The conspiracy to cover up his dangerous and wicked past was set aside in a brilliant documentary film entitled, *Traitor King*.[11]

That a weak, selfish and pathetic character should ascend the throne at a uncertain time when Europe was darkened by the shadow of Hitler, may have been beyond the creative mind of even Shakespeare himself. His father, George V, predicted accurately that Edward would ruin himself within a year of ascending the throne. Mercifully, he fulfilled that prediction within eleven months. That the Prime Minister, Stanley Baldwin, was able to force his abdication over his love for Mrs Simpson was a piece of rare fortune. For the real reason was that he was not fitted to be a constitutional monarch with access to State secrets.

Evidence seems to indicate that he had betrayed his former people on several occasions during the Second World War. He seems to have given comfort to Hitler after the outbreak of the Second War in the following ways. First, in the autumn 1939 the Duke of Windsor was appointed a Major-General on the General Staff in Paris, where he were in daily contact with Charles Beddeau, a known Nazi sympathiser. The duke allowed Beddeau to pay his hotel bills. Through regular visits to the Hague, Beddeau briefed the German ambassador who reported to Berlin accurately the duke's thinking on his dissatisfaction with his own position and on the war. Second, in January 1940 Hitler had decided to attack France through the Low Countries but, days before the launch of the onslaught, his battle plans were lost in an aircraft which crashed over the German border. Hitler stood down sixty divisions in doubt and waited for intelligence. Within a month the German ambassador in the Hague reported to Berlin that the Duke of Windsor had let it be known that the 'War Council of the Allies' had spent a day discussing an attack through Belgium in the light of papers found in a crashed aeroplane and made detailed plans for the defence of that border, which the ambassador enclosed. Hitler acted by switching his attack through the

---

[11] Video obtainable from Heart Ryan (0171-403-6363).

undefended forest of Ardenne. Third, he adhered to Hitler's ambassadors and Nazi sympathisers in Madrid and Lisbon. German papers reveal that he was resisting calls to return to London and that he was opposed to Churchill and war, and was heading a peace movement of British people. A secret memorandum, based on intelligence, was written by the Private Secretary to the king, Alec Harding, corroborating this role of Edward in Madrid. Fifth, the German ambassador in Lisbon wrote in 1940 to Berlin that Edward was certain that continual heavy bombing of Britain would force them to accept peace. Sixth, he left Lisbon for the Bahamas on the day Hitler ordered the bombing of London. On arrival he fell in with Axel Wenner Gren, a rich Nazi backer, and ignored Churchill's warning that this man was in communication with the enemy. Seventh, he summoned an American journalist, Fulton Ousler, to communicate to his [Ousler's] close friend President Roosevelt to bring peace in Europe and to inform him that if he made that move he would himself support the move by causing a revolution against war in Britain. Oustler trembled in disbelief but President Roosevelt commented that he ceased to be surprised that so many leading figures in Britain and the British Empire wanted to make peace with Hitler. It seems that Hitler promised to re-enthrone him if Britain were conquered or surrendered. In pursuing that end the duke put the survival of the nation at stake. Even when that possibility had vanished after Pearl Harbour in 1941, he enriched himself by making substantial illegal transfers of money into US dollars.

The evidence disclosed by this film would have made a strong case for the prosecution of the Duke of Windsor for treason but, without a defence on his behalf and a verdict, the issue must remain speculation.

The reason for the suppression is the feeling that the conduct of Edward would have undermined the monarchy. Indeed, if there had been an occasion in the last half century when the merest hint of such an evil, the monarchy would probably have suffered greatly. But in that time Britain has been served by Edward's brother and his daughter, the present Queen, who have conducted themselves with exemplary dignity and the damage done by Edward has been completely erased. They have no reason to fear any reaction against the villainy of Edward. This evidence has now emerged. Whilst it points to the wicked character of Edward, it enhances the reputation of the two monarchs, who followed this tragedy.

Now it is time to face this constitutional danger situation constructively. There is always a danger inherent in any hereditary institution that a particular holder will prove incompetent or unsuited to the position and there is a rare danger that, in addition, to being hopeless he or she might also be wicked. The great difference between the times of Edward VIII and the present is that the media are ready to expose any official. The media refused to publish Edward's wild philandering. When an individual in Britain cannot hurl abuse at outrageous behaviour, is a day, maybe of taste, but also of danger. The danger of wrongful accusation by the media is common place but the danger of silent compliance with the authorities is a greater danger.

The role of monarch could be filled by a president elected from beyond the political world without political involvement for a period of a few years. It is an arduous position to hold; much work, much criticism. But the British people seem to prefer to continue the tradition of monarchy.

Democracy involves dignity and the people of Britain have to rid themselves of feeling that they are unfitted to take responsibility, as the electors and more importantly as political thinkers, for the governance of their nation. To have pointed out the actual role of the monarchy has been necessary to distinguish monarchal sovereignty from parliamentary and political sovereignty. To suggest that the monarch is the servant of the nation is not an attempt to demean it, for service runs through the Creation. Both the Creator and Nature serve man.

2

Sovereignty of Parliament

Having seen that the monarch lacks substantial political power, Parliament can be considered as the sovereign body in Britain. Before considering the reality of parliamentary sovereignty, a rough guide of certain aspects of Parliament's historical development should be sketched briefly first. The history of this sovereignty is one of the leading developments in British history.

The historical development of Parliament

The evolution of the British Constitution is marked by the political decline of the monarchy in step with the rise of the Commons. It mirrors the wresting of power from the Crown, which was at various times dictator, tyrant and despot, and from the Lords, who endured as an hereditary obstacle; this evolution heralds the democratic advance of the people.

The antecedents of Parliament were present in the Anglo-Saxon witenagemot, or council of wise men. But in the tenth century it was replaced by feudalism which spanned society like a spider's web. Under feudalism there was no choice, no freedom and no chance of evasion. The king raised revenue from profits of demesne land, feudal dues, profits from justice, sales of privileges and offices, ecclesiastical dues, tallages, or taxes, of demesne land and customs. He raised his revenue as he wished; much as a modern Chancellor does. However, in 1188 he imposed the Saladin Tithe, which is reckoned by some historians to have been the first attempt to tax private property. It was imposed to finance a crusade. Subsequent impositions were resisted and in 1215 the strait-jacket of feudalism was unbuckled by Magna Carta, which restored former liberties. In 1265 Simon de Montfort struck the first note in the history of Parliament by calling together an English Parliament, which thirty years later was split into three divisions: clergy, Lords temporal and spiritual and Commons of the knights of the shires, citizens and burgesses of the cities and boroughs.

The king retained awesome legal power and he could raise sufficient revenue throughout the greater part of the thirteenth century. But in 1297 Edward I was forced to agree to the principle of taxation by consent of a few of his wealthier people. On behalf of counties and towns, they struck separate bargains with the king.

The subsequent development of Parliament is described in five steps.

CONTROL OF TAXATION

The monarch's continual need of finance proved the first step in the development of Parliament. It gave rise to annual summons and statutes on taxation during the fourteenth century. But later the monarch could manage without raising revenue and he dispensed with Parliament. This was particularly so under the Tudor monarchs during the sixteenth century and the Stuarts in the seventeenth. The Crown levied taxation by proclamation. In *Bate's Case*[1] the Court of Exchequer upheld the king's imposition. Hawkeshill disputed the judgment in the Commons. A Bill was carried that there should be no imposition without the consent of Parliament. But the Lords rejected it. Again the Commons restated their opposition in the short Parliament of 1614. Thereupon James dissolved Parliament and raised money by the sale of monopolies. Towns were sold their freedoms repeatedly. The Commons in their last Parliament declared that the sale of monopolies was and had been illegal.

Charles I made sparing use of Parliament. During his first Parliament the Commons refused to grant tonnage or poundage for his life. After he dissolved his third Parliament in 1628 there was not another until 1640. They were prepared to grant tonnage and poundage for one year. But the Lords would not agree to that condition. Charles had recourse to forced loans. But he accepted the Petition of Right in 1628 which declared against loans, benevolences, taxes or any other like charge being imposed without the consent expressed by act of Parliament. Yet in 1634 Charles levied ship money and in *Hampden's Case* his right was upheld; a tax levied for the defence of the realm was deemed outside the Petition of Right. The judgment was reversed by the Long Parliament in 1641. This marked the victory of Parliament in the matter of taxation. The control of taxation has proved the backbone of Parliament. The need of money obliged both Charles I and Charles II to submit and no monarch has managed to rule without Parliament since.

THE ESTABLISHMENT OF ITS OWN LIBERTIES

The Commons were sometimes bold and often supine. But its Speaker often stood for its liberties. Speaker Peter de la Mare complained on behalf of the Commons in 1376 at the cost of the Hundred Years War and demanded public accounts. For his bravery, however, he was gaoled by Edward III, who summoned a new Parliament in order to reverse the resolutions of the previous one. De la Mare was released after a year by the new king and installed in his former chair. In 1397 a Bill was laid before the Commons attacking Richard II. The Lords declared the mover of the Bill, Thomas Haxey, a traitor and demanded his death. He was spared and the first Parliament of Henry IV annulled the judgment on the petition of the Commons, who claimed it contrary to their liberties. In 1453 Speaker Thorpe was imprisoned. The Commons

---

[1] (1606) 2 St. Tri. 371.

when they next met demanded the release of their Speaker under ancient privilege. The establishment of the privilege of the freedom of speech within the Commons followed the imprisonment of a member, Richard Strode, in 1512.[2] In 1621 the Commons issued a Protestation that the ancient liberties of the Commons allowed it to debate whatever it pleased. James VI & I responded by dissolving Parliament.

The freedom of members from arrest was claimed throughout the sixteenth century. In 1603 Sir Thomas Shirley was arrested for debt and was delivered from gaol by the sergeant of the Commons. In the same year the immunity of members from arrest was recognised by statute.

SUPREMACY OF LEGISLATIVE POWER

This grand struggle for sovereignty came to the fore in the seventeenth century. Parliament had acquiesced in the oppressive rule of the Tudors, who were resolute tyrants. But James VI & I, who ascended the English throne in 1603, was a Catholic, disputatious and slightly ridiculous. Parliament was fortified by a number of courageous men who championed their cause.

The king claimed absolute sovereignty to override law by his own Proclamations. Such power had been asserted in the Statute of Proclamations (1539), which had given Henry VIII wide power to legislate without reference to Parliament. But it was a limited power; he could not transgress common or statute law, alter the laws of property or inflict the death penalty. The Act was repealed in 1547 but the power to issue Proclamations continued to be used by Mary and Elizabeth. James VI & I made full use of the power to govern by Proclamation. Parliament protested, claiming that laws concerning the property or lives of the people were to be made only by the common law or by the assent of Parliament. Chief Justice Coke was consulted by the Crown in 1611. He stated that the king could not create any offence which was not one before, that he could admonish by Proclamations his subjects to keep the law and that an offence not punishable in the Court of Star Chamber, which enforced Proclamations, could not be made the subject matter of a Proclamation.

James sometimes sat in the Court of Star Chamber which had wide powers, except that of imposing the death sentence. It could and did inflict torture. It was not befuddled by a jury, but even punished them for what appeared to the Court perverse verdicts. Thus it controlled the administration of justice. Yet Coke spoke of it with respect. There was also the Court of High Commission which interfered in religious matters. This was a Tudor institution to regulate people's beliefs.

In 1616 Coke was one of the judges hearing the *Case of Commendams*. During the proceedings the royal prerogative was brought into question. James ordered the trial to discontinue. Coke replied that his oath as a judge forbade him to have regard to that command. James dismissed him as Chief Justice of the King's Bench. Coke believed judges could also declare a statute void, if they held it was against reason and natural law.

---

[2] This will be discussed in Ch 5.

In 1640 an Act of Parliament abolished the Court of Star Chamber. Having trimmed the royal prerogative power, they severed the neck of a monarch who had caused rebellion against his nation.

After the Restoration of Charles II in 1660 matters were re-established as before. But the declaration of new prerogative powers by James VII & II resulted in an explicit declaration of the rights and liberties of Parliament. When James VII & II fled William summoned the Convention of the Estates who presented the Declaration of Rights, later enacted as the Bill of Rights and offered him and his wife jointly the throne. The Declaration of Rights secured freedom of speech within Parliament and the freedom of its members from civil arrest. When Parliament was summoned two years later it made the throne dependent henceforward on statute.

Both James VI & I and James VII & II had been kings of Scotland and then of England but the two nations were separate. After the Restoration union of the kingdoms was promoted and in 1707 it came about on conditions involving the two legal systems and the respective religions. The nation of Great Britain came into being.

On the face of it William and Mary had been installed in 1688 as constitutional monarchs by a Parliament, it is often supposed, representing the people. But in fact the Commons represented landed interests and the Crown. For the knights of the shires were the nominees of the landowners and rural nobles and the borough members were returned by the Crown and nobles and the city members were bought by bribery. Members of Parliament attacked the prerogative of the Crown not to advance the liberties of the people but because the Crown threatened their interests. Thus until the end of the reign of George III in 1820, Government was controlled by the Crown and the landed interests. But publication of Parliamentary debates in 1771 helped to stir public agitation which followed the French Revolution.

REPRESENTATION OF THE PEOPLE

Pressure was building in the late eighteenth century for reform of the system of representation. The people became seized in the eighteenth century of the notion that they might take a part in political life. James Burgh, a political writer, wrote in 1774:

> Eight hundred individuals rule all, themselves accountable to none. Of these about 300 are born rulers, whether qualified or not. Of the others, a great many are said to be a handful of beggars instead of the number and property,who have the right to be electors.[3]

The demand for parliamentary reform was discussed in the Corresponding Societies, which were formed at the end of the eighteenth century to overcome the prohibition

---

[3] *Political Disquisitions*, J. Burgh, vol 1, p. 36.

of public meetings. Pitt's Reform Bill (1795) proposed to abolish thirty-five rotten boroughs and extend the franchise to forty shilling copyholders. But it was defeated in the Commons by a majority of forty-three. The mood of the country became revolutionary after the end of the Napoleonic Wars and even Robert Peel, on behalf of the Tories, objected to the idea of reform but acknowledged that danger would be unleashed if it were not introduced. Thomas Macaulay, the historian, appealed to the Commons:

> Save property, divided against itself. Save the multitude endangered by its ungovernable passions. Save the aristocracy, endangered by its own unpopular power . . . The danger is terrible. The time is short.[4]

The Bill passed its Second Reading by one vote in the largest House within living memory. The Bill was lost when the Government were defeated in committee. But the Government was returned in a General Election with a larger majority. Richard Carlile, a radical writer, warned that the Act would extend control of legislation to the full complement of 'land stealers, merchants, manufacturers and tradesmen'. The second Bill was passed by the Commons but rejected by the Lords. When the news reached Birmingham the bells were muffled and tolled. Riots broke out in Nottingham, Derby and later in Bristol and London. The magistrates and newly formed police in the capital lost control and allowed the mob to break into prisons, burn a bishop's palace and a number of buildings. The cavalry restored order. A third Bill was introduced and the peers were subject to pressure from the king, William IV, and Brougham, the Lord Chancellor. The result was that bishops changed their minds and on the Second Reading in the Lords the majority in favour was nine. But the Lords refused to accept the detail and when the king refused to create fifty new peers, the Government resigned. Amid public danger, financial collapse and fears of an outbreak of cholera the Liberal administration returned within a week, as the Tories were divided. But in order to bring the Liberals back the king had to agree to create peers if needed. The Lords, appraised of this royal commitment, passed the Third Reading after a month. The Reform Act (1832), acclaimed with banquets, illuminations and bell-ringing, disenfranchised fifty-six boroughs returning 111 members. Twenty-two towns were granted two members each and twenty smaller towns were accorded one member and sixty-five additional members were created. It also extended the voting qualification from the existing qualification of the forty shilling freeholder to copyholders in the counties of £10 and tenants at will worth £50. The 1832 Act had introduced a new order by increasing the representation and the electorate by 50 per cent, so that 1.4 million adult males possessed a vote. But despite featuring in the Cabinet Committee for Reform, provision for secret ballot did not appear in the 1832 Act. It was granted finally in 1872. For the first time voters were listed. When the

---

[4] *The Age of Reform 1815–70*, E. Woodward, p. 79.

Liberals spoke about extending the vote in 1866, Disraeli doubted the wisdom of involving the working class in the Constitution. Again the process was pushed along by a large meeting called in Hyde Park, London. The Cabinet closed the park but the demonstrators broke down 1400 yards of railings and disturbed local residents. But the Tories in both Houses raised objections. Eventually the decision was taken to reform again, or as Thomas Carlyle put it 'Shooting Niagara'. Lord Derby saw it differently, and described it as 'a leap in the dark'. The franchise was extended to cover another 1.12 million males, so that about half the adult males could now vote, by the Second Reform Act (1867) and again by the Third Reform Act (1884), which enfranchised 68 per cent of males in the counties. The Fourth Reform Act (1918) increased the franchise from eight to twenty-one million by extending the vote to men over twenty-one and to women upon attaining the age of thirty, in response to a decade of activity by the suffragettes. It was not until 1929 that they were entitled to vote at the same age as males.

The extension of the franchise was an essential element of democracy but, as will be argued, does not in itself constitute democracy.

POWERS OF THE TWO HOUSES OF PARLIAMENT

Hitherto, it has been supposed that Parliament comprised both the Lords and the Commons. They are not, however, equal legislative assemblies. Indeed, what until 1999 had been a largely hereditary body, contained a large number of people quite unskilled in debate, who can be supposed to be reactionary and seldom in the vanguard of progress. They opposed the 1832 Reform Act until William IV accepted Grey's advice to create sufficient peers to carry the measure. Relations between the two Houses continued uncertainly throughout the nineteenth century. The further Reform Acts and the Irish Home Rule Act proved to be contentious measures.

The Lords were dominated by an overwhelming majority of Unionists, or Conservatives. Thus they became obstructive when the Liberals held a majority in the Commons. In 1906 the General Election returned a Liberal landslide. A number of Bills concerned with alcohol, voting, education and landowning were rejected by the Lords. But in 1909 Lloyd George introduced a Budget, in which he had the temerity to introduce misconceived measures to tax the value of land. The Lords contemptuously rejected the Budget and two elections were held in 1910 in order to establish the will of the people, which the Lords disingenuously purported to uphold. It was plain, however, that they were more mindful of their own liability to the taxation of land value. In the Parliament Act (1911) their lordships were deprived of their right to interfere with a Bill which had been certified by the Speaker of the Commons to be a money Bill; that is a Bill dealing with taxation, public accounts and public loans. That alone was a considerable loss of power. But the Parliament Acts (1911) and (1949) contained a further limitation. When the Lords have rejected in two successive sessions a public Bill, other than a money Bill or one to extend the life of Parliament beyond five years, and that Bill has been passed twice with a year's interval between its Second

Reading for the first time and its Third Reading for the second time in the Commons, then it only requires the automatic stamp of royal assent.

Reform of the Lords is a perennial question. In 1909 Churchill described it as a 'feudal relic'. It possessed, however, an independence of mind which is not to found in the House of Commons. Labour Governments attempted to address the problem in 1948 and 1968 but both attempts broke down. At the end of the 1998–99 session the power of hereditary peers was abolished. But as a transitionary measure they were allowed to elect ninety-two of their number to remain until the form of the new chamber is yet to be decided by a Prime Minister, who will go down in history for his mania to control everything which moves in the political world. The present transitional house, however, may endure for some years to come.

The history of Parliament reveals a remarkable story of how what might be described as the democratic hardware has developed over centuries.

The Sovereignty of Parliament

The doctrine of parliamentary sovereignty was promulgated principally by A.V. Dicey in his book entitled *Law of the Constitution*, which was first published in 1885. He formulated it thus:

> Parliamentary sovereignty means neither more nor less than this, namely that Parliament has the right to make or unmake any law whatever; and further, that no person or body is recognised by the law of England as having a right to override or set aside the legislation of Parliament.

Since that time the dominion of the British Empire has all but vanished, the power of the Lords has been trimmed, the Commons has become a veritable manufactory of statutes full of detail and devoid of principle, and the monarchy has become less a national focus. In these changing circumstances Dicey's constitutional doctrine need examination.

According to Dicey, Parliament had the sovereign right to make whatever law it wished. Being so possessed, it was not bound by any law, so much so that Parliament at any time was not bound even by its earlier enactments. Dicey quotes de Lolme, the Swiss jurist, who wrote, 'The power and jurisdiction of Parliament is so transcendent and absolute, that it cannot be confined, either for causes or persons, within any bounds.' This had been the outcome of the momentous struggle in the seventeenth century between the throne and the Commons.

Dicey stressed that he was dealing with sovereignty from a legal point of view. Yet by citing the legal sovereignty of Parliament as the most important of three leading characteristics of the British Constitution, Dicey inferred that Parliament possessed an omniscience, which amounted to more than legal sovereignty. Such an approach supplanted the evident fact that Parliament is both the creature and the servant of the British people. It has already been observed that the Prime Minister possesses various powers under the Royal Prerogative, without needing to consult Parliament.

Dicey mentioned three limitations to the sovereignty of Parliament. The first two had been formulated by the jurist, Sir Leslie Stephens. He postulated that there were internal and external limits. The former was that the legislature itself was the product of certain social conditions, and was, therefore, limited by the nature of society. The external limit was the instinct in society to obey its laws. The third limitation was more profound. Dicey mentions another limit twice. This limit is of much greater importance than those already mentioned. He quotes Blackstone who wrote in his *Commentaries*, Parliament 'can, in short, do everything that is not naturally impossible'. Then Dicey quotes Jean Louis de Lolme, 'It is a fundamental principle with English lawyers that Parliament can do everything but make woman a man, and man a woman.' Such sentiment had been uttered by Edward Coke, the seventeenth-century judge. Dicey reckoned this statement was a 'grotesque expression', but he conceded that it had become 'proverbial', though he failed to develop the point. In setting a limit to the absolute sovereignty of Parliament, Coke had stumbled across an important fact. For though Parliament has the legal sovereignty to enact any law, it lacks the power to command Nature, any more than King Canute could by His Majestic will subdue waves. Further, if Parliament intends its legislation to have a certain effect it must ensure that its measures are in harmony with Nature, otherwise the results will be unpredictable and often the opposite of what was intended.

In vain, does Parliament legislate without regard to the natural order of the Universe. For example, for six centuries it has been confronted by the problems of poverty and yet the causes of the problem have been allowed to persist. Instead of reform, Parliament has attempted to mitigate the effects of poverty and in this century it has unloosed ruinous taxation to finance the welfare state. The natural order does not allow Parliament to tax the nation into prosperity. The welfare state will never patch over the injustice which gave rise to the widespread condition of poverty. Until Parliament deals with the causes of this injustice, its actions will be futile, unnecessary and the cause of greater poverty. Parliament may attempt to impose equality on society but it will never succeed, because Nature does not strain for equality. Parliament may attempt to enact an injustice and, even though they have the authority of law to enforce it, Nature will retaliate.

It is implied in Dicey's constitution that Parliament can ignore both people and Nature. It does so continually. The conservative mind imagines that society is entirely man-made. But an impartial mind sees a different picture. Accordingly, parliamentary sovereignty must be interpreted reasonably as a legislative sovereignty and no more. It has no political sovereignty and no sovereignty over Nature.

Sometimes politicians forget the limitations placed upon the sovereignty of Parliament and infer that Parliament is possessed of a political sovereignty which obliges the people to be bound by the Acts of Parliament. It will be argued that the people possess natural rights and when Parliament overrides these rights its laws lack the sanction of Nature and the mischief is endless and incalculable.

Two consequences of the sovereignty of Parliament are that a Parliament cannot bind a successor Parliament by any law nor can it pass retrospective legislation. Though that may apply as a general principle in peacetime, in the aftermath of the Two World Wars Indemnity Acts were passed to to render illegal acts on behalf of the state during the wars unactionable. These exceptions, however, are justified by the supreme duty imposed on the state during war to ensure survival by almost whatever means. War is not waged according to the rules of constitutional cricket.

The courts will not concern themselves with an Act of Parliament or the procedural matters of Parliament. If two statutes are in conflict the courts will give precedence to the later one.

THE RULE OF LAW

Dicey highlighted a second feature of the British constitution: the rule of law. The concept of the rule of law can be traced to ancient Greece. It was familiar to Roman lawyers. It signified some universal law, existing above human law. In the sixteenth century there grew up the belief that the sovereignty of nations was expressed, in a great degree, by a nation's laws. The idea of natural law, meaning the law based on the nature of the individual and of societies, contains a universality above human law, for man's nature remains similar throughout mankind. But lawyers made the concept of natural law into a medieval, dry doctrine, which has become redundant since the sixteenth century.

He ascribed three meanings to that concept. First, that no one could be punished physically or through diminution of his property except for transgression of the law and by a court of law. There was in Britain no arbitrary power invested in the crown or any non-judicial body to inflict punishment. Traffic wardens, for example, have no powers to exact penalties at their discretion. Dicey contrasted Europe during the eighteenth century when freedom could be devastated by press gangs, Secretaries of State and thugs of many descriptions. But in France it was worse and *lettres de cachet* were employed as weapons to defeat rivals and to arrange the disappearance of enemies. However, having made his point, Dicey did acknowledge that by the twentieth century most European countries were living under the first aspect of the rule of law.

The second meaning of the rule of law ascribed by Dicey, was that individuals of whatever rank and condition were subject to the same law. Again, he had recourse to Europe in the eighteenth century, where law applied only to the unprivileged. But his concept lacked contemporary validation. In modern Britain legislation, particularly fiscal law, describes different species of person and purports to apply differently to each of them. Taxation is levied under the rule of politics which allows Government to raise as much revenue from the pockets of the people as possible. It cannot be pretended that the Budget is consistent with this second meaning ascribed to the rule of law. Nor does the concept allow the payment of public subsidies to a particular body. The social welfare provisions depend on differences of personal detail. The second feature of the rule of law highlighted by Dicey has applied with less and less force throughout the twentieth century.

The third meaning was that the law affecting the legal rights of individuals in Britain resulted from both the courts and Parliament. Yet the vast number of laws and regulations to which Britons are subject are parliamentary statutes. Dicey imagined British liberties were secured largely by common law. In fact, statute law has so invaded every aspect of life, that most individuals have to accept the policeman's or bureaucrat's opinion than face the expense of seeking that of a judge.

But, in addition to the statutory outpouring of Parliament, Britain is deluged with directives from Brussels. Parliament is no longer the sole fount of legislation in the United Kingdom. For it has enacted the European Communities Act 1972. The EU issues regulations and directives by the hour on the most detailed subjects. Sections 2(1), 2(4) and 3 of that Act have been construed to mean that, in a conflict between a European regulation and a UK statute, the former will be given effect. For as long as Britain remains bound by the Act, so it will be subject to a legislative power outside Parliament. In 1974 Lord Denning held that the Treaty of Rome was 'like an incoming tide. It flows into the estuaries and up the rivers. It cannot be held back.'[5]

The sovereignty of Parliament and Community law were in conflict in the case *R v Transport Secretary, Ex p Factortame Ltd.*[6] Spanish fishing interests alleged that the Merchant Shipping Act 1988, which excluded them from British fishing grounds, were contrary to EU law. The House of Lords upheld the Spanish claim. The assertion by Sir William Wade, the constitutional jurist, that a revolution had taken place[7] seems to have been the case. But whether the EU will endure, or Britain remain a member, is an uncertain political question. In any event there is nothing to prevent the exercise of British parliamentary sovereignty in repealing that Act whenever it wished and it could be done by a majority of one Member.

If the rule of law refers only to human law, it is a meaningless concept. Then it suggests that people must obey any law passed by Parliament. It may appear at first that this is a precept of a civilised democracy but such a precept could become a duty which tyranny attempts to impose. Parliament should remember that the limit imposed upon its legislative sovereignty was that it should have regard to the instinct of the people to obey law. Locke allowed people to 'appeal to Heaven' or revolt. One such occasion occurred in 1990 when an unjust poll tax was laid on people, with the effect of relieving the freeholder at the expense of the tenant. The riot in Trafalgar Square was a healthy reminder of the limits on Parliament. As Sir Kenneth Jupp, a retired judge of the High Court, writes, 'The word "law" has come to mean little more than the "will of the powerful".'[8] Law becomes indistinguish-

---

[5] Bulmer v Bollinger [1974] 3 WLR 202.
[6] [1991] 1 AC 603.
[7] *Constitutional and Administrative Law*, A.Bradley & K. Ewing, p. 159.
[8] *Stealing Our Land*, K. Jupp, p. 4.

able from regulation. It is stretching the meaning of the word too widely to embrace measures to regulate the dimension of a banana and another to declare war on another nation.

The third feature of the British Constitution highlighted by Dicey, along with the sovereignty of Parliament and the rule of law, was the role played by convention, as distinct from express enactment. It is one thing to state that Parliament does not pass retrospective laws declaring what was formerly legal to have been illegal, but it is not true to say that Parliament cannot enact, and has not enacted, legislation retrospectively. But it is not necessary to explore more fully the constitutional conventions here.

The rule of law is a constitutional concept of faded elegance. Even when in tatters, it is still theoretically attractive. It was intended to set a standard for law. But there is no standard, except the majority will of the House of Commons. In other words, the objectivity of the ancient concept of the rule of law has been been replaced by the subjectivity of the nation state. It is sufficient say that a majority in the Commons reflects a majority in a nation. But human majorities, even unanimous majorities, can disregard the law of nature and the birthrates which it has created.Indeed, the rule of law is used as authority to override Nature. So employed its meaning has been perverted from its original sense. When it believed that a human legislature is omnipotent, natural liberties will be extinguished.

Summary

The sovereignty of Parliament mean that in Britain there is one supreme legislative authority. That is a necessary step in the evolution of a democratic nation. For it means that every individual in Britain stands, for the most part, on the same legal ground as their fellows. Dicey's legal concepts have been taken beyond his limitations to suggest that above individuals stand the majesty of Parliament and its enactments. The natural rights of individuals have been displaced by the power of the State. It has been seen how puffed up is this majesty of state by the fiction that the monarchy is included in Parliament.

The rule of law was promoted by Dicey with reasons that were outdated. It means something substantial only in a society existing in a state of lawlessness. Then it represents an essential step from tribalism to nationhood. In a developed society it implies that the people are bound to obey any enactment by Parliament, thus affording Parliament a political sovereignty to do what it pleases. There is no reason why people should obey half-witted or unjust regulation. They have a deeper right, identified by Locke as the right 'to appeal to heaven' – the right to revolt, in order to put an end to an ill.

It is time to set aside the constitutional gloss of constitutional jurists, such as Dicey, Anson and Jennings. It was meat and drink to those who subscribed to the rule of the masses by the élite and of mankind by the British Empire. But their doctrines obscures free or serious political thought.

Parliamentary sovereignty is not the pinnacle of democracy; merely a component of its machinery. It should be seen as the creature of the people, rather than of Dicey's mind. It is not deserving of blind veneration, as if it were an exhibit under glass in a museum. It needs to be employed to remove injustice in society.

In the second half of the nineteenth century the image of the monarchy, which was no longer seizing public imagination, was refurbished by pageantry. The opening of Parliament and trooping the colour dates from that time. During the same period Dicey made people feel good about the Constitution by giving it the appearance of mystique, grandeur and antiquity. It is like the practice of retaining a classical façade of an old building as the outer shell of a modern office in order to give the appearance of tradition.

The idea that British people owe their liberties to Parliament is quaint but it is seldom the case in history. It is redolent of the harsh doctrine of Hobbes, the political philosopher, that the people enjoyed only the rights the king was minded to allow them. In seeking a basis of essential human rights, it is necessary to look far beyond the sovereignty of Parliament and the rule of law, as presently understood.

One of the the handicaps which Members impose on Parliament is their acceptance of party discipline, often without demur, and the cross-party acceptance of political correctness. Both reduce Parliament and political thought in Britain to a level of mediocrity. Thousands visit Parliament every day and are most impressed with the the sense of history and with the building but if they tarry for a debate, they are mostly bored comprehensively. They leave with the sad conclusion that this department of the nation should be delegated to experts in boredom.

3

Sovereignty of Nature

It has been shown that political sovereignty of Britain does not reside in monarchy and that Parliament possesses only a legal sovereignty. To imagine that Parliament has been, or is, the source of the liberty of the individual in Britain is an illusion. Before considering where effective political sovereignty in Britain lies, it is helpful to consider the government of a democratic society.

Maximilian Caspari[1] wrote that in Greece during the fifth century BC:

> Pericles sincerely contemplated the good of his fellow-countrymen, and we may believe that he endeavoured to realize that ideal Athens which Thucydides sketches in the Funeral Speech – an Athens where free and intelligent obedience is rendered to an equitable code of laws ... In accordance with this scheme Pericles sought to educate the whole community in political wisdom ...[2]

It was possible in Athens during Pericles's life to involve free males in government. In a society consisting of a population numbering millions, adults cannot expect to take any active share in government. Therefore, the election of representatives to parliament becomes necessary.

But as soon as the representative enters a parliament he or she submits to the tight control of political parties and thereafter they come to represent their parties, even when pursuing policies that injure the rights and liberties of those who elected them, unless they are members of particularly strong character and clear thinking.[3] Political parties are cemented together by the ambition of politicians to hold power and to represent sectional interests. They can only pretend to advance the objective interests of the individual, above those of their most powerful supporters. They maintain a façade of the national interest to keep the electorate in a state of aquiesence. The acceptance of the concept of 'political correctness' allows political mediocrity to pass without real criticism.

---

[1] Reader of Ancient History at London University and lecturer in Greek History at Birmingham University.
[2] *Encyclopaedia Britannica*, 11th edn, 1911.
[3] See *Enemy of Injustice*, M. Hill.

The domination in Britain of Parliament by political parties has added to parliamentary sovereignty a political sovereignty. The people are required to vote and to delegate thereafter political sovereignty to political parties. Briefly they exercise sovereignty and while standing before a voting booth, they resemble a consumer deciding which chocolate to buy from a vending machine. Once the coin is released they receive whatever the machine determines.

Parliament has been weakened as political parties have grown stronger. No government brought to power by political parties and held in power by them can be considered democratic. Even though they achieved power by the vote of the majority of the people, such government bears more the traits of an oligarchy. Democracy in Britain resembles a game which the spectators have never played, according to rules which are endlessly varied. The people have been forgotten what the aim of the game ever was.

Pericles realised that participation in public administration alone would not secure democracy. He had hoped as well to introduce public education in political wisdom, but this object was thwarted by the continuance of the Peloponnesian War. In modern terms it might be said that computer hardware will not itself advance efficiency. The software required to produce substantial democracy is political wisdom, which Pericles had wished to include in education.

Dividing government into what has to be, and what should not be, delegated by a democratic people, it can be argued that the prime function of government during peace is the administration from day to day of the State. This has been likened to travelling down a fast-flowing river which is continually disturbed by rapids, floods, earthquakes, assassinations, wars, scandals, famines, plagues, outbreaks of violence, world-wide elections, rumours, recession and the like. The individual who earns a living or brings up a family does not have the time to develop the skills to deal with this business. It is wise, therefore, for people to delegate administration of the State to politicians, as it is wise to delegate local administration of rubbish collection, lighting and drainage to local authorities. Administration is a daily business spread over a wide range of issues, which are impossible to predict.

When a nation is forming itself, it needs a great leader. Such an example was Count Camillo Cavour, the nineteenth-century Italian statesman, who overcame the strife, the petty division and domination by foreigners which afflicted the Italian states. He converted the Risorgimento into nationhood. President Mandela led South Africa from the terrible, inhuman system of apartheid, which had imprisoned the nation for four decades. It is rare, however, that a nation needs a leader after it is formed or recovered from internal strife.

In the exceptional times, for example, when Britain's survival was threatened and all seemed lost in 1940, Churchill led the nation with unshakeable courage. Or in more recent times President Sadat of Egypt who led his nation with great courage to war and then to peace. In peacetime, however, a Prime Minister of a democratic nation serves more as manager of administration. When the Second World War was brought to an end, the British people preferred to elect the epitome of a manager. Churchill appreciated the distinction by remarking, 'a large empty car drew up to Downing Street and Mr Attlee stepped out.'

The second sphere of the political world during peacetime, unconcerned with political administration, is the culture of political thought in a society. For that, rather than a government, determines the framework of society. When political thought is vague politics degenerates into the superficial world of appearances and deeper issues are hidden by being swept out of sight. But when political thought is sharp and alert government can be directed to higher ends. Then, and only then, pillars of justice, liberty and democracy can be established on objective grounds. It is through their culture of political thinking that a society may restrict government to an administrative function. This division was put simply by Cavour: 'In the system of the Universe they are two orders utterly distinct from each other – the order of principles and the order of facts.'[4] Whereas principles are objective and endure, facts change with the hour.

Though distinct, the two realms of politics influence each other. It is natural that society should consist of the two partners in a democracy: the governed and the government. It is desirable that the governed should control government and highly undesirable that government should control the political thinking of the governed. Political thinking can determine the shape of administration, particularly in the fields of taxation, foreign affairs, home issues and defence. It is impossible for a democracy to flourish without the intelligent participation of a people in the creation of a political culture. This realm of political thinking cannot be delegated to politicians, because their role as public administrators does not allow time or perspective to think about anyone so remote as the individual.

The complete realisation of democracy rests on a partnership between public representatives elected to administer the State, and the people who project by their political thinking the ends and the framework of society. A people have a real interest in restricting government to its minimum, in order to strengthen their liberties. To accomplish this end the people have to direct government to maintaining justice in the main branches of its activity.

Having gained universal suffrage in the twentieth century, the British people need to assume practical control of political thought by instituting education in political wisdom, as Pericles wished to have done. Youth is a special time when in the later teenage period and early twenties the aspiration for justice and humanity tends to be strongest. If that period is not inspired by an education in political thought, or political wisdom, young persons will lack clear principles of political thought and fall prey to the prejudices inherited from their elders and take on material responsibilities and burdens, which come with rearing families and earning a living. As they undertake these responsibilities the individual will fit into the habit of what Churchill called the British preference for 'business as usual'. The good of a whole society will disappear

[4] *Cavour*, E. Dicey, p. 46.

in thinking behind self-interest. The idealism of youth will be replaced by dull, mechanical, party-political thinking. If he or she is interested in politics they will drift into political parties without knowledge or interest in Nature's bequest of liberty and birthrights. In other words, the young adult, uneducated in political thought, is woefully unprepared for a political role, either as an administrator or voter. Yet a few may in time hold ministerial office. But even they will retire ignorant of Nature, justice or lacking a deep understanding of the democratic relationship of peoples and politics.

A democracy needs a culture of political thinking based on universal or natural principles. A culture of political wisdom can only be built from a foundation of classroom education in political thought. Without such a culture politics will continue to be brokered by politicians, equipped only with pragmatism. Instead of justice and prosperity, there will be increasing government regulation and diminishing freedom for society. Profound, simple law will be replaced by complex, superficial and largely unnecessary regulation. In Britain government will oscillate between one party and another.

But objective principles of a just society are not taught in schools because teachers are not trusted to rise above the petty rivalry of party politics. Instead, students are taught political history, which is a wholly different subject. It concentrates on the 'politically correct' interpretation. Young people need something more inspiring, more interesting, more incisive and more simple. Whereas political thought about a just society is concerned with principles, political history is composed of ever-changing events and personages. But young people have no need to digest the history of political parties or the long catalogue of trivialities and tawdry compromises by which politicians have prolonged their administrations. But if they have been taught nothing else they will vote in an election on such criteria as the shape of a candidate's teeth, the curl of hair or the seductiveness of a smile.

They need to be taught something about human society beyond politics, which will remain with them through life.They need to discern the natural rights of man and the natural development of society, essential principles of reason and justice, the balance between the liberty of the individual and the power of the State, the natural extent and limits of government. Such teaching would satisfy their hunger for inspiration, develop understanding of justice and humanity and make them aware that these principles apply to societies across the world, whatever their size or stage of development.

The reason why education in political thought does not arise in the classroom is due to the fact that Government controls education. That is a mistaken delegation in a democratic society. Politics should be taken out of education completely, as it has been ejected from arithmetic, by removing it from the control of Government. It should be restored to local government to provide school premises and the teaching be restored to its natural parties: teachers and parents. Public education was introduced at the end of the nineteenth century because it appeared that the mass of society could not afford education. The political question of why able-bodied adults could not afford to educate their children was avoided. In place of that question Government provided education at the expense of the taxpayer, not as is supposed at the expense of the rich but at the expense of rich and poor. For taxation is not paid by the individual as Parliament particularise but the burden is shifted into prices. So the poor are taxed more heavily than the rich.[5] The people, who could be the natural masters in a democracy, are bored comprehensively by politics, except some scandalous tit-bits, and the political activists are motivated to move into the vacuum with their own interests. Young people should know that Parliament rests in their hands, without them ever needing to go within a hundred miles of Westminster. The grand drama of achieving a just, democratic and prosperous society, which has not appeared before in recorded history depends in the first place upon them. In a healthy society a minority will be drawn to the administrative side of government; but every person would love to become acquainted with the political thought upon which their freedoms, prosperity and welfare depend.

Disregard of political education about a just society is dangerous. Apathy provides an excellent seedbed for frustration born of poverty and unemployment to develop into irresponsible and violent revolution. Lacking a formal education in the principles of political thought a young person is confronted by the muddle of politics comparable to a subject in which there was no agreed language or arithmetic.

Laws of Nature will be seen as belonging only to animals who eat each other in jungles. Indeed, animals and plants are governed largely by natural instincts. But man and human society are governed by different laws.

It is a strange but reasonable speculation that students would show a keener appreciation of Nature, humanity and justice than a Parliament of adult experts or politicians, whose interest in such things is rarely evident.

It is impossible to define the law of Nature comprehensively because it is not a law devised by humans and thus not dependent on succinct formulation. Edmund Burke described a higher order of law thus:

> The principles which guide us in public and private, as they are not of our devising, but moulded into the nature and essence of things, will endure with the sun and moon – long, very long after whig and tory, Stuart and Brunswick, and all such miserable baubles and playthings of the hour, are vanished from existence and from memory.[6]

The law of Nature is a superior law to which human law is ever subject. Justice is an instinct implanted in Man without being formulated. Rather it is sown in every human breast, so deeply that only the most determined enemy of mankind can claim not to understand it. If that were not so, the summoning of trial juries would become a farce.

A starting point in modern British history is the political thinking of John Locke, the seventeenth-century philosopher, who expressed the spirit of English liberalism, its

---

[5] See *Tyranny of Taxation*, M. Hill, [due to be published in 2001].
[6] *Correspondence*, E. Burke, vol I, p. 332–3.

tolerant temper, its reasonableness, its modesty, its simplicity. He is principally known as the author of the *Essay Concerning Human Understanding* (1690). So reasonable a work that it is difficult to imagine that it was ever opposed. But *Biographica Britannica* records that:

> there was a meeting of the heads of the houses in Oxford, where it was proposed to censure and discourage the reading of this Essay; that after various debates, it was concluded that, without public censure, each head should endeavour to prevent it being read in his own college.[7]

He explained his political thought principally in the *Two Treatises of Government*, which was published in 1690. The *First Treatise*, which has already been discussed, demolished the theory of the divine right of kings. His purposes seem to have been to justify the English Revolution of 1688 and to refute the argument of Hobbes that individual rights were those only accorded by human law by showing that man derives his rights from Nature. The Hobbesian argument is not far away from the idea that the British people owe their rights to Parliament.

His political thought was set out in the *Second Treatise*. He began with a powerful first paragraph:

> To understand political power right, and derive it from its original, we must consider what state all men are naturally in, and that is a state of perfect freedom to order their actions and dispose of their possessions and persons as they think fit, within the bounds of the laws of nature, without asking leave, or depending upon the will of any other man.[8]

To suggest that legislators should consider the natural order before enacting a statute is, in an uneducated political culture, an unfamiliar notion.

His study of society was inspired by returning to the early state when the rights of man in peace derived from Nature rather than human command. He believed in 'the idea of a supreme Being, infinite in power, goodness and wisdom, whose workmanship we are' and that state of Nature human beings were equal and independent creatures of a Maker. It is a state of perfect equality. Every individual has the power to punish to the extent that may hinder further transgression.

Individuals are constantly living in a state of war with each other, which Locke describes as a 'state of enmity and destruction'. The will to have absolute power of another results from a state of war, which in turn leads to a state of slavery. To develop beyond this state, men are impelled to form societies.

---

[7] *An Essay on the First Principles of Government*, J. Priestly, p. 99.
[8] *Political Writings of John Locke*, Penguin edn, p. 262.

Locke affirmed that the foundation of a commonwealth, or society, lay in the consent of free, independent men. Precisely what Locke meant by consent is not clearly defined. According to J. W. Gough:

Government by consent may remain . . . as an historic and serviceable, if loose, description of a constitutional type of Government, not because individuals ever agreed to accept it, but because it is sensitive to public opinion, with which it is kept in touch by representative institutions and a free press, and does not have to stifle opposition by force.[9]

Though he gave up liberties, like that of punishing the wrongdoer, he gained from a society the preservation of his liberties and his properties. This step required a judge to adjudicate and settle quarrels.

'Behind the supreme legislature stands the superior power of the people,' wrote W.S. Carpenter in his Introduction.[10] If such a tyrannical ruler abuses his power the people, having no appeal to any authority on earth retain the right 'of appeal to Heaven', by which Locke meant revolution. Locke rejected the alienation of independence to a sovereign, as argued by Hobbes, and maintained instead that a ruler was subject to the laws of Nature.

Locke believed the two fundamental purposes of society to be to secure civil liberties and the preservation of private property of the individual. Locke started from the reasonable proposition that the earth was given in common to man, to counter the argument that God made a gift of the earth to Adam and Eve. Everything removed from that common pool of Nature by a man's labour becomes private property. The labour could just be picking a wild berry. Locke applied the similar reasoning to the acquisition of property in the earth itself. As a man mixes his labour with the earth in tilling and cultivation, so he appropriates the soil to himself. But he can only acquire property in common land by the consent of his fellows. Yet when the spread of cultivation, the increase of population and the use of money led to land becoming scarce and valuable Locke imposed the limit of self-restraint on this progression – whereby men would remove from the common fund only what they needed. It was simplistic in Locke's time when the power of money was becoming apparent. Men could enclose more than they needed for themselves. This is the least convincing part of the *Second Treatise*.

Locke became well known in Paris after Voltaire had discovered his writings on his visit to England in 1727. Locke, stated Voltaire, 'expounded human understanding as an excellent anatomist explains the mechanism of the human body. At all points he seeks the light of physics, he sometimes speaks affirmatively, but he also dares to

---

[9] *John Locke's Political Philosophy*, J. Gough, p. 79.
[10] *Two Treatises of Government*, Everyman ed. J. Locke. Introduction.

doubt.'[11] Voltaire introduced Locke and Isaac Newton to Turgot, who was to become a celebrated statesman and thinker. When Turgot[12] embarked on the study of public administration, as he termed government, and the economic nature of society, he adopted the foundation of his thought from Locke. The ends of society, Turgot fully agreed, were to protect the liberty of the person and private property of the individual. Turgot developed the thinking of Locke from the state of society in the time of Locke to the emergence of the system of capitalism and the Industrial Revolution. He made one fundamental change in Locke's argument.

He regarded Nature as underlying the order of human society in a developed, rather than a primitive, state. Locke had argued that the formation of society had ousted the state of Nature. There was in Turgot's thinking no notion of man being perfectly natural only whilst he was primitive. Rather, he demonstrated both in his learning and conduct that Nature was the the power with which man had to co-operate in every field of life. To interpret Nature from observing the animal world was a worm's-eye view of a power that ordered also the mental, emotional and spiritual nature of man. Man is both an animal but also a spiritual being capable of reason, justice and humanity. In his youth Turgot had adopted Locke and Newton as his leading authorities.

He applied Nature to the economic sphere as a field, which is an important part of man's existence. He adopted the idea of Locke that a society existed to protect the civil and economic rights of man. He was not happy with Locke's argument about property and developed this in a reasonable and natural way.

Locke's concept of a natural order was similar to that of François Quesnay, who has been reckoned the founder of economic science in the West.[13] He had adopted ideas of a natural order from ancient Chinese thought. Quesnay attracted followers, who came to acknowledge him as their Master. Turgot was attracted by his thinking but he detested sects and their doctrines and recoiled from the idea of moulding his thinking to fit in those followers of Quesnay, who styled themselves Physiocrats. Quesnay's ideas were purged of what Turgot termed his complex 'algebra' and were formulated with precision and simplicity by Turgot in his *Réflexions sur la formation et la distribution des richesses*.[14] This principle he illustrated in his work as an intendant, or provincial administrator, and later as *contrôleur-général*, the most powerful minister in France under the *ancien régime*. The office would comprise in Britain as Chancellor of the Exchequer, Home Secretary, Minister of Agriculture, Transport and Local Government.Throughout his adult life he was engaged in public administration. He wrote little, apart from his official papers and the *Réflexions*, which he stated modestly, was intended to explain the economic thinking of the French *économistes* to two Chinese students in Paris, who were returning home. He set down

---

[11] *Letters on England*, Voltaire, Penguin edn, pp. 68 & 63.
[12] See *Statesman of the Enlightenment*, M. Hill.
[13] *The Wealth of Nations*, J. R. McCullock, 1828 edn, Introduction. p. lviii.
[14] See *Formation and Distribution of Wealth, Reflections on Capitalism*, K. Jupp (ed.).

his argument with simplicity and precision which were the hallmarks of his wide scholarship.

The belief that Adam Smith founded the science of economics is widely accepted. By the time, however, that Smith met the économistes in Paris in 1766, they had established a complete system of economic thought. Smith had just had the idea of beginning his economic work. In 1769 Turgot's essay, *Réflexions*, was published and the first two parts were catalogued in Smith's library.

When his *Wealth of Nations* was published in 1776, two features stood out. First, Smith's writing and comprehension were uneven. In places there were some clear pieces on free trade. It would be wrong, however, to imagine that Smith was a champion of free trade, as were several of his predecessors and contemporaries. Even in a matter so simple, he managed to be ambiguous, in order to please both free traders and the protected interests. The stronger passages on free trade seemed so close to the phraseology of Turgot, as to stand out with a special luminosity from the general tone of his writing.

Second, the treatment of that more important matter, taxation, was superficial. In Paris the fiscal question had been held as the most important economic question twenty years before Smith's work was published. Smith trod carefully around radical ideas, lest they should make his work unpopular with the vested interests in Britain. He reiterated four canons of taxation. They were plausible but superficial. He treatment of taxation was lacking in both profundity and justice. In short, the popularity Smith gained as an author was enjoyed at the expense of his thinking.

The distinction between private and public property lay, Turgot believed, at the bottom of political thought. The question of property was to define private property, belonging to the individual exclusively, and public property, belonging to no one in particular but to society in common. Plainly labour was the mother of individual, or private, property; for, as Locke explained, it appropriates from the common store the raw materials afforded by Nature and suggested that labour could appropriate land in the similar way as its produce. The cultivator, by 'mixing', as Locke put it, 'his labour with the soil', appropriated not only the crops but also the soil in which they grew. This appropriation did not convince Turgot, who was determined to resolve the question of property which Locke had adumbrated.

He needed to examine the question of property, in order to collect revenue for the purposes of government from public, rather than private property. For he believed that to tax private property was to violate something which society had come into being to protect. Taxation should be aimed at public property which belonged to no one in particular, because it belonged to everyone equally.

Turgot showed that the capitalist system was not an ideology but a mechanism whereby self-interest could flourish as a mainspring of economic activity. He also emphasised that in order for the individual to be free to meet his or her responsibilities government must set a just framework of taxation. He described how the private appropriation of land caused the landless to constitute a pool of unemployed in search of a job. Their competition drove down the level which was the least an unemployed individual would accept. In a later correspondence with Benjamin Franklin, the American leader, he showed how taxes became passed on through prices, causing a rising and inflationary price level.

At the end of the eighteenth century the French Revolution obscured this fine political thought with mindless butchery. It obliterated the foundations which Turgot had laid for the Industrial Revolution. In place of justice and prosperity for an entire society arose widespread poverty which industrial invention seemed only to make more wretched. Cities were disfigured by squalid slums. Turgot had given a visionary insight into a just society, which mankind has never put into effect.

During the nineteenth century the contrast between man's inventive prowess and his political ignorance became apparent. Britain excelled in technological development but languished in medieval political thought. A few entrepreneurs made fortunes and the mass remained poor.

The Victorian order was wanting. It was sustained by belief that man had a duty to look after himself, and family and by a rigid social orthodoxy which outlawed radical political thought. Poverty was extreme and its mitigation was entrusted to starch-collared Poor Law Guardians. But it was the seedbed of socialism and Marx, neither of which set sights on the high ground, towards which Locke and Turgot had been travelling. Similar ideas to those promoted by the *économistes* of the eighteenth century were promulgated by an American writer, Henry George, whose book *Progress and Poverty* (1879) became a world best-seller. His ideas took root in Britain, and particularly in Scotland, during the last two decades of the nineteenth century.

During the brief period, between 1906–8, while Sir Henry Campbell-Bannerman's Liberal administration was in power, there was a serious possibility of reform of these perennial afflictions of poverty. There was a desire in Government to reform the causes of poverty. Churchill was a champion of that spirit.[15] But following Sir Henry's death in 1908, the determination to deal with causes gave way to dealing with effects. Lloyd George persuaded Churchill that there was more popularity to be enjoyed with voters by mitigating effects. Churchill was easily persuaded that the limelight was the most important consideration for a politician with ambition How just was Asquith's observation during the Cabinet struggle over dreadnoughts that 'Lloyd George lacked principles, Churchill lacked convictions.'[16] The foundations were laid of the welfare state. Measures of national insurance for sickness and unemployment were added to the pensions introduced in 1907 by Asquith, as Chancellor of the Exchequer.

The twentieth century closes with political thought less appropriate to a just and prosperous democracy than ever before. The light of Nature has been scrupulously excluded by government regulation and ignored in education. There is no framework for human law except the will of the majority. It has been a century of war and

---

[15] See *Churchill His Radical Decade*, M. Hill.
[16] *Winston S. Churchill*, R. Churchill, vol II, p. 247.

intervals of hopeless problems of recession and unemployment. In terms of political thought, little has been established to advance natural liberties. It has been a perfect habitat for experts. They gather round the economic wreckage of society like vermin round uncollected rubbish. The culture woven by little, expert minds has been largely emotional.The culture of the victim has evolved.The last conceivable oppressor is reckoned to be the Government.

The question of sovereignty in Britain can now finally be considered. Sovereignty is shared briefly at certain moments by the monarch, often by the Prime Minister and Government, sometimes by the media, occasionally by sportsmen or popular heroes but seldom by the people, who have to wait for that precious moment on the day of a General Election. Sovereignty in Britain is splintered between many and people suffer – as a consequence there is ineffective government.

Britain has been governed for centuries by the attitudes of middle-minded reactionaries, who do not want any revolution in thinking to upset their nests.They dismiss the notion of the sovereignty of the people as the prelude for violence and political licence, as if to imply that the people are too unintelligent to think about justice and democracy. Talk of revolution in Britain has been branded as incitement to violence. They point to the wild explosions of revolution in France and in Russia as terrible examples. Indeed, both were murderous and devoid of justice and vision. Neither achieved profound reform. The word revolution has been branded as unthinkable. The meaning of the word revolution, however, is complete change. Change can be reasonable and just. Change wrought by violence will always fail to effect profound change attainable by change of thinking. The first step is to cast aside the veil which seeks to render party politics respectable.

It has been said that Jean-Jacques Rousseau's book, *Social Contract*, pointed to the distinction between sovereignty and government and to the fact that the sovereignty of a people was inalienable.[17] Priestly and many others since also believed that: 'All civil power is derived ultimately from the people.'[18] However, it is plain that the British people can become quiescent and exercise sovereignty through political thought. Dominated by earning a living and struggling against poverty, taxation and the fear of unemployment, given to an inexhaustible appetite for entertainment and on account of being overwhelmed by a feeling of impotence, the British people have failed to exercise a control over Government. They have allowed to slip from their control the important fields of Government and particularly the important fields of taxation and education.

Nature pervades the planet earth, not only controlling gravity, the weather and animals, but operates through the nature of man and the nature of society, to control the economy, trade, taxation, inflation, poverty and unemployment. Nature's universal sovereignty cannot be ousted by Parliament's legislative sovereignty.

---

[17] *Les Oeuvres de Turgot*, G. Schelle, vol ii, p. 660.
[18] *An Essay on the First Principles of Government*, J. Priestly, p. 28.

Rather, legislation which ignores Nature will not give effect to the results intended by Parliament. If Parliament sat everyday of the year on a twenty-four-hour basis for a decade, even then measures to mitigate poverty would not even begin to touch the fringes of the problems. Natural justice demands that the cause of these human ills of society are eradicated; mitigation and compassion will not suffice when the causes are allowed to remain.

In order to make democracy manifest, to clear away the melodramas of party politics, to set aside the constitutional mist surrounding the monarchy and House of Lords, to strip the principles of political thought clear of the daily administrative cares of Government, to set aside the personal ambitions of politicians and to focus attention on the distribution of wealth and taxation the people of Britain have need of a culture of political thought based on principles of Nature and justice. From those two sources will give rise to liberty and prosperity. But to aim for liberty and prosperity without justice is to aim too low for either to be achieved.

When the people harmonise their political thinking with Nature's laws they are capable of exercising the highest sovereignty which human government can attain. The people, however, can only exercise their sovereignty within a living political culture. Such a culture does not exist anywhere in the globe nor has at any period of modern history. Everywhere politicians are competing to win votes in elections. In large areas of political administration there are few principles. People can study any subject, however unimportant and inconsequential, but it is a surprising fact that at school a student is fortunate indeed to meet a teacher of political principle. In history teachers of political thought have been extremely rare. Statesmen of leading societies who have carried principle into action without compromising the integrity of their ideas are rarer still. The history of governments can be read, but the study of political thought which concerns political thought above party or Parliament is omitted in schools.

Locke stated that the two ends of society were the promotion of civil liberty and the preservation of private property. The remaining chapters are concerned with examining to what extent some of these liberties have been secured in England.

CIVIL LIBERTIES

4

Freedom from Arrest

Policing a society, or preserving the peace, is an art and a profession, for it involves managing people whose disorder exists side-by-side with the rights of an orderly citizen. As well as being technical, because it involves freedom and legal constraint, it also involves quick thinking and sometimes decisive action. It also involves taking society as it is, with its traditions, classes, minority groups, injustice and poverty.

Policing is made no easier when Members of Parliament refuse against self-evident reason that poverty is a fertile seedbed of disorder, simply because there are no statistics to prove it. Rather than regarding the police as the force to clean up society, government are responsible for setting a reasonable framework for society. Police may apprehend the odd criminal but they cannot suppress wide-spread drug-taking or theft. But policing is not a realm of administration which can be delegated to the police alone. For by its nature in a democracy policing involves a whole people, whose thinking sets the basic framework of society. For as has been remarked by an ex-Chief Constable: 'The state is the product of society not society of the state.'[1] A great danger is when the State becomes the controller of police. Such a convergence is bad for government, bad for the police and bad for the people. Cooperation with the police is desirable and criticism of them is also healthy. Two decades ago it was troubled by terrorism and disorders flowing from economic causes and in the 1990s it has been afflicted principally with racial tensions and drugs. Racial tension in Britain was inevitable because the economic conditions were so insecure and poverty so extensive. The latest exposure of racism in the Metropolitan police in London needs to be kept in perspective and the police does not need to be branded for the fault, which it now openly admits. For it is superficial to imagine that racism is as deep seated as poverty.

Towards the end of the twentieth century a number of celebrated trials were dismantled on appeal when it emerged that police evidence was unreliable. These included the *Bridgewater Three, the Guildford Four, the Birmingham Six, the Broadwater Farm*. These shook public confidence in the police. This led to the requirement of taping police interviews, except for terrorist offences and offences under

---

[1] *Law and Disorder*, J. Alderson, p. 25.

the Official Secrets Act. So even if had been a taping requirement during the 1970s, the *Birmingham Six*, who suffered the worst injustice in British criminal history, would have been regarded as terrorists. Since that time criminal prosecution have been taken out of the hands of the police and placed in those of the Criminal Prosecution Service. Much of the procedure for dealing with suspects has been controlled by the introduction of the the Police and Criminal Evidence Act 1984 [PACE] which replaced the host of common law principles. In the nature of a police force has to deal with some ugly suspects and a measure of menace and force depends on the character involved. While injustice in police conduct cannot be tolerated, it should be understood as a tendency when a body is given so much power in a society in which injustice is so general. Failures of the police have to be accepted in part as a consequence of the failure of society to eradicate poverty and injustice. The determined and courageous individuals who have exposed excesses of the police are doing a great service to society and also to the police. Policing from the moment of the first apprehension of a disorder to the delivery of the verdict of the court is a long process, though a professional force makes it look easy. But the pressures from society, Government, Parliament and the media are intense. The police force in Britain is a relatively young institution and society receives the quality of policing it itself deserves. The political thinking of society is largely superficial and muddled and, therefore, Government in important fields poor and dishonest. To blame the police for what should in fairness be blamed on poor political thinking is simplistic and unjust.

The constable emerged in the twelfth century as a military figure of senior rank. But the position declined in importance in the next century. However, by 1285 the constable had become a permanent official of peace keeping. The word police was adopted in England during the eighteenth century but was disliked as a form of oppression. In the sixteenth century Charles V, the Holy Roman Emperor, introduced a system of police. He said it was 'to increase the happiness and security of his people'. To dispense happiness is not a normal function of State and a number of specialists have been trained to expunge it from people's lives. But by 1800 London, outside the City, had doubled its population to a million within the eighteenth century. The capital was assailed by highwaymen on the roads, sneak-thieves, pickpockets, shop-lifters, armed footpads in the streets, burglars and thieves, who operated even on the river Thames. They were supported by pawnbrokers, who operated without control. Drunkenness, particularly on home-brewed gin, was especially prevalent in the capital during the first half of the eighteenth century. The Government sought to ban its consumption by the Gin Act 1736. But the measure was resisted in Parliament and by rioting outside. The cry of the rioters was 'No Gin, No King' but by 1756 it had been almost taxed out of existence. Corruption extended from the petty criminal to the Government itself. In short London was disorderly and dissolute.

In the second half of the seventeenth century a number of paid night-watchmen, known as 'Charlies', so-named after the king, were recruited to assist unpaid constables. Armed only with poles and generally chosen from the poor and infirm, they proved no match in speed, strength or intelligence for the criminal. Throughout the eighteenth century up to almost seventy constables[2] were employed by the magistrates at Bow Street, London. They became known as the Bow Street runners. They were succeeded in 1782 by the Bow Street Foot Patrol, who numbered sixty-eight men. But it became evident that prevention of crime and detention of offenders could not be left to local authorities. In 1785 Pitt's government attempted to introduce a Metropolitan Force. His plan was taken up forty-four years later by Robert Peel. In 1829 a full-time police force was introduced in London and the duty was imposed on Counties and Boroughs. Since 1856 Central Government has provided a grant to police costs.

Although the management of police outside London is exercised by local government, the Home Secretary holds supervisory powers, whose exercise tends to central control. The Home Secretary is himself also the police authority within the Metropolitan area of London. Any attempt of a Home Secretary to use his authority to direct police operations, as Churchill attempted to do in the siege of Sidney Street, East London, in 1911, would be unlawful. For as Salmon L.J. held in *R v Metropolitan Police Commissioner, ex p Blackburn*:[3] 'Constitutionally it is clearly impermissible for a Home Secretary to issue any order to the police in respect of law enforcement.' But apart from his role as the police authority for Metropolitan London [which does not include the City of London], the Home Secretary has considerable supervisory powers over other forces. He may determine policy objectives, performance targets, require police authorities to report to him, order inspections by the Inspectorate of Constabulary and lay down requirements for the management and conduct of police forces. The justification for his influence over police is that he determines the funding of the greater part of their expenditure.

In 1962 a royal commission examining the constitutional position of the police advised that a national force would lead to a totalitarian 'police state'. Under the Police Act 1996 the country outside London is divided into forty-one police areas, which can be altered by the Home Secretary to promote 'efficiency and effectiveness'. The main duty of a police authority is to secure the maintenance of an effective and efficient police force within its area. The police authorities appoint, retire and can institute proceedings against chief constables but their decisions in this regard are subject to the approval of the Home Secretary. The police authorities are the local paymasters, but they pay less less than half of police expenditure.

The position of chief constables was clarified by the Police Act 1964. The Act places the local police force under his direction and control. No authority can require him to behave in a certain way, but he can be required to assist another force. Appeals against his internal disciplinary decisions lie with Home Secretary. The chief constable must report annually to the Home Secretary and the local police authority.

---

[2] *History of the Bow Street Runners*, C. Armitage, p. 123–4.
[3] [1968] 2 QB 118.

There is a limit to what can be laid down by statute. It depends upon the qualities of those involved. One clear principle emerges from this framework. Government must leave the police to conduct their duties as they think fit.

The procedure of complaints against the police was laid down in PACE. There are three levels of complaint, the informal complaint demanding meeting and apology, complaint of a more serious nature and finally complaint about serious injury or death. The level of investigation for each category is detailed. The Police Complaints Authority becomes more involved with the serious complaints.

Nothing is more odious and dangerous than police being deployed as the batons of Government. For their role is to tread between upholding communal order and private freedom to protest. One gross example of this misuse was the visit of the Chinese President, Jiang Zemin, in 1999. The police were operating an unusual and arguably unlawful policy of hiding public protest from this dictator. They were acting, not on their own motion, but under the active advice of the Foreign Office. Scenes of banners and flags being torn down or confiscated and protesters being hidden behind ranks of police was covered by the thinnest pretence of legality. Park regulations were employed to justify suppression of peaceful protests, which right the police are bound to protect. A local by-law may banish swearing but a man has a right to express himself forcibly when his liberty is being suppressed. An individual who ran into the royal procession was rightly seized but when the noted Chinese dissident, Wei Jinsbeng, who had suffered for eighteen years in a Chinese jail for political offences, attempted to unfurl a flag demanding in Chinese characters the release in China of political prisoners, he was restrained by police, resembling state thugs. When in Cambridge protesters were obscured by police vehicles, Britain hung its head in shame. Bowing to the dictate of one last communist leader in order to allow the British Government to take the credit for signing export contracts, is a clear proof of poor Government. The responsibility for the scenes of ugliness rest with a Prime Minister, who made plain his attempt to control society by giving a false impression of the native distaste of dictators, in order to win commercial contracts. As the contracts become valuable the deception initiated by Blair will become more necessary. Dishonesty always begets more serious dishonesty. The most shaming denunciation of this thuggery was delivered by Wei Jinsbeng, when he deplored the lack of liberty and democracy in Britain. This episode was nothing less than the prelude of a police state. But it was not the fault of the police. Few individuals ever meet or fall foul of Home Secretaries or Chief Constables. For most people, the police mean those on the beat. His or her status *vis à vis* members of society is most important. At common law he is personally liable and can be sued for damages for unlawful acts while in uniform. A constable cannot rely on the defence to a charge of wrongful imprisonment or of trespass by pleading that he was obeying superior orders. Attempts to make the local police authority liable for acts of constables have failed. In *Fisher v Oldham Corporation*[4] it was held that the constable

---

[4][1930] 2 KB 364.

was a servant of the State and as the local authority had no power to control his acts, it could not be held liable. In *Lewis v Cattle*[5] it was held a constable was bound by the Official Secrets Act because he was a person holding office under His Majesty, but as he was neither appointed nor paid by the Crown, vicarious liability for his acts did not bind the Crown. However, the Police Act 1996 made a chief constable liable for the civil wrongs of constables, in the same way masters are held responsible for the acts of their servants. They are now liable for damages arising from acts of constables.

The powers of the constable and the liberty of the individual are governed largely by PACE, which consolidated the many sources of common law. These powers are illustrated in relation to:

i] Police powers short of arrest.
The position at common law was determined in three cases. In *Jackson v Stevenson*[6] it was held to be unlawful if a constable held a suspect in order to establish grounds of arrest. In *Kenlin v Gardiner*[7] it was held that in order to hold someone for questioning that person must first be arrested. In *R v Lemsatel*[8] it was held that police cannot require individuals to accompany them to a police station in order to help them with their enquiries.

Various statutes give police powers to stop and search persons or vehicles for drugs and stolen property or for a traffic offence or road check, provided they have reasonable suspicions. But the grounds of suspicion cannot be based on dress, hairstyle, colour, age nor on previous convictions. PACE governs the procedure of a search. The police must identify themselves and their station, specify the grounds for the search, record the details of the search and use only reasonable force.

ii] The powers of arrest.
The powers of arrest can be exercised by anyone to end a wrongdoer's liberty and the person lawfully arrested can be detained. The power of arrest arise when a person is reasonably suspected of being in the act of an arrestable offence, which include crimes broadly carrying a sentence fixed by law, sexual offences, theft or when an offence has been committed and the person arrested is reasonably suspected of it. If there are reasonable grounds for believing that an offence has been committed, a private person who arrests, even on reasonable suspicion, will face an action for damages, if no offence has actually been committed. But a constable is protected in these circumstances, if he has reasonable grounds for suspicion. A constable can arrest a person whom he suspects is about to commit an offence. Though an unlawful arrest gives a right of action in damages. This common law right confirms that individuals are responsible for the peace of

---

[5] [1938] 2 KB 454.
[6] [1879] 2 Adams 255.
[7] [1967] 2 QB 510.
[8] [1977] 2 All R 835.

society. Arrests by police can be made with or without warrant. At common law the power of arrest by police arises when the peace is breached. The powers were laid down in *R v Howell*.[9] It was held that the person making the arrest must have been present at the breach of the peace; or if the person making the arrest reasonably believed that such a breach would be committed in the immediate future; or if a breach had already been committed and it is reasonable to believe that there was a threat to renew it. The case also established that a breach of the peace amounted to harm to person or property or fear that such harm would be done. In *Wershof v Metropolitan Police Commissioner*[10] a solicitor advised a jeweller not to hand over a ring to a police officer without a receipt. The constable refused to sign a receipt. The solicitor argued with him and was arrested for obstructing a police officer. The solicitor was frog-marched down the road. The solicitor sued for wrongful assault and won damages of £1,000. It was held that arrest for obstruction of duty needed the person arrested to have caused or about to cause a breach of the peace. Arguing was not breaching the peace and the constable should have realised that no breach was threatened.

Most arrests are made by police under warrant. These are issued by magistrates at the initiation of criminal proceedings. Warrants are sought by police on a written application on oath. The magistrate may endorse the warrant for bail. A constable acting in good faith is protected[11] from mistakes by magistrates in issuing a warrant. He or she may enter premises and search them in order to make the arrest and use reasonable force.

The manner of the arrest is also an important element. The person arrested must be told that they are under arrest and the reasons for it given. In *Christie v Leachinsky*[12] a person was arrested wrongly. The police argued that they held information about Leachinsky which would have justified arrest for another offence. The House of Lords rejected this defence. Indeed Lord Simmonds said that: 'it is the corollary of every citizen to thus be free from arrest that he should be entitled to resist arrest unless the arrest is lawful.'[13] It is an important principle that a public body be kept strictly within its precise powers. In another case *Alderson v Booth*[14] a driver, having shown positive for a breathalyser test, was told: 'I shall have to ask you to come to the police station for further tests.' He was acquitted because he had not been arrested before going to the station.

iii] Powers of detention
Up to 1984 the police had no express powers to detain suspects for further questioning. Such powers were granted by PACE. The arrested person must be

---

[9] [1982] QB 416.
[10] [1978] 3 All ER 540.
[11] Constables' Protection Act 170.
[12] [1947] AC 573.
[13] At 591.
[14] [1969] 2 QB 216.

taken as soon as possible to an approved police station, where there must be a custody officer, who will authorise the detention. Between the person detained and the investigating officer is interposed the review officer who must review the detention after six hours and then again every nine hours. PACE lays down that a person can be detained for twenty-four hours without charge or release and in a serious arrestable offence – murder, manslaughter, rape and the like – the period can be extended to thirty-six hours and up to ninety-six hours maximum, before application must be made to a magistrate for further detention. The prisoner can attend and may be legally represented. The duty officer records the details of a search. Samples and fingerprints may be taken. but intimate samples only with consent. But if it is withheld without good cause, a court may be invited to draw an inference. The introduction of DNA testing raises serious questions concerning the balance between personal liberty and the need to police society. Samples from which a DNA profile can be created can be collected from persons charged with a recordable offence. But prints and samples must be destroyed if a person is acquitted.

The remedy for unlawful detention by anyone is by writ of habeas corpus which requires the detention party, be they police, individual or parent. The writ effects the release of the person detained but damages for wrongful detention have to be sought in a separate action. Now that PACE has specified times and manner of detention by police it should be employed less frequently. But Donaldson LJ stressed that it is 'a real and available remedy.'[15]

iv] Rights of suspects

A suspect or an accused has the right of silence. The police have to produce evidence sufficient to overcome the presumption of innocence.[16] Although a failure to give evidence without good cause entitles a jury to draw 'such inference as appears proper.' There is no obligation to give evidence. There is no obligation to answer police questions, but failure to answers questions about incriminating objects on the clothing or body or about presence at or about the time of the offence may permit an inference to be drawn. Statements have to be taken in accordance with requirements of the Judges Rules 1964. They provide that as soon as an officer has reasonable grounds for suspecting a suspect has committed an offence the suspect should be cautioned and reminded of the right to remain silent and of the fact that any answers may be used in court.. Again the caution should be repeated when the charge is made.

A suspect has the right to to consult privately with a solicitor at any stage of an investigation, providing that no unreasonable hindrance is caused to a investigation. A suspect is entitled to have a solicitor throughout his interrogation by police. Police interviews have to tape-recorded.

---

[15] *R v Holmes ex p Sherman* [1981] 2 All Er 612.
[16] Except failure to provide samples may invite a negative assumption to be taken.

A suspect cannot be held *incommunicado* but has the right to ask the fact of arrest to be communicated to a friend or relative as soon as practicable. Exceptions exist in cases where commination would cause danger to evidence or witnesses.

A suspect held for twenty-four hours is entitled to continuous rest for an eight hour period.

v] Powers of entry and search

The rule of *Entick v Carrington*[17] was strict: 'No man can set foot upon my ground without my licence, but he is liable to an action though the damage be nothing.' However, an implied licence allows any person on legitimate business to walk up to the front door and request entrance and to leave in a reasonable time.[18] Under PACE a police officer may enter to execute a search warrant, arrest a person for an arrestable offence or certain public order offences or to recapture a person unlawfully at large.

Searches by warrant were governed until the 1980s by about fifty statutes. The powers used by the Inland Revenue were described in *R v IRC ex p Rossminster* by Lord Scarman as 'a breathtaking inroad on the individual's right of privacy and right of property.'[19] Indeed the Revenue investigating a tax fraud vacuumed every conceivable piece of paper from homes and offices. Arming tax gathering bodies with excessive powers is undemocratic.

PACE set down conditions for searching under a general warrant which is obtainable from a magistrate. A constable has to prove that there are reasonable grounds for believing a serious arrestable offence has taken place and that material likely to be of substantial value in police investigations may be on certain premises. Privileged evidence, such as letters between suspect and lawyer cannot be searched or seized, or fluids taken as medical samples, or confidential journalistic material. A circuit judge may give orders allowing the search of such material. This power was reviewed in *R v Maidstone Crown Court, ex p Waitt* when it was observed that the special procedure: 'is a serious inroad upon the liberty of the subject . . . The responsibility for ensuring this procedure lies with circuit judges.'[20] The actual manner of the search is covered in detail under the provisions of PACE.

A search without warrant is allowed in three circumstances. Following an arrest a suspect can be searched if there are reasonable grounds for believing the person has anything dangerous or anything with which he may escape custody. Possession can be taken of any article which might be used as evidence. After the person under arrest is taken to a police station there may be strip and intimate searches. Second, premises ancillary to an arrest can be searched without warrant. The premises must either the premises in which the person was at or before arrest.

---

[17] (1765) 19 St Tr 1030.
[18] *Robson v Hallet* [1967] 2 QB 939.
[19] [1980] AC 952, 1022.
[20] [1988] Crim LR 384.

The right of search exists only at the time of arrest. Third, the home of a person can be searched. However, in *Jeffrey v Black*[21] the police arrested a person for stealing a sandwich in a public house and demanded to search the person's home. They were let in reluctantly and they discovered cannabis and the person charged. The court held that the search was unlawful, but a search for sandwiches might have been allowed. PACE allows a search of premises occupied and controlled by a person arrested for an arrestable offence if there is reasonable grounds for believing there is evidence there.

If a person is searched there is right to retain anything reasonably suspected of any offence. Whether a search is by warrant or not, there is no general right to seize. Either what may be seized is specified in the warrant or is evidence reasonably believed relating to the arrestable offence. The principles governing the power of the police to seize private property were laid down by the Court of Appeal in *Ghani v Jones*.[22] The police must believe that a serious crime has been committed, that articles seized are the instruments of or evidence of the crime, that the possessor of the article is implicated in the crime or that his refusal to hand over is unreasonable, that seizure is only for such time as is reasonable and the question of their lawfulness of seizure must be judged at the time. There is no right to seize communications with lawyers, for those communications deal with matters of legal defence.

This brief account of the power and duties of the police is intended to show that they are restricted in their powers to walking a tight line between upholding individual freedom while apprehending those who abuse the freedom of others. It is also intended to show that the common law of Britain ensures that individual liberty is unlimited, while the power of the State is limited to precise bounds.

The police may be a a professional and highly-trained body, but they will reflect the quality of the society from which they are drawn It will emerge in the third part of this book that society is bedeviled by poverty and injustice, which condition makes policing much more difficult. It is self-evident that these conditions have been the cause of crime for centuries in Britain. Poverty breeds frustration and unemployment intensifies the condition. Crime feeds on itself. Police are required to handle a problem whose causes Parliament have not attempted to eradicate in the last six centuries. The problem of drugs, similar to alcoholic addiction, cannot be solved by police even when assisted by a curious figure called a Tsar unless the underlying causes of the problem are eradicated by Parliament. The role of the police is determined to a great extent by the framework of a just society, which can be set only by Parliament. Since its origin Parliament has allowed injustice to prevail and policing a society riven by injustice is a rough and tough business, because it involves the police being employed a role for which they are not suited.

---

[21] [1978] QB 490.
[22] [1970] 1 QB 693.

5

Right to a Fair Trial

The Establishment of the Judiciary

Locke considered the formation of society to be marked by the point when the individual put punishment of a wrongdoer out of personal power and relied on the determination of a judge.

In Britain the monarch is described as the fount or source of justice. What is now done in the name of the monarch by the judges was done at times down to the twelfth century by the monarch sitting as judge in his own court. About the end of that century kings gave up their judicial role, in order to administer affairs of State and to defend or promote interests interests on the field of battle. The hearing of petitions was delegated to justices.

The justices began to extend their jurisdiction into areas of local and ecclesiastical law. They developed law by reason and argument, so that it acquired a structure and an objective texture. They began to see themselves as the servants of justice rather than the appointees of monarchs; they acknowledged that in the exercise of their power they became accountable only to God and their conscience. Possessed of these powers and being thus answerable for their use, it is not difficult to understand how reasoned judgments prevailed over *ad hoc* decisions, how succeeding justices adhered to precedents and also how the corpus of the common law was fashioned.

In the Middle Ages the courts were divided between the Court of Common Pleas, hearing suits between individuals, the Court of Exchequer, cases concerning the king's revenue and the King's Bench, hearing pleas of the Crown and criminal offences. Over the last three centuries the administration of justice has come to be transacted by courts of common law, eventually named King's or Queen's Bench and the Courts of Chancery, which allow the doctrine of equity to ease, it was said, the harshness of common law. The difference at present is one of classification of cases, but the general doctrines of common law and of equity are available in both courts.

The justices claimed, consciously or unconsciously, exclusive powers in law and independence in their exercise. Inevitably, the nature and the needs of their office required clarification of their relationship with the Crown. Clarification could only mean independence, but, from the viewpoint of medieval government, independent judges were as potentially subversive and quite as dangerous as independent ideas and independent religions. In 1328 the Statute of Northampton enacted that royal commands should not disturb common justice and justices could not be commanded to do other than right in any point. The constitutional relationship between the Crown and the justices fell to be settled finally, along with much else, during the upheavals of the seventeenth century.

James VI & I, given to theological study and political argument, claimed to be God's appointed monarch, subject only to His will and judgment. Such a claim was essentially the same argument as that employed by tyrants to justify the possession of absolute power together with an absolute discretion over its use. In 1605 James supported Archbishop Bancroft by hearing his complaint that the common law courts were interfering with ecclesiastical tribunals. He summoned the judges to remind them that they were merely his delegates and that, therefore, it belonged to him to decide which court had jurisdiction in any matter. But the common law had developed beyond the point when that argument might have commanded respect. Coke, at that time one of the judges, observed that:

> True it was, that God had endowed His Majesty with excellent science and great endowments of nature; but His Majesty was not learned in the laws of his realm of England, and causes which concern the life, or inheritance, or goods or fortunes of his subjects, are not to be decided by natural reason, but by the artificial reason and judgment of the law, which law is an act which requires long study and experience before a man can attain to cognisance of it: that the law was the golden met-wand and measure to try the causes of the subjects; and which protected His Majesty in safety and peace.[1]

Coke and Francis Bacon, one of the celebrated thinkers of the Rennaisance, had been rivals since the close of the previous reign. In 1595 Bacon had failed to become Attorney-General and prevent Coke obtaining the appointment and, because of the animosity of Elizabeth, he also failed to become Solicitor-General. He lost no time, therefore, in making himself privy to the affairs of King James.

The king regarded the suggestion that he was under the law as nothing less than treason. Coke recalled the opinion of Bracton, one of the earliest authorities on common law, that the king should be answerable only to God and the law. In 1611 the Court of Common Pleas held in the *Case of Proclamations*[2] that royal proclamations could not create new offences. James examined the judges seriatim; some gave way but Coke refused to yield.

---

[1] *In Prohibitions del Roy*, (1607) 12 Co Rep; 65.
[2] (1611) 12 Co Rep 74.

In 1613 on the advice of Bacon, James made Coke Chief Justice of the King's Bench. Bacon told the king:

> My lord Coke will think himself near a privy councillor's place and thereupon turn obsequious . . . Besides the removal of my lord Coke to a place of less profit . . . will be thought abroad a kind of discipline to him for opposing himself in the king's causes, the example whereof will contain others in more awe.[3]

Coke left the Court of Common Pleas reluctantly and in tears. It was thought he would be able to do less mischief in the King's Bench. In 1616 Coke was hearing a case against Edmund Peacham involving the grant of benefices by the king to the Bishop of Lincoln and it was contended that the king had no power to make the grants. Peacham was tortured and then charged with treason. Bacon, then Attorney-General, sought the opinion of the judges of King's Bench. Coke refused to advise. Later matters came to a head in the *Case of Commendams*, involving the living granted by the king of the Bishop of Coventry and Litchfield. James, through Bacon, ordered the trial to be halted until he had spoken to the judges. But the trial continued and Coke declared that he was bound by his oath to disregard the order. The other eleven judges agreed that the king had power to halt a trial but Coke refused to assent to such a proposition. Other controversies, public and within his family, began to engulf Coke. He was summoned before the Privy Council. His answers did not satisfy the king and he was dismissed. At that time an anonymous letter written, it has been supposed,[4] by Bacon painted an observant account of his defects of character in the exercise of his public role. Unsurprisingly three months later Bacon was appointed Lord Keeper and in the next year Lord Chancellor.

Though the point was not conceded by James, the common law had overtaken the royal prerogative and overturned the dependence of the courts on their royal foundation. The struggle was to continue but it had taken the boldness of James and the courage of Coke to bring the extent of royal prerogative into the realm of public debate.

A less open method of retaining a measure of royal control over the administration of justice was through the establishment of special courts presided over by crown servants. The most celebrated of these royal creations were the Court of Star Chamber and the Court of High Commission, created by Henry VII in 1487. In theory the former was said to complement the common law in criminal, as the court of Chancery did in civil law and the latter ecclesiastical law. It was staffed by members of the King's Council to try crimes such as riots, perjury, misconduct of sheriffs and bribery of jurors. Its jurisdiction, though defined in the statute, expanded to take cognisance of other crimes, but it was limited by its incapacity to inflict capital punishment. The

---

[3] *Life of Bacon*, Spedding, vol VI, p. 381.
[4] Ibid, vol VI. p.121.

accused could be examined on oath and was encouraged to incriminate himself by torture, if necessary. Yet until the reign of Charles I the court was respected. Thereafter, it became more tyrannical and later a wicked instrument of the king – more a means of enforcing policy, rather than of operating a court of law. In 1641 Charles was forced to assent to the abolition of the court. Its foundation had been obscure. It was said to derive from from the king's original authority. Its abolition closed an attempt by the crown to establish its jurisdiction against the progress of the common law.

During the reigns of Charles II and James VII & II the Bench underwent one of its darkest periods. This was caused by the manipulation of the judiciary by the Crown, in promoting a dreadful trio of judges: Sir William Scroggs, Baron George Jeffreys and Sir Robert Wright.

Scroggs, who started as a butcher's son, came to notice in 1678 when as a judge of the King's Bench he was summoned to assist the House of Commons in the trial arising from the popish plot. Titus Oates, a clergyman, was telling untruths about about the plot. Acting as prosecutor, more often than a judge, Scroggs, displayed great cruelty and partiality and convicted many people informed on by Oates. The judicial murders resulting from that trial have been described as worse than the massacre of St. Bartholomew in France.[5] After intervening with questions to intimidate Staply, a Catholic banker, Scroggs summed up in a violent manner which left him out of breath. After the accused had been interred, Scroggs ordered the body to be taken from the grave, because a mass had been said for his soul. In accordance with his order the body was exhibited upon the gates of the City of London. What was clear from his unflagging efforts is that he hated papists as if they were either deranged or vermin. Despite being 'a great voluptuary, his debaucheries egregious, and his life loose',[6] Scroggs became Chief Justice in 1678. His reputation in judicial history is unambiguous. '. . . in his abominable[e] cruelties he was the sordid tool of others, and in subsequent career he had not the feeble excuse of gratifying his own passions or advancing his own interest.'[7] In 1680 he was impeached on eight counts by the House of Commons. In the following year the matter was carried to the House of Lords for treason, high crimes and misdemeanors, but when the House dissolved he escaped conviction. He was dismissed three months later, amid much rejoicing.

Jeffreys was also involved in the prosecution of the popish plot, both before Scroggs and as a recorder at the Old Bailey. Several criticisms were made of his conduct in court. In the House of Commons Henry Booth said that 'he behaved more like a jack-pudding than with the gravity that beseems a judge'.[8] The Commons resolved in 1680 that, 'by traducing and obstructing Petitioning this Parliament he hath betrayed the rights of the subject' and should be removed from every public office. Charles II

---

[5] *The Lives of the Chief Justices of England*, J. Campbell, vol II, p. 256.
[6] Ibid p. 252.
[7] Ibid p. 235.
[8] *Debates*, Chandler, vol II, p. 163.

commented that he had 'no learning, no sense, no manners and more impudence than ten carted street-walkers', but did not demur to his appointment in 1683 as Lord Chief Justice of England.[9] Next year he condemned Sir Thomas Armstrong to death for treason. When the prisoner claimed his statutory right to a trial, Jeffreys replied that he would have the benefit of the law. 'That you shall have by the grace of God. See that execution be done on Friday next, according to law. You shall have the full benefit of the law.' Two years later Jeffreys was put in the House of Lords by James VII & II – the first Lord Chief Justice for four centuries. Two days after the Battle of Sedgemoor in 1685 Jeffreys was appointed to head a commission of four other judges to travel to the West country to try the followers of the Duke of Monmouth. They 'set out on that circuit', wrote Macaulay, 'the memory of which will last as long as our race and language.'[10] In trials at Winchester, Salisbury, Dorchester, Taunton, Exeter and Wells a number, estimated at two hundred, were executed for high treason. In addition, more than eight hundred were given to court favourites to be sold as slaves to the owners of American plantations and many others were whipped and imprisoned. To plead 'Not Guilty' was to risk life in a court hung with scarlet. Jeffreys boasted that he had hanged more traitors than his predecessors since the Conquest. The fine, imposed on Edmund Prideaux of £14,500 as the price for his life, enabled Jefferys to buy an estate. The king made him Lord Chancellor. After the flight of James VII & II in 1688 Jeffreys fled to Wapping, East London, hoping for a boat to France. But he was recognised by a scrivener, or copyist, who had once retreated from Jeffreys's court muttering in terror, 'as long as I live I shall never forget that terrible countenance.' Jeffreys was seized and accompanied to the Tower by a crowd, who would gladly have ended his existence without further formalities. Jeffreys was visited by John Tutchin, whom he had sentenced, though still a boy, at Dorchester to be flogged every fortnight for seven years. Jeffreys stated, 'I was bound in conscience to do so'. 'Where', asked Tutchin, 'was your conscience when you sentenced me?' 'It was set down in my orders to show no mercy to men like you', replied the former Lord Chancellor. James VII & II himself pleaded that the violence of the 'Bloody Assizes' was due to Jeffreys, who died in 1693 at the age of forty-one and was buried next to the grave of Monmouth in the chapel at the Tower.

The last of the trio was Wright, who was was appointed a Baron of Exchequer in 1684, after he had acquired a reputation as a poor lawyer, dissipated an estate, fraudulently re-mortgaged and was suspected in 1678 of implication in the popish plot. However, Chief Justice Jeffreys was greatly impressed with his ability as a mimic. Francis North, Lord Keeper of the Great Seal, objected. But the recommendation of the Chief Justice carried sufficient weight with Charles II. Wright, despite such misgivings, was promoted as Chief Justice of the Common Pleas within three years.

[9] *Correspondence*, Clarendon, vol 1, pp. 82–3.
[10] *The Life and Works of Macaulay*, Edinburgh edn, (1896), vol 1, p. 496.

After only five days in that position, James VII & II appointed him Chief Justice of the King's Bench, in order to obtain a judge who would instill martial law by hanging deserters without compunction. He gave further proof of his attachment to the king and to his judicial zeal. He fined the Duke of Devonshire, an opponent of the royal court, the sum of £30,000 for striking Col. Thomas Colepeper with a cane on the ear in the royal presence, after his victim had insulted him and declined to face him outside. The fine was underwritten by imprisonment until paid. The duke escaped from prison and when the sheriff of Derby arrived at Chatsworth to recapture him, he and his force were seized by the duke. The fine was then paid. The duke avenged himself later by caning Colepeper more thoroughly. In 1687 Wright was appointed an ecclesiastical commissioner to effect the expulsion of all but three of the Fellows of Magdalen College, Oxford, for resisting royal authority. In 1688 he presided over the trial of the *Seven Bishops*, in which he declared their petition to the king a libel. They were asking relief from the duty of reading a declaration in their churches that the king suspended Acts of Parliament on ecclesiastical matters. The king attempted to pack the jury. One, Michael Arnold, the king's brewer, observed, 'Whatever I do, I am sure to be half ruined. If I say Not Guilty, I shall not brew for the King; and if I say Guilty, I shall brew no more for anyone else.' Wright was overawed by the national and local sentiment which protested at their imprisonment before trial and dogged the actual proceedings, which were punctuated by abuse and hisses. He had no course but to conduct the trial impartially. The jury were divided between eleven who wanted to acquit and the obstinate brewer, who held out for a contrary verdict until six in the morning. The bishops were acquitted of the charge of seditious libel amid shouts of joy which reverberated in the streets, on the Thames and from church bells. After the flight of James five months later, Wright went into hiding. He was found in Old Bailey, London, and committed to prison for subversion for having suspended laws. The House of Lords held that his fining of the Duke of Devonshire was a breach of the privileges of Parliament. Wright evaded further vituperation by perishing from fever while in prison. He stands out in judicial history as a colourful figure among a body otherwise conspicuous for gravity and worthiness. Wright was merely an airy mimic and a pawn of a wicked king.

The important questions concerning the tenure of judges were settled finally after the Revolution of 1688. Judges had previously held their office during the pleasure of the Crown. It was the most insecure basis that could be imagined and it afforded the sovereign control of weaker men than Coke.

William III commissioned the judges during their *good behaviour*. The Act of Settlement (1701) determined that basis henceforward, but made it subject to an Address in both Houses of Parliament to vote for the dismissal of a judge. It also fixed the remuneration of judges as a charge on the Consolidated Fund, which had the effect of making it a prior charge upon the revenue, without the need of an annual vote by Parliament.

It is not clear today, however, what *good behaviour* means in relation to superior judges. Circuit judges and stipendiary magistrates can be dismissed by the Lord Chancellor for *inability or misbehaviour*. Lay magistrates hold their office at the pleasure of the Lord Chancellor, and, as he is not required to show cause for a dismissal, they hold office by the thinnest thread, but in practice the Lord Chancellor is slow to dismiss a magistrate.

It might be supposed that *good behaviour* in a senior judge means the constant display of virtues, which common opinion attaches to their office: impartiality, even-temper, courtesy, patience, sobriety and the like. But the opinion of constitutional experts is that it implies much less: no more than behaviour which falls short of criminality. Thus it appears that judges of the High Court can be dismissed only after a criminal conviction or after an address in both Houses of Parliament. A less cumbersome procedure is the tap on the shoulder from the Lord Chancellor. It was employed to effect the retirement of Lord Atkinson in 1928. The Lord Chancellor called him to explain that 'the scurrilous press of Quebec had abused the the Privy Council and said that the members were all fogies, that I was the oldest of the old fogies and had better resign.' It was known to have been used to bring to end Justice Hallett, who was known during the 1950s for interrupting trials continuously. On appeal in 1957 it was complained that the judge prevented counsel cross-examining. The judge's name appeared 544 times in the transcript of evidence. A rare power of dismissal available to the Lord Chancellor was placed on a more formal basis in 1981. Section 11 of the Supreme Court Act allows him to declare that a judge's office has been vacated when he is satisfied by a medical certificate that a judge is permanently infirm and temporarily unfit to resign. The Chancellor needs a corroborating opinion from one senior judge. This rare occasion arose in 1970 when a judge in the Court of Appeal was for over a year too ill to tender his resignation .

In a democracy the judge occupies an anomalous position: vested, as a public servant, with powers for whose exercise he is not administratively accountable. He may be professionally incompetent, he may indulge partiality, testiness, impatience and yet continue in an office, for which such failings render him quite unsuited in the eyes of any reasonable man or woman and even a child, who expects a judge to behave as impeccably as Father Christmas. Barristers, hoping for judicial office themselves, are either too timid to complain about poor behaviour or too ambitious. So a judge who misbehaves continues in office and the Lord Chancellor continues to have faith in him, though it is plain to practitioners in his court that he ought to be dismissed. In 1997 Harman J, a Chancery judge, resigned after being criticised by the Court of Appeal for faults in his conduct. These had been talked by barristers even before his appointment in 1982.

In seeking to secure judicial independence, the Act of Settlement[11] has secured that judges be irremovable. For though Parliament – by an address in both Houses – retains

---

[11] As amended by the Supreme Court Act 1981.

John Locke

Turgot

Edward VIII

A. V. Dicey

Francis Bacon

Thomas Macaulay

William Scroggs

George Jeffreys

the power of dismissal, it has made such sparing use of it, that, for practical purposes, it does not exist. During the nineteenth century there were few attempts in Parliament to remove judges but only one was successful; that involved an Irish judge, Sir Jonah Barrington, who had misappropriated litigants' money and abandoned his duties for a period of several years. In 1906 Members of Parliament, numbering 347, signed a motion against Mr Justice Grantham, who was an outspoken Tory. More recently a motion was put down in Parliament to dismiss Sir John Donaldson as head of the controversial Industrial Court and signed by 187 Labour Members. He had seques-trated, or impounded, the political fund of a leading Trade Union. This was really a protest at the political creation of the court and was not debated.

In *Fox's Case* Lord Grenville had warned:

A judge may be in a situation of notorious incapacity from age, and yet, it may happen through peevishness natural to age, or ill humour, or some other cause, that he may wish to adhere to his situation after he has been rendered unfit for his duties. That this may be a painful necessity for the interference of Parliament none would doubt.[12]

However, it was not until 1959 that Parliament steeled itself to act against the dangers of judicial senility, by obliging judges to retire at the age of seventy-five, which was later reduced to seventy. The example of Lord Denning, who continued as Master of the Rolls in the Court of Appeal well into his eighties, suggests that judicial ability depends more upon the strength and character of the individual judge, than upon arithmetic.

In 1973 the Amalgamated Engineering Union was fined £100,000 for being in contempt of court and 180 Labour Members signed a motion for the dismissal of the judge. But their front bench colleagues did not support the motion and it was not debated. In the previous year the Court of Appeal had held that a trade union was not responsible for the actions of its shop stewards and in effect threatened the Government's Industrial Relations measures. Ministers were profoundly shocked by the decision. Lord Denning recalled that:

[I]n Government circles the downfall of the Act was attributed to the Court of Appeal . . . Sometime afterwards I was told by one in a high place: 'Your decision was a disaster for the country which will last until the end of the century'. I was shaken to the core, [he continued.] But I was not downcast. I just thought: Thank goodness, the judges of the Court of Appeal are independent.[13]

The same thought was expressed in Parliament by Churchill.[14]

---

[12] (1805) 7 Parl Deb 751.
[13] *Closing Chapter*, Lord Denning, p. 177.
[14] House of Commons, 23 March 1954.

The independence of the judiciary has been regarded as a tradition. But legislation since 1971 and the growth in the Lord Chancellor's Department have adversely affected the independence of the Bar and the powers of the judiciary. The resulting position has been rightly called 'a constitutional mess'.

Sometimes judges are pitched into the political arena by contentious legislation, which requires them to make decisions of a political nature. A Bill of Rights would seek to set up a constitutional court which would have the task of deciding on the legality of legislation by comparing it with a tabulation of vague and general rights, which are capable of as many interpretations as they are lawyers to fabricate them. Such a proposal would bring the constitutional court into conflict with Parliament.

The Industrial Relations legislation of the 1970s brought judicial pronouncements from the ordered quietude of law courts into the glaring headlines of the media. The Industrial Relations Court gaoled three dockers for contempt of a court order, imposed under the Industrial Relations Act, which forbad them obstructing the entry of lorries into a container depot in London. The dockers in the major ports came out on strike immediately. An appeal was launched on behalf of the three dockers by the Official Solicitor, who shot from anonymity to fame and back again within a few hours, and the Court of Appeal released them from gaol. The dockers were determined to ignore the orders of the Industrial Relations Court and within weeks a further five dockers were committed for their defiance of court orders. The House of Lords gave judgment the following day in another case and held that fines rather than imprisonment were the appropriate penalty. The Industrial Relations legislation sought to regulate a contentious issue, on which there was little political agreement. Lord Devlin concluded:

> The prestige of the judiciary and their reputation for stark impartiality . . . is not at the disposal of a Government: it is an asset that belongs to the whole nation.[15]

One of the most depressing reflections on law throughout the globe is that so often it is administered by corrupt persons. Before turning to the virtual absence of judicial corruption in Britain since the seventeenth century, however, the observation of Dr Johnson should be heeded: 'A judge may be corrupt, but there may be no evidence to prove it.'[16] Evidence has come to light of only three cases of judicial corruption, involving senior members of the judiciary, in almost four centuries.

The first involved Francis Bacon. It was as frustrating in his time to wait several years for a case to come on for trial, as it still is. Bribery provided a shortcut. Bacon had been receiving gifts from litigants, who believed they were buying justice. The case of one briber, Aubrey, still remained in the lists, waiting to be heard, and he

---

[15] *Sunday Times*, August 1972.
[16] *The English Judge*, H Cecil, p. 49.

complained to Bacon. In his reply Bacon scolded him. Eventually the case was heard and, in accordance with law and the evidence, Bacon found against Aubrey. Imagining that he had already purchased the decision, Aubrey demanded it to be reversed and entered for him. Bacon agreed but failed to keep his word. In 1617 Bacon was created Baron Verulam and appointed Lord Chancellor. In the spring of 1621 Aubrey, aggrieved by the futility of his investment made his allegation at the bar of the House of Lords. A similar case immediately came to light in which Edward Egerton was suing his brother. He had presented the Lord Chancellor with a basin and ewer valued at £50 and then £400 in gold sovereigns. At first Bacon recoiled from such generous gifts but his love of wealth and luxury soon allowed him to accept it. Nevertheless he awarded the case to Egerton's brother. Other cases came to light but no one suggested that Bacon had decided them in accordance with the bribes. He was investigated and tried by a select committee of the House of Lords on twenty-eight charges of corruption involving £11,000 . He was fined £40,000 and imprisoned in the Tower of London and barred from public office. In character he wrote that his fall would purify the courts of corruption.[17] The king remitted the fine and ordered him to be released after four days. In his remaining six years of life he completed literary works. In 1625 he published the final version of *The Essays*, which included a piece on the judiciary. He wrote of judges:

> Above all things, their integrity is their portion and proper virtue. Cursed (saith the law) is he that moved the landmark. The mislayer of a mere stone is to blame. But it is the unjust judge that is the capital remover of landmarks, when he defineth amiss of lands and property.[18]

His contribution to culture was of transcendent quality, although he was modest of his role in directing minds away from religion towards science.

The second Lord Chancellor found guilty of corruption was Lord Macclesfield at the beginning of the eighteenth century. Despite legislation forbidding the sale of judicial offices, he had sold positions in the Chancery Division. The sales came to light after the collapse of the South Sea Bubble stock. He was impeached, fined £30,000 by the House of Lords, and imprisoned for six weeks until the fine was paid.

In 1865 Lord Chancellor Lord Westbury resigned after being censured by the House of Commons for having been lax and inattentive in regard to the granting of a pension to a clerk to the patents who had appropriated public money, and to appointments in the Leeds Bankcrutpcy Court, including his son. His offence was to have misled Parliament.

There are many factors which have preserved judges at the highest level from corruption. In part it is due to the professional training of judges, in part to their virtue

---

[17] *Letters and Life*, F. Bacon, vol VII, p. 242.
[18] *The Essays*, F. Bacon, Penguin edn 1985, p. 222.

and character and in part to the British people's respect for the law. But the most positive factors, perhaps, lie in the instinctive understanding of justice in Britain and the general expectation that judges will conduct themselves to the standard that justice demands.

The evident fact that politics is disingenuous and dishonest is not to degrade Parliament or its Members; rather it is to say that the people's political lethargy has allowed this to be so. Yet the British people have a stricter sense of civil liberty than of economic liberty which engages much concern of Parliament. Hence their keen understanding is focused more upon judges than upon politicians. So it is as Algernon Sidney, an eighteenth-century politician, wrote: 'The strength of the Nation is not in the Magistrate, but the strength of the Magistrate is in the Nation.'[19]

Judges are held immune for liability in respect of their judicial acts. Not only would liability undermine their fearless pursuit of duty, but proceedings would necessarily involve a re-trial. There would be no end to litigation. The immunity is accorded not as a privilege, but on grounds of public policy. They must be free to do their job without fear of personal consequences. Most complaints against judicial acts are covered on appeal against their conduct during trial. But two cases have been brought to test the position when a judge was alleged to have acted in the first mala fide and in the second mistakenly. In *Anderson v Gorrie*[20] it was alleged that the judge, while imprisoning the plaintiff for contempt of court, had set harsh and excessive bail in order to prevent his release. The Court of Appeal held that no action would lie against a judge acting within his jurisdiction, even though he was acting maliciously and contrary to good faith, for without immunity a judge would forfeit his freedom and independence to act judicially. The case of *Sirros v Moore*[21] was an action brought against a judge who committed the plaintiff to prison by mistake. The plaintiff was an immigrant, who had been recommended for deportation by a magistrates' court. He was allowed, however, to be freed from custody pending his deportation. He appealed, but the court confirmed the order. The judge saw him leaving the court and ordered a policeman to detain him. He was held over lunch in the cells and the judge later refused him bail. He was released from prison on a writ of habeas corpus the next day. He sued for false imprisonment. The Court of Appeal held that the judge had made a mistake and was acting within his jurisdiction and could not be sued for the reasons given in the earlier case above.

One of the most severe powers available to a judge is to punish a contempt of court summarily, that is on the spot, without an indictment, without a jury and, before 1950, without right of appeal. The power to do so is afforded to enable a judge to maintain the authority of the court and is like the original power of a schoolteacher to administer an immediate punishment on occasions of extreme contempt. The power

---

[19] *Discourses Concerning Government*, A. Sidney, pp. 437–8.
[20] (1895) 1QB 668.
[21] [1975] QB 118.

arises under common law when contempt is committed by scandalising the court, by open contempt in court, by disobedience of court orders, by interfering with jurors, witnesses or litigants.

The offence of scandalising the court was introduced in the case of *R v Almon*.[22] The accused sold books in Piccadilly and stocked one which attacked Lord Mansfield for his pursuit of Wilkes; it alleged that the Lord Chief Justice had conducted himself 'officiously, arbitrarily and illegally'. The case of scandalising the court was brought against Almon but the charge had been made out in the name of Wilkes by mistake. The judge asked counsel for Almon 'as a gentleman' to allow the mistake to be rectified but he refused to comply 'as a man of honour'. The Government fell and the case was not brought. The judge, however, had already written his judgment in which he stated that, 'A greater scandal could not be published.' He claimed the power to punish the scandal originated under common law, the great repository of legal actions, from time immemorial. The power, no sooner discovered, fell into disuse and in 1899 the Board of the Privy Council concluded:

> Committals for contempt of Court by scandalising the Court have become obsolete in this century. Courts are contented to leave to public opinion attacks derogatory or scandalous to them.[23]

However, in the following year the editor of a Birmingham paper was charged with contempt for writing about a judge:

> If anyone can imagine Little Tich upholding his dignity on a point of honour in a public house, he has a very fair conception of what Mr Justice Darling looks like warning the Press against the printing of indecent evidence. No newspaper can exist except upon its merit, a condition from which the Bench, happily for Mr Justice Darling, is exempt. There is no journalist in Birmingham who has anything to learn from the impudent little man in horsehair, a microcosm of conceit and empty headedness ... One is almost sorry that the Lord Chancellor had not another relative to provide for on the day he selected a new judge from the larrikins of the law.

The eloquent journalist admitted that his article was 'intemperate, ungentlemanly and void of the respect due to His Lordship's person and office'. He was fined £100. In 1928 the *New Statesman* complained that Marie Stopes, the protagonist of birth control, was unlikely to enjoy a fair hearing before Avory LJ, a Roman Catholic, and it complained that 'there are so many Avories'. By a skillful and humble apology the editor was required only to pay the costs. In 1930 the *Daily Worker* complained of the

---

[22] (1766) 87 ER 94.
[23] *Macleod v St Aubyn* [1899] AC 549 at 556.

severity of a sentence of nine months imposed on Comrade Thomas for a trivial offence. The editor called the judge, a former Tory Member of Parliament, a bewigged puppet chosen to put communists away after the general strike in 1926. The editor and publisher were jailed for 'a gross and outrageous contempt'. A few years later Lord Atkin propounded[24] a more liberal approach when he said:

> provided that members of the public abstain from imputing improper motives to those taking part in the administration and are genuinely exercising a right of criticism, and not acting in malice or attempting to impair the administration of justice, they are immune. Justice is not a cloistered virtue; she must be allowed to suffer the scrutiny and respectful, though outspoken, comment of the ordinary man.

There have been no successful prosecutions for scandalising the court since. Though a former Lord Chancellor was prosecuted privately in 1968 for an article in *Punch* in which he had claimed that the legislation on gaming had been wrecked by 'unrealistic, contradictory and, in a leading case, erroneous decisions in the courts including the Court of Appeal . . .' Lord Denning, disagreeing with several predecessors, who judged mere criticism of the Bench a contempt, said:

> we will never use this jurisdiction as a means to uphold our own dignity, that must rest on sure foundations. Nor will we try to suppress those who speak against us. We do not fear criticism, nor resent it. For there is something far more important at stake. It is no less than the freedom of speech itself.[25]

The court ruled that the attack did not constitute a contempt. Salmon LJ held that, '. . . no criticism of a judgment, however vigorous, can amount to a contempt of court, providing it keeps within the bounds of reasonable courtesy and good faith.'[26] In the following year Salmond chaired the Committee on The Law of Contempt, which reported that 'the right to criticise judges . . . may become one of the safeguards . . . to ensure their high standard'. Judicial thinking seems to have returned, after a renaissance in the offence of scandalising the court during more authoritarian days, to the position it in which it found itself in 1899.

In 1985 Lord Devlin wrote a book about the trial in 1957 of Dr Bodkin Adams. A leading feature of the book was his attack on the Attorney-General, Manningham Buller, who had died five years previously. Devlin attacked him personally, professionally and for his want of judicial competence and drew condemnation on all sides.

The second variety of contempt is contempt in the face of the court. For example in 1631 a felon threw a brick at the judge during the assizes at Salisbury. His offending

---

[24] *Ambard v A-G for Trinidad* [1936] AC 332, 335.
[25] *Times* 16/7/32.
[26] *R v Coms of Police* [1968], 150, 155–6.

hand was severed from the arm and he was hanged from a gallows erected in court. If the contempt occurs before the eyes of the judge, the truth of the offence is manifest and no trial is needed. Three years later a more fortunate felon threw a stone at a judge in Chester. His hand was severed in court but his life was spared. The hand was attached above the entrance to the castle for a few years where it served as a warning against contempt. A similar case arose recently, when the Court of Appeal refused relief to a persistent litigant, who represented herself. She hurled a law book, generally more substantial than a brick or a stone, at the Bench. It missed. Lord Denning and his fellow judges chose to ignore the incident.

A third contempt is the disobedience of court orders or of undertakings given in court. The court can punish such contempt by fines, sequestration of property or imprisonment. Once imprisoned an offender is required to purge the contempt by unconditional apology to the court and by agreeing to abide by the court's orders in the future. Some refuse to purge their contempt and their release has to be obtained by the magic of the Official Solicitor. Such examples of contempts occur regularly and are not worth examining. But one refusal to obey a judge was interesting and unusual. A tribunal was set up in 1963 under Lord Radcliffe to investigate how a spy, W. Vassal, had penetrated the Admiralty. The tribunal summoned two journalists, Mulholland and Foster, to explain the source of their allegations that Vassal had avoided top security checks through the intervention of a senior official in the Admiralty. Lord Radcliffe asked them for their source, for it was clearly a most important matter, and they refused to provide it. They were imprisoned for contempt for six months. They appealed, claiming privilege of the Press to withhold their sources. The appeal was dismissed and Lord Denning said:

> A judge is the person entrusted, on behalf of the community, to weigh the conflicting interests – to weigh on the one hand the respect due to confidence in the profession and on the other hand the ultimate interest of the community in justice being done or, in the case of a tribunal such as this, in a proper investigation being made into these serious allegations. If the judge determines that the journalist must answer, the privilege will not avail him to refuse.[27]

A fourth species of contempt involves the publication of material which will damage the legal interests of litigants or influence juries or witnesses. These contempts are covered by the Contempt of Court Act 1981.

Superior judges are selected by the Lord Chancellor's Department. The process of selection is not published. It is wide open for personal malice and gossip. In 1986 John Parris, an aspiring barrister, obtained his file through a friend. Its contents horrified him by its meticulous recording of reports of his private life. He left the Bar because any hope of advancement would be based on shaky foundations:

---

[27] *AG v Mulholland* 2 QB 477 at 489.

[W]hat really finished me off were getting on for a hundred scrappy notes addressed to the Lord Chancellor, many of them from one particular judge I had crossed swords with. Some of them were downright bloody lies. The most damning one was from this judge saying: 'Sleeps with divorce clients!' It was totally untrue.[28]

Judges used to be selected from barristers, but since 1990 solicitors may be appointed judges in the High and Appeal Courts. Judges of the High Court, circuit judges and recorders are appointed by the Crown on the advice of the Lord Chancellor and judges of the appellate courts are appointed by the Crown on the advice of the Prime Minister, who in practice takes the advice of the Lord Chancellor (although Lloyd George did not). In July 1999 the Lord Chancellor approved the basic selection process but agreed to submit his appointments to an independent auditor who would review the decisions and suggest improvements. In 1986 Lord Hailsham, the Lord Chancellor, robustly removed the idea of a Judicial Appointments Board from the political agenda.

It would not be subject to parliamentary accountability; it would be a permanent mafia of judges appointing one another or the Bar appointing themselves to higher office. I don't think the public would approve of that.[29]

Since 1977 the remedy of judicial review has provided another growth of common law in response to the volume of administrative law which has been generated by Parliament. Judicial review replaced the prerogative orders of mandamus, prohibition and *certiorari*, by which the courts ensured justice was done by inferior courts and tribunals. Acts of Parliament sometimes deny appeal from the decision of a tribunal but the words that decision's shall be final' does not oust judicial review. Parliament can oust the courts by clear provisions to that effect, but the courts will lean over backwards to make judicial review available.

In addition to the judges, the Lord Chancellor watches over about 27,000 magistrates of whom about eighty are Stipendiary (paid) Magistrates and their Deputies. Magistrates judge 98 per cent of criminal cases. They are drawn from the community and their legal knowledge is assisted by a trained clerk. There are about a thousand Recorders and assistant Recorders and almost four hundred Circuit Judges.

Before the war, there were a number of curious appointments to the Bench. None more so than one of Lloyd George's appointments. He knew the price of ambition and vanity and believed that offices in his gift could be awarded on his terms. In 1921 he appointed the Lord Chief Justice to be Viceroy to India. He had promised the vacancy to Gordon Hewart, the Attorney-General, but could not spare him from the Commons. Therefore, he decided to appoint a caretaker, Lord Trevethin, aged

---

[28] *Law Gazette*, 28/8/85, 2335.
[29] *A Matter of Justice*, M Zander, p. 112.

seventy-seven. But in order to hold the position in his gift, he obtained, against the spirit and letter of the Act of Settlement, an undated letter of resignation from the caretaker. Lord Birkenhead, the Lord Chancellor, complained that the object of the Act of Settlement had been defeated. 'That object was to secure that judges should hold office independently of any political or other influence and should be removable only for the more serious judicial behaviour and then in the most public and open manner.'[30] In due course Hewart could be spared and the letter of resignation was dated. The serving Lord Chief Justice was engaged in a case when his attention was drawn to the notice of his retirement in *The Times*. Hewart succeeded to the office which he determined to hold until death stole it from him. He proved a poor judge. He was bad tempered and when he thought that the Lord Chancellor's department lost control of the appointment of judges in King's Bench he termed it 'larceny' and contrary to Magna Carta.[31] He detested the delegation of quasi-judicial matters to the civil servants in the Lord Chancellor's Office. Unfortunately, he became ill and incapable. But he refused to resign. He was accorded the courtesy of a telephone call from the Prime Minister's office that his notice of retirement was being published the following morning, the Act of Settlement notwithstanding. There were a number of appointments in recognition of political service between the wars and even as late as 1956 23 per cent of superior judges had been MPs or parliamentary candidates. However, Attlee, the post-war Prime Minister, brought that tradition to an end.

In many countries a judicial career is open to graduates but in England only to practitioners of proven abilities. The judges and magistrates receive limited training, which is designed primarily to promote uniformity in sentencing of criminals. The idea of judicial training made Lord Devlin recoil:

> Once you start training him in anything he loses the essential character of the English judge. He no longer speaks and reacts as the ordinary man, he sits on the bench as what would never be more or better than a half-trained expert.

Two criticisms have been made against the judiciary. It is often said to be remote from every day life. Judges, like bankers, are generally discreet figures. They seldom make good media figures, although Lord Denning gathered a public reputation which was earned naturally and was of positive value to everyone. Judges normally observe the rule, laid down in 1955 by Lord Chancellor Kilmuir and in 1986 it was reaffirmed by Lord Hailsham, that they do not appear on radio or television. It seems a rather restrictive measure when the public have great interest in hearing such public servants speak. The ban was challenged by Judge Pickles, who became something of a hero for defying Hailsham. When he burst free of the official bridle, however, he had little to say. Indeed, as Dr Johnson observed, 'A popular judge is a deformed thing.'

---

[30] *Judges*, D. Pannick, p. 91.
[31] *The New Despotism*, Lord Hewart, p. 214.

A second criticism has been that members of the judiciary hold homogeneous social attitudes, owing to having been educated for the most part in public schools, universities and professionally trained at the Bar. The admission of solicitors, the emergence of suitable female candidates and from the immigrant communities should gradually return a judiciary which will reflect society more closely. But the process, if it to preserve its high standards of public surface, can only be gradual.

The current role of the judiciary and its position in the administration of society is hardly that imagined by Locke. It has been restricted largely to civil liberty. Locke, however, thought to have both personal liberty was of lesser importance to society than the preservation of property.

The common law has been increasingly supplanted by statutory law. Much of the law enacted by Parliament savours more of bureaucratic regulation than law. Law devised over centuries by a judiciary, who are independent and answerable only for the reason of their judgment is the operation of a mature society. Law enacted at the behest of Government, often impelled by a mania for both power and control, in a Parliament of representatives, intent on gaining and retaining popularity, is bound to be less objective than law determined by a judge in a court.

This restriction of the judiciary is due not to any defect of the institution, but rather to the virtual absence in Britain, as in other nations, of a culture of political thought. If this culture comprehended both liberty and individual property, there would be a sea-change in the administration of society. In such a state it would be reasonable to expect the judiciary to determine in a much wider sense the division of property into its public and private aspects.

In Britain the judiciary has developed a tradition of public service. Provided the people are vigilant, it has been an institution particularly fitted for a larger control over the administration of the state.

Lord Bingham, the Lord Chief Justice, described in reasonable and just words his opinion of one of Britain's grandest institutions:

> I am not an unashamed apologist of our existing judiciary, which I believe are as good as are to be found anywhere in the world.[32]

The evolution of the jury

It is unnecessary to define justice, for it is implanted in every human breast. Arising without thought or formulation, it does not depend upon education or sophistication. Adults in England and Wales are eligible to determine justice as juror in a criminal trial. Without preparation of any kind an individual is given the responsibility of acting justly towards fellow members of society.

In a criminal trial there are two contending interests. The person accused retains the rights of an individual, according to the particular circumstance, in a democratic

---

[32] *The Times*, 5 November 1999.

society until he is found guilty. The other party is society. Though a crime may be committed against another individual, it is reckoned in law to be a crime against society. Many wrongs are derided loosely as 'criminal', and in earlier times were punished summarily in the stocks and pillory but at present criminal acts can only be charged in a court if particularised either by common law or by the provisions of a statute, for the individual is possessed of liberty of an unlimited nature. By contrast, the powers of society to apprehend, detain, arrest and interrogate are defined precisely. In England and Wales, society is represented by the twelve members of the trial jury who will decide on the guilt or innocence of the accused.

The jury seems to have been imported into Britain about seventy years before the Norman conquest.[33] It consisted of a body of sworn men charged to supply information to the Crown. Innumerable juries were sworn throughout the country to return the information collected in the 'Domesday Book'. The jury was first introduced into the trial process by Henry II, who offered litigants, in disputes over land, the choice of trial by combat or by twelve jurymen. The jurors came to court apprised of the facts and decided on their verdict. The oath, it is said, commanded consciences powerfully in the Middle Ages, before science and reason had disturbed the power and mystery of religion.

At the Fourth Lateran Council in 1219 Pope Innocent III prohibited trial by the barbarous ordeals of fire or water. A new method of proof had to be found. Thus trial by jury was extended to cases other than those involving disputes over land. The jurors were required to act on their knowledge of the facts and resembled witnesses more than judges of fact. The claimant proved his case by vouching a number of witnesses and the defendant responded by vouching, if possible, a greater number who swore to the contrary. Gradually witnesses gave their knowledge to the jurors and by the end of the fourteenth century judges were directing juries to pay regard only to evidence produced in court. If the twelve jurors were unable to agree on their verdict a new jury was sworn.

Grand juries, who were responsible for bringing wrongdoers and suspects to court, had existed as a native institution centuries before the Conquest. They fell into disuse after the foundation of the police during the middle of the nineteenth century and were finally abolished in 1933.

The jury established its independence from Crown, litigants and overbearing judges in a struggle marked by seven leading cases.

The first case in the sixteenth century involved the jury's independence from the trial judge. Judges were often appointed to uphold an official line, to find guilt and punish severely. The jury, though they were picked and packed by local representatives of the established order, had a tendency to judge according to evidence, morality and fairness. For centuries down to the present they have stood between the State, acting through the judge, and the individual. The menace of judicial interference with the jury

---

[33] *Anglo-Saxon England*, F. Stenton, p. 651.

was shown clearly in a case in 1554, in which Sir Nicholas Throgmorton was charged with treason for having been involved in Wyatt's rebellion, which had been raised to prevent the marriage of Queen Mary to Prince Philip of Spain. The rebels under Wyatt marched from Kent and reached Southwark Bridge in London before they were finally halted and dispersed. Wyatt was executed and Sir Nicholas put on trial for his life. 'By eloquence, readiness of wit, and adroit flattery of the jury he contrived to secure his acquittal in the face of the open hostility of the judge – a unique achievement at a time when the condemnation of prisoners whom the authorities wished to convict was a matter of course.'[34] But the jurors who found him 'Not Guilty' of treason were fined and imprisoned and Sir Nicholas was still held in prison for several months. Their later release started the movement to secure the independence of the jury.

The second case concerned John Lilburne, a radical, who was tried in 1653 at the Old Bailey for seditious political activity. He conducted his own defence and told the jurors that they were the equals of the judge in deciding both law and fact. Despite the interventions of a hostile judge, Lilburne was acquitted. However, the next day the jurors were summoned by Parliament to explain their decision. The foreman explained they had acted according to conscience and believing themselves equal judges of law and fact. Owing to the popular support engendered by the trial and the desire not to risk incurring the unjust reputation earned during the reign of Charles 1, the matter was dropped.

The third case was the celebrated trial of the *Seven Bishops* in 1688. The bishops had refused to read the Declaration of Indulgence, which granted equal toleration to Christians, from their pulpits. They were charged with sedition. James VII & II not only packed the Bench but also the jury. While the nation held its breath, the jury dared to return a verdict of 'Not Guilty' and struck a blow from which James never recovered.

The fourth case, *Bushell's Case*,[35] which partially secured the independence of the jury from the judge, arose out of the trial of two Quaker preachers, William Penn and William Mead. The Quakers rejected violence, luxury and did not acknowledge priests. Their passive non-conformism challenged the might of the established order, not in open and contentious struggle, which they would be sure to lose against superior force, but on the uncertain ground of conscience. The two preachers were arrested for addressing a crowd of about 400 one morning in August during 1669 in London. They were charged with holding an 'unlawful and tumultuous meeting which caused great terror and disturbance of [the king's] liege subjects'. As one might expect of devout Quakers, the meeting was orderly and the preaching mild and devoid of colour and passion, but it was, despite all this mildness, uncomfortably disturbing to the authorities. The trial at the Old Bailey opened badly for the preachers when they failed, in accord with their practice, to remove their hats in court. The judge was incensed by

[34] *Encyclopaedia Britannica*, 11th ed, vol xxvi.
[35] (1670) 6 St Tr. 999

their deplorable contempt and fined them heavily. When the trial began Penn enquired of the authority in law for the indictment. The judge had him removed for impertinence. Mead began to appeal to the law and to divinity and was also excluded. The fate of the two preachers lay in the hands of the justices and the jury. They acquitted Mead, but held doubt in regard to Penn. The question arose whether the fate of the jurors also lay in the hands of the justices. In the absence of the accused Quakers the judge directed the jury to convict in accord with the oaths which they had sworn. Unsurprisingly, after such a direction, four members of the jury refused to do what the judge required. The judge fined the foreman, Bushell, for having been an 'abettor of faction'. The jury then agreed on a verdict of 'Guilty of speaking in Gracechurch Street'. 'Is that all? ' exclaimed the judge. He refused to accept this phatic opinion. The jury were sent back but they returned again with the same verdict. The judge sent them out again and demanded: 'We shall have a verdict by the help of God, or you shall starve for it.' Despite being locked up overnight they delivered their finding twice unaltered on the following day. The judge threatened the factious Bushell with a fine and the Mayor threatened to cut his nose. On the third day the jury announced a bolder verdict of 'Not Guilty'. The judge upraided them for 'having followed your own judgment and opinions, rather than the good and wholesome advice which was given to you'. The jurors were fined and jailed and the preachers were dispatched with them for having failed to pay the fine for wearing their hats. The next day Bushell applied to another court by a writ of habeas corpus and was freed and the case established that no court could inflict punishment on a juror for his verdict.

The jury had now gained a measure of independence from the judge, but the fourth case extended it further in an area that allowed judges still to browbeat juries. It had become understood that judges determined questions of law and the jury gave their verdict on the facts of a case. But there was often no clear delineation of fact and law and nothing to prevent a judge acquiring cognisance of facts by ruling that they were matters of law or inextricably mixed with law.

The fifth case, *R v Shipley*, in 1784[36] illustrated the problem and presaged its resolution.It concerned a charge of publishing a seditious libel against Dr Shipley, the Dean of St Asaph. The Dean's brother-in-law, Sir William Jones, a judge in the Supreme Court of Bengal, had written a pamphlet of nine pages, entitled *A Dialogue between a Gentleman and a Farmer*, about the reform of Parliament and the representation of the people. The pamphlet had been attacked by the court party and the Dean passed it to a Welsh translator. The local sheriff did not like it and summoned the Dean to a committee meeting, at which he declared the pamphlet to be treasonable. The Dean then read it and, finding it to be quite reasonable and interesting, published it himself. Both the Attorney-General and the sheriff declined to prosecute.

---

[36] 4 Doug 166

But a private prosecution was brought. On the opening the trial the judge, Buller J, ruled that the issue before the jury was whether the Dean had published the pamphlet. Whether the pamphlet constituted a seditious libel was reserved to himself. Thomas Erskine appeared for the defence and argued, in what Charles Fox described as one of the finest pieces of reasoning in the English language, that the jury had cognisance of the whole matter: publication as well as its libellous content. Not only was the pamphlet written by an eminent judge, but it contained the foundation of the Prime Minister's proposals to reform the representation in Parliament. At the conclusion of his argument he addressed himself to the jury for the final time.

> [I]f you find the defendant guilty, not believing the thing published a libel, or the intentions of the publisher contentious, your verdict and your opinion will be at variance, and it will be between God and your conscience to resolve the contradiction.

The judge was astonished by this intemperate finale and directed the jury to find the Dean guilty of publishing, in order that he could complete his task. The jury returned a verdict of 'guilty of publishing only'. Buller J, the judge, sought to erase the 'only' and, during a lengthy interchange, Erskine strove to have it recorded. At one point the judge cautioned Erskine, 'Sir, I will not be interrupted.' To which Erskine replied, 'I stand here as an advocate for a brother citizen, and I desire the 'only' to be recorded. ' Buller retorted, 'Sit down Sir, remember your duty, or I shall be obliged to proceed in another manner. ' 'Your Lordship', replied Erskine on the point of being gaoled,' may proceed in what manner you think fit; I know my duty as well as your Lordship knows his. I shall not alter my conduct.' The report of the trial discloses that the judge did not 'afterwards repeat the menace of commitment'. The verdict eventually recorded was 'Guilty of publishing, but whether a libel we do not find'. But the Dean was found guilty on all counts. Erskine appealed. Lord Mansfield heard the argument but Erskine describes how he 'put me aside with indulgence as you do with a child lisping its prattle out of season '.

The sixth case, *R v Jones* in 1723,[37] confirmed that a person acquitted by a jury cannot be charged on the same grounds; that is to say, the prosecution cannot appeal against a verdict of acquittal by a jury. The appeal system constitutes a threat to the decisions of juries. Generally, however, the appeal judges are loathe to re-hear evidence which was placed before a jury or re-try a case in which there is an appeal from a jury's finding of guilt. In 1972, however, it was enacted in Section 38 of the Criminal Justice Act that the Attorney-General can refer to the Court of Appeal a question of law which arose in a criminal case resulting in an acquittal. The person acquitted is entitled to be represented but his acquittal stands. It allows, it might be thought quite reasonably, the lawyers to eat the last crumbs of a profitable feast. But, in fact, the Attorney-Generals have not indulged their appetites often in this way.

---

[37] 8 Mod 201

The seventh case was *Floyd v Baker* in 1807.[38] It was established that no action would lie against the jury at the suit of the parties in a case. Plainly, if such actions ensued, jurors would be fearful of giving a verdict, and reluctant to give unpaid public service at the risk of personal bankruptcy and ruin. Furthermore, actions against jurors would postpone finality in law, already delayed by a host of procedures and devices which involved massive transfers of wealth from litigant to lawyer.

But in picking out a few celebrated cases in history is to exaggerate for as Professor Jackson, an authority on the jury wrote, '. . . for every acquittal there was a conviction to balance it.'[39] Although he was referring particularly to trials of seditious libel in the eighteenth century, it was probably a good general point about the jury.

The right to trial by jury is open to persons charged on indictment for a criminal offence. About 85 per cent of such cases are tried by magistrates and only about 6000 per annum go before juries. Up to 1913 about 50 per cent of cases in the High Court were tried before juries but during the First World War it became impossible to empanel sufficient numbers of jurors. The expedient was adopted in 1918 of withdrawing civil cases from juries apart from those involving fraud, libel, slander, malicious prosecution, false imprisonment and the dastardly breach of a promise to marry [no longer actionable]. In 1933 the expedient became the permanent order. Today less than two per cent of civil actions are heard before a jury. Trial before a judge is usually quicker and less expensive – that is not to infer, however, that it is cheap – and the outcome is more readily predictable. For a jury have to be conducted through the admissible evidence slowly and subjected to the flourishes and arts of advocacy, whereas a judge can spare himself the tedium and the entertainment with a few incisive questions.

There have been moves to restrict the right of an accused person to elect trial by jury in recent years on administrative grounds of expense and convenience. Such attempts are met invariably with a celebrated passage from Blackstone. In 1750 he warned:

> So that the liberties of England cannot subsist so long as this palladium remains sacred and inviolate; not only from open attacks (which none will so hardy as to make), but also from all secret machinations, which may sap and undermine it; by introducing new and arbitrary methods of trial.[40]

Sometimes writers, who feel deeply on some question and wish to convey that intensity, employ their art to draft opinions which come to stand as declarations of eternal verities. But it is posterity which succumbs to the spell thus created. The jury exists today not merely because it has survived through at least seven centuries, but

---

[38] 12 Co Rep 23.
[39] *The Machinery of of Justice in England*, R. Jackson p. 391.
[40] *Commentaries*, W. Blackstone, Bk iv, Ch XXVI.

rather because it is today a useful guardian of individual liberty against the State. But its use must be tested as the needs of different ages require. At the time when Blackstone wrote, in about 1760, the catalogue of capital crime was extensive, the power of the Crown considerable, the motivation of judges questionable, the uniformity of law non-existent and the reporting of cases irregular and unreliable. Plainly, it was better to be in the hands of twelve jurors than at the mercy of the State.

The first inroad on the role of the jury is the idea of removing the right of jury trial from petty offences. In 1975 the James Committee recommended[41] that about 8000 cases per annum should be removed from the Crown Court to hearings before magistrates and that the right to trial by jury should not be available to a person charged with various driving offences and with theft valued then at £20. The latter recommendation was rejected by the House of Commons and it had been resisted strongly by traditionalists. One of the most effective arguments was that the value of an offence was no guide to its gravity. It would be more serious in personal terms, for example, for a bishop to be caught stealing a penny from a blind box, than for crooks caught stealing diamonds. It was put so forcibly that one might suppose the bishop was thrown to the dogs without trial or conviction, when in fact he would appear before unpaid magistrates, who, far from being constitutional upstarts, had been judging their fellow subjects for over six centuries. If they misjudge, an appeal lies to the courts. The question was again considered by the Government in 1986 and in 1997 and again withdrawn. Change was recommended by the Law Commission in 1993. But in 1999 the Queen's Speech contained proposals to eliminate 'middle-ranking' offences, such as possession of drugs, theft, burglary and assault, despite the opposition of the Bar and Law Society. The decision of which court would hear the trial would be taken by magistrates rather than the defendant. Defendants put off conviction by electing jury trial and wasting time by changing their plea of 'Not Guilty' just before the trial by jury. They hope the delay in the trial being called will affect memories and the jury will be more tolerant than magistrates. The proposal will cover about 18,000 trials per year, which cost on average about five times as much before magistrates. In order to prevent magistrates becoming a police court appeal against their decision would lie to a Crown Court judge. The Government is responsible for the administration of justice on behalf of the rest of society and has the right to decide on any matter concerning the efficiency of that system.

The second inroad mounted against the jury was delivered by the Roskill Committee, which recommended in 1986 that trial by jury in cases of fraud was inappropriate; the report described the use of a jury in a fraud trial as outdated as 'an 18th-century ramshackle machine drawn by oxen'. Society is permeated by fraud and it must be admitted that much of it has been encouraged by the increase in bad laws which have fostered its remarkable growth; fiscal laws of such complexity and scope invite fraud, social security laws of similar complexity are open to it and institutional

---

[41] Cmnd 6323

arrangements of impenetrable obscurity, like those of the Common Agricultural Policy [CAP] of the EU, are themselves corrupt and fraud is interwoven in their establishment. The Roskill Committee stated that the present fraud trials allow the accused to escape conviction simply because the complexity of their activities lie outside and beyond the comprehension of the generality of jurors. It recommended, however, not that fraud should be reserved to a judge rather than a jury, but that it should be tried by a judge sitting with two lay experts. For judges often lack the experience of commercial dealings, in which much serious fraud is often wrapped and experts in the relevant fields would not only simplify the task of the judge but also expedite the trial; for when a judge relies on counsel, similarly inexperienced as himself, to explain the evidence, there is much talk, without penetration or understanding. Indeed, the only person in court with knowledge of the details of the fraud is often the accused.

The recommendation was sufficient to prompt the traditionalists to cite Blackstone's celebrated warning that, 'the liberties of England cannot but subsist as long as this palladium remains sacred and inviolate'. The Commentator, however, had been in complete agreement with the argument of the Roskill Committee. He did not believe the jury was suited for cases 'depending on complicated questions of account, in which figures and documents must be frequently referred to. With these a jury is obviously unable to deal.'[42] Unfortunately the Government were persuaded not to implement the recommendations of the Roskill Committee; one minister explained that they would not remove a major criminal offence from a jury 'lightly'. Thus, it is possible that a juror might have little or no ability to read English, that counsel have little understanding of the nature of the fraud and the judge not much more, while the accused may happen to be the only expert in a court, that is bound to acquit him at considerable expense to the taxpayer. It is not only that the Crown mistakenly rejected the recommendations of the Roskill Committee and allow fraudsters to go undetected, but also the fact that its annual output of complex and ill-considered legislation actually lays out greater inducements to varieties of fraud, many as yet undreamt.

In July 1999 the Lord Chancellor did not accept that the jury was an inappropriate institution to hear cases of fraud. 'Juries can understand', he stated, 'the essence of these cases, and it is the job of the prosecution to make these cases as simple as possible for juries.' He was inclined to the idea to allow defendants in 'serious charges' to opt for trial before a judge sitting alone.[43]

The decisions of the jury had to be unanimous. But in 1967 majority verdicts of ten out of a jury of twelve were introduced. This slight diminution in advantage to the accused has been reckoned a worthwhile reform.

Juries were assembled before 1825 from the local squires by the petty constable of the parish. Then the Jury Act introduced a requirement of the ownership of a dwelling with an annual value above £20 per annum and so it remained until 1967. Women were

---

[42] *Commentaries*, W. Blackstone, Bk iii, Ch XXV.
[43] *The Times*, 26 July 1999.

first eligible to serve as jurors in 1919. This property qualification returned, in Lord Devlin's words, jurors who were predominantly 'male, middle-aged, middle-minded and middle class'. The Morris Committee recommended[44] in 1965 that the jury qualification should be extended to anyone who had attained legal majority of eighteen. At that time only seven million owners of property were eligible. In 1974 the eligibility to jury service was opened to any person, saving broadly lawyers, police and criminals, on the electoral register, being between the ages of eighteen and sixty-five, and having been resident in the United Kingdom for at least five years since the age of thirteen. Juries are selected on a random basis.

The essential qualifications for jury service are disinterestedness and fair mindedness; the jury box is certainly not the place for representation of interests or beliefs or for personal views on society or politics. These qualities are hardly the virtues of youth. Indeed eighteen is an age in which many young people pass through a period of open revolt against society. It is more important, it would seem, to preserve, in a reasonable manner, the quality of disinterested jury service than to enfranchise youth with responsibilities of citizenship at the age of eighteen; the age of twenty-five would seem to be better. The Morris Committee recommended that no person should be qualified to serve on a jury who 'cannot read, write, speak and understand English without difficulty'. The Juries Act 1974 went some way to meet this suggestion by providing in Section 10 that, 'where it appears . . . that on account of . . . insufficient understanding of English there is some doubt as to his capacity to act effectively as a juror' the juror can be stood down. In other words a juror need only understand English. The Roskill Committee, which reported in 1986, reaffirmed the need in trials involving perusal of documents to insist on the full recommendation of the Morris Committee.

There has been a traditional right for the defence to remove a person from the jury panel by exercising, what is called, the right of challenge. As the jurors present themselves to the court the defence can challenge without showing cause before the oath is sworn. As Blackstone observed:

> As everyone must be sensible, what sudden impressions and unaccountable prejudices we are apt to conceive upon the bare looks and gestures of another; and how necessary it is that a prisoner [when put to defend his life] should have a good opinion of a jury, the want of which might totally disconcert him; the law wills that he should not be tried by any one man against whom he has conceived a prejudice, even without being to assign a reason for such his dislike.[45]

The right of this peremptory challenge without cause was an important right at a time when the accused had no right to be represented, when he could not give evidence on his own behalf, when the jury was selected from local squires and when death was

---

[44] Cmnd 2629
[45] *Commentaries*, W. Blackstone, Bk iv, Ch XXVII.

the general punishment for offences of no great seriousness. But the extension of these rights has seen the right to make peremptory challenges fall from 35 challenges in 1500 to nil in 1988. The right has been used to in recent years, according to a White Paper:[46]

> [A]s a means of getting rid of jurors whose mere appearance is thought to indicate a degree of insight or respect for the law which is inimical to the interests of the defence. This is contrary to the interests of justice as well as offensive to the individual juror.[47]

The Criminal Justice Act 1988 abolished the defendant's right to peremptory challenge and withdrew the offences of driving while disqualified and common assault from trial by jury. The Crown retained its right to stand-by jurors, the equivalent of a challenge. The right to jury trial had been removed in respect of cases involving criminal damage less than £100 [in 1997 £2000].

It has been the practice of police to check a panel of jurors against their files in important criminal trials. If their files hold information which might disclose a bias in a juror, the prosecution may exclude such a juror from a panel by asking him to stand by for the Crown; in other words to drop to the end of the list of potential jurors. This practice came to light in a number of trials during the early 1970s, but was not officially admitted until 1978. The Attorney-General restricted vetting to cases in which the Director of Public Prosecutions so recommended and he himself authorised it. The Attorney-General allowed in 1988 a juror to be stood down without cause to remove a manifest injustice and in cases involving terrorism and security when he had authorised jury vetting. Cases involving security were subject to the guidelines issued by the Attorney-General in 1988. In these cases the search of police files should be conducted under the authority of the Criminal Prosecution Service and the list of names on the jury panel should be sought from the trial judge. Judges ask jurors to stand down if they hold, say, racial prejudices in a trial involving racial element. But the basic principle remains that of random selection.

A juror is obliged to rely on the directions of the trial judge on matters of law. His judicial role is to ensure that the trial proceeds according to law, which affords the greatest opportunity that the verdict be given according to the evidence presented to the jury. If the judge is satisfied at any stage of the trial that the evidence against the accused is insufficient, he can withdraw a civil case from the jury and direct the jury in a criminal case to acquit the accused. If the judge decides that a verdict has been given plainly against the evidence he is empowered in a civil case to order a new trial or substitute a contrary verdict. In a criminal trial a judge has no power to set aside a verdict when he believes it has been given against the evidence. The prosecution cannot appeal against an acquittal, and if the accused appeals against conviction on

---

[46] Criminal Justice Cmnd 965
[47] *Ibid* para 32.

the ground that the verdict is unsound, then he must prove that no body of men could have reached that verdict: a high standard of proof.

Appeals in criminal cases generally concentrate on the evidence presented to juries or on the directions given to them rather than on the jury's decision on such matters. In 1907 the Criminal Appeal Act afforded three grounds for appeal against a criminal conviction: verdict cannot be supported having regard to the evidence or that it was unreasonable: an error of law had occurred during the trial; and a miscarriage of justice had occurred. The last ground of appeal presented the greatest threat to the verdict of the jury, for it empowered the Court of Criminal Appeal to supplant the decision of twelve jurors, who had seen the accused and the witnesses, by their own. The Court of Criminal Appeal, however, was wary of trespassing on the ground accorded to the jury and made no use of this general power to do so. The Criminal Appeal Act 1968 opened the door wider by providing that the court of appeal could set aside a conviction, which 'in the circumstances is unsafe and unsatisfactory'. In *R v Cooper*[48] the Court of Criminal Appeal examined a witness, who had turned Queen's evidence and incriminated three, in order to clear up confusion as to the identity of two of the three. Having heard him, they released one. In the course of his judgment Lord Widgery formulated the statutory test in the 1968 Act as, 'Do the circumstances of the case leave me with lurking doubts, causing me to wonder whether justice has been done?' In the later case of *Stafford v DPP*[49] Lord Kilbrandon declared the 1968 Act to say, 'Have I a reasonable doubt, or perhaps a lurking doubt, that this conviction is unsafe or unsatisfactory ?' In the view of Lord Devlin the right of appeal 'has overthrown the supremacy of the jury and replaced it by a diarchy which is an unstable form of Government, and sooner or later one of the two rulers try to get the upper hand.'[50]

Appeals in criminal cases are lodged in the great majority of cases on some factor which emerged during the trial or on a point contained in the judge's summing up. For once the case is complete and put into the hands of the jury the only ground of appeal involves, as described above, a high standard of proof. Similarly an argument can be overthrown by exposing the flaws in the assumptions more easily than by questions only the conclusions based on them.

The direction of the judge is required to advise the jury, *inter alia*, on the construction of documents – the plain meaning of words must prevail over eccentric constructions, on the scale of damages, on the weight and reliability of evidence, and on the remoteness of damage. For example, can a person, who throws an egg at the monarch on the other side of the world, be sued by the husband of a staunch royalist wife, who seeing it on television in Britain, died of shock? There are numerous matters of evidence and procedure, such as the admissibility of evidence; there is a great

---

[48] [1969] 1 QB 267
[49] [1974] AC 878
[50] The Judge, Lord Devlin, p. 174.

difference between a witness who actually heard words and a witness who heard someone gossiping about what had been heard. In his summing up a judge has to present the issues upon which they must decide, the rights of the accused before them and the balance of proof to be applied by them. Provided the summing up is fair to the accused, the judge may express his opinion on the evidence: there is no requirement that his summing up should be neutral.

But there is no reason why a jury should share a judge's views about facts. This seems to have happened in the acquittal of Clive Ponting, who was charged with an offence under the Official Secrets Act in 1985, arising from the sinking of the Argentine battleship, *The General Belgrano*.

Jeremy Thorpe, the Liberal leader, tells of their intrepid presence in the constitution. He was defending counsel for an individual facing a charge of drunken driving at Bridgwater Sessions. The prosecution evidence was formidable and undisputed: he had struck the car carrying the Police Superintendent and his Deputy and was followed by another car filled with four more policeman. 'After a two-day fight', Thorpe recalled, 'the jury must have obviously felt: "But for the grace of God, there go we." And he was acquitted.' He then concluded from this singular example, 'I felt this was a suitable moment to retire and remind myself to be very careful when driving through Bridgwater.'[51]

The rate of acquittal in trials by jury is around 50 per cent of contested cases. It is a rate which police think unduly high, even after allowing for cases of benefit of doubt. However, 60 per cent of cases in the Crown Court result in pleas of guilty and nearly half the number of acquittals in contested cases are ordered by the judge.

Lord Devlin has been one of the keenest advocates of trial by jury. He has presented powerful arguments for its continuance. First, it introduces conscience into the law which arises more naturally in the breast of a juror than in the trained mind of a judge. For as Blackstone observed, 'Mankind cannot be reasoned out of humanity.' In exercising an instinctive faculty a jury – sometimes to ignore a law or a ruling from a judge when it is perceived to be unjust – no harm is caused to the law. But were a judge to adopt a similar approach, the law would descend to the uncertainty of subjective criterion. Second, the jury stands against harsh law and tyrannical power, for it involves a people subject to the rule of law in its implementation. Third, the jury allows justice to be seen to be done. Fourth, judges who sit without a jury can 'construct a mystique that cuts them off from the common man', as well as confound evidence with law. Finally, jury trial provides an alternative to which litigants can turn when judges lose the confidence of lawyers and public alike.

The author once served on a jury in London in the early 1970s and the memory of those two weeks corresponded with those recorded in a book written at that time.[52] In particular, after two weeks of trials a few impressions seemed to be general in about a

---

[51] *In My Own Time*, J. Thorpe p. 38.
[52] *Members of the Jury*, eds D. Barber & G. Gordon.

dozen cases. Juries were curious bodies. Rather than pieces of constitutional clockwork, they resembled political committees. Several minority convictions were surrendered late in the afternoon to a verdict of 'Not Guilty' in order to avoid too much overtime. Women tended to reach a decision quickly, usually of guilt, whereas the older men were bothered by the 'beyond reasonable doubt' [today a jury are asked if they are sure]. In the jury room it came to mean beyond doubt of whatever quality the mind can imagine. Those afflicted by habitual doubt considered themselves to be following scrupulously what the judge had told them. The burden laid upon the police seemed heavy, who had to stay around for a brief confrontation with a barrister, usually of a flowery type, to tear their evidence to shreds and then to see an accused no doubt with previous convictions released.

The jury is a traditional survival that defies scrutiny or objective assessment. But it is a British institution which has been woven in its history and without which the nation would feel ill-protected against civil injustice.It is drawn from the people of Britain and it stands between the individual and the State. A fair trial in higher courts than that of magistrates in England means in the mind of the people a trial before judge and jury.

In the 1760s correspondence was maintained between Turgot and Condorcet about the British jury system. Condorcet could not persuade Turgot that they were preferable to investigating magistrates used in France. Turgot's principal objection was that the jury would be unsuitable for trials involving protest and unrests, which were then prevalent in France. In fact, in France today juries of nine, chosen from the electoral roll, are employed in serious criminal trials presided over by three judges.

Perhaps the supreme value of the jury, when it is the chosen method of trial, is that involves the people in the administration of justice by demanding them to exercise a duty towards society.

6

Freedom of Speech

The fight against the monarchy: the sixteenth century

The freedom of speech is the parent of many other freedoms.In that sense it may be considered as the most precious in a democracy. Man without the freedom to speak is like a bird without the use of wings: a caged animal.

The introduction of the printing press in 1476 by William Caxton, after an apprenticeship abroad, introduced a new epoch in the spread of ideas and learning, although he himself published little of the new learning. Printing immediately attracted the attention of the Tudor monarchs. It was not sufficient that they held the reins of government and political power, that they were the overlords of justice, supreme masters of religion and the licensors of commerce. They required as well control of the expression of thought, in order to ensure that it did not diminish royal authority or disturb the peace of the realm. There was nothing strange about this. In 1485 the shadow of royal control was introduced by the appointment of Peter Actors under royal patent as the Stationer to His Majesty and the office became known as the King's Printer. Publishers were granted monopolies by the patent of the king. Ideas, particularly new ideas and the ideas of progressives aiming for a distant dream of free thought, threatened the cohesion of society itself. The spread of ideas conveyed in print was watched by the Council, later the Privy Council, and the Court of Star Chamber, ready to imprison author, printer and bookseller for 'unseemly words', 'unfitting expressions', or 'evil opinions'.[1] A contemporary described this court as 'the curious eye of the state and the king's council prying into the inconveniences and mischiefs which abound in the commonwealth'. It operated without the presence of either a jury or, until the end of the trial, the accused. The only power they lacked was the sentence of death, but their powers to inflict imprisonment, fines, whipping, branding, pillory, and to cut of ears and slit noses were sufficient to make life seem as death.

The Tudor monarchs divided commerce into monopolies. But as the monopolist recoups the price paid for the monopoly in prices, it is the public, who, in fact, pay for the monopoly. Thus the new law books, bibles, prayer books, catechisms, Latin

---

[1] *Freedom of the Press in England 1476–1776*, F. Siebert p. 29.

grammars, schoolbooks, statutes and chronicles, which comprised the range of reading material in Tudor England, were produced by monopolists who operated under a grant of letters patent. They were controlled by King's Censors. The technology of printing was novel, the reformation was revolutionary, but the censors had a partiality for established and older ideas.

In 1512 Richard Strode, a burgess of Plympton, made an early call for freedom of speech. He had been imprisoned by a stannary court in Cornwall for things uttered in the House of Commons. It was enacted by Parliament in 1513 that everything done to Members was illegal in so forthright terms that many lawyers felt it a general enactment extending to all Members. Henry VIII when dealing in 1532 with the Pope thought it expedient to state that the Crown had no power over that body. Yet in 1541 when Speaker Moyle claimed the right of free access and free speech, Henry VIII, no longer in delicate negotiations, conceded only the former.

The Church shared the anxieties of the administration; it suspected that scriptural mysteries set in print would invite more scrutiny than those glorified in stained glass and that the Bible, once translated into the vulgar tongue, could be read as a textbook of heresy or revolution. In 1521 the clergy demonstrated against heresy at St Paul's, London, at which the writings of Luther were burned. This was the first bonfire of books which Cardinal Wolsey presided over and he repeated the same ceremony twice in 1526, causing Cardinal Campeggio, the Bishop of Salisbury to observe 'no holocaust could be more pleasing to God'.[2] Henry VIII published his answer to Luther, which was entitled the *Assertion of Seven Faiths*, and Pope Leo X was impressed with the gold-bound work. Five months later the pope decorated Henry with the title *Defender of the Faith*.

William Tyndale's translation of the New Testament appeared in 1525. He had 'perceived by experience that it was impossible to establish in the lay people any truth except the scripture plainly laid before them in their mother-tongue.' It was smuggled into England after being printed on a Lutheran press in Germany. There was a great demand for the work. A scholar wrote that, 'Englishmen were so eager for the gospel as to affirm that they would buy a New Testament even if they had to give a hundred thousand pieces of money for it.' Unsurprisingly it was suppressed. In Oxford groups of Lutherans formed into groups of 'Brethren'. Their books were seized and they were gaoled. Henry desired to arrest the spread of the New Learning. One of his keenest supporters in this task was Thomas More, his Chancellor between 1529–32. More loathed Tyndale's work, not because it was poorly translated, but only because it was judged heretical. Tyndale wrote that More was 'the most cruel enemy of truth'.[3] But the Tyndale Bible circulated among learned folk, despite containing unseemly words', 'unfitting expressions', or 'evil opinions'. In 1528 by royal decree in the Court of Star Chamber Henry VIII regulated foreign printers; they were not allowed to set up new

---

[2] *The Early Tudors*, 1485–1558, J. Mackie p. 345.
[3] *Ibid*, p. 347.

shops or employ more than two foreign servants. In 1534 a statute forbade the import of any bound books.

From 1525 he wanted to win favour with the Pope, who alone could release him from that frustrating bond to his first wife, Catherine. To accomplish this ecclesiastical seduction he needed to appear to suppress Reformation heresies. To make his suppression seem more effective, he encouraged their circulation surreptitiously; for there was little glory in unfurling his majesty and colours upon a vacant field. In 1529 Henry VIII was denied relief in what was to be known as his 'great matter'. What was especially irritating to Henry was that his marriage to Catherine had been made possible after papal dispensation of the fact that she had been married previously to Henry's late brother Arthur. Now he argued that the dispensation had been granted in defiance of scriptural law as outlined in the Old Testament. Throughout his life he had obtained what his will had desired. His wrath at being denied was considerable. His determination to be independent of political and ecclesiastical foes was fired to a deeper extent than his want to be released from his wife, for he regarded lack of a male heir to be a punishment of God – a matter outside his power. With the help of the clergy, Henry issued a list of prohibited books. In the 1530s a number of booksellers were burnt to death and several executed. After the break with Rome in 1533, the offence of free speech did not become obsolete. For Henry used that as an occasion to strengthen his hand with Parliament and Church The booksellers incurred guilt by dealing in Roman, rather than Reformation, works.

The king, however, was assisted, after the Act of Supremacy in 1534, in his marital difficulties with the pontiff by Protestant translators of the Bible. But, as soon as he was freed of the control of the Rome, he made sure that the free thinkers in Britain would not also employ their wits to do without him as well. Tyndale's translation of the Bible had been particularly useful in that it had not confirmed the spiritual supremacy of the Bishop of Rome. Henry let it be known through Archbishop Cranmer that it no longer was banned and frowned upon. But, yet, after some perusal, it did not confirm, as had been supposed, the ecclesiastical supremacy of the king. Worse – it contained a number of annotated passages which appeared a little too democratic. Furthermore, it contained far too much new Protestant theology. Henry was intent on controlling the Church, not on effecting a reformation of theology. In 1534 he had founded a new Church on the occasion of his need of another wife. Having taken control of the Church, Henry set about bringing the existence and wealth of the monasteries within his control. In 1534 the Treason Act had been extended from deeds to words and also a denial of royal supremacy. However, the offence of treason by words was repealed thirteen years later.

He was not minded to allow the keen interest in affairs of State to ferment in private minds, and private investigation into the business of government was discouraged by the censorship of opinion on matters touching the Government, State, religion or anything that caused the Crown unease. In 1538 Henry introduced a licensing system by which unlicensed printing would not only occasion his 'most high displeasure and indignation', but would also expose the offender to loss and forfeiture of goods and chattels and, according to royal pleasure, the risks of fines and imprisonment. He began by suppressing and stifling thought and then ventured into the manufacture of acceptable forms of learning by prescribing the books to be used in schools, where young minds could be conditioned to pursue the less contentious studies in an uncritical spirit. In 1544, for instance, he suppressed publications which 'leaked' news of the king's victories. Indeed, news was a valuable pawn in the diplomatic game played by kings; rather than something to be punted about by scribblers of little renown.

Cranmer commissioned Miles Coverdale to produce an edited version of the Tyndale translation with the purpose of rendering scripture more favourable to temporal authority. It appeared in 1535 and on the title page a drawing depicts the sacred work being donated by the king to the archbishop, who distributes it to the clergy and laity massed on a lower level. The drawing, intending to demonstrate the heavenly amplitudes of eternity and infinity being delivered to human kind, reveals only the realities of earthly governance.Henry had to terminate the sovereignty of the pontiff and fill no less imperiously the vacuum which he had created, in order to oust by title and might the merely intellectual authority of Luther. Coverdale's translation was reissued and in 1539 ordered to be read in churches.

The intellectual maneuvering was outlawed in a statute of 1543; English translations could not be cluttered any longer by preambles and annotations and those 'craftye false and untrue' translations of the Bible, such as that by Tyndale. Reading the Bible was forbidden by the classes of ordinary women, apprentices, serving men or persons of base degree. Noblemen, gentlewomen, gentlemen and rich folk could read in their private boudoirs. Clergymen who preached against the king's doctrine of 'pure and sincere teaching', which the king's doctrine, were liable to be accused of papacy and heresy. Penalties for an erring cleric were death by burning and for laity life imprisonment.

A Royal injunction declared that the new edition should be read decently and without comment. But soon it was read boldly and became the focus of lively and passionate discussion. Maidens were engrossed in studying it during matins. The 'most precious juel the worde of God,' Henry VIII told Parliament in 1545, 'disputed, rimed, sung, and jangled in every alehouse and taverne.'[4] In his last proclamation of the following year Henry condemned Tyndale's and Coverdale's translations. As the king was dying in January 1547, beyond powers of speech, Cranmer assured him of the mercies of Christ and Henry squeezed his hand in gratitude.

Edward VI and Mary developed the censorship bequeathed by Henry VIII. In 1557 the Stationers' Company, a body in existence since 1403, was incorporated by royal charter to preside over the regulation of the printing trade. The founding charter of the Stationers formulated its purpose: to suppress 'scandalous, malicious, schismatical and heretical' works. This company was made up of master printers, who alone were

[4] *Ibid* p. 432.

granted a monopoly over printing, so that a work could not be printed by anyone else. The charter provided that the privileged status of master printer could be passed down to sons and to those lesser printers who wooed and married the widows of former masters. By 1583 there were twenty-three master printers working fifty-three presses. The status was conferred on printers, whose instinct was to conform and leave unthought ideas at odds with their privileges. Indeed, the fear that the status could be withdrawn without investigation remained a sure corner stone of censorship. By 1558 it has been estimated that there were ninety-one stationers, mostly in London and a few in Oxford, Cambridge and St Albans.[5] Queen Mary in 1558 directed the licensing machinery against Protestants instead of Catholics. Protestant books were described as 'hereyse, sedityon and treason'. Elizabeth achieved the contrary result by making Protestant ecclesiastics the licensors.

New works had to be submitted to and licenced by various authorities, depending on the nature of the work, before publication. Existing and new regulations were laid down by orders in Council and by decree of the Court Star Chamber in 1586, whose preamble mentions 'enormities and abuses of dyvers contentyous and disorderlye persons professinge the arte or mysterye of pryntinge' were increasing. The ordinances were designed to prevent printing outside London, except in two universities, to compel all printers to register with the Company, to require prior perusal and authorisation of the Archbishop of Canterbury or Bishop of London, to allow officers of the Company to search for illegal presses and printed material and seize the same, to make arrests, deface illegal presses and to diminish the number of printers to a figure acceptable to the two bishops. In 1569 the licensors described various books in the study of John Stow, an annalist, as papist and 'unlawful'. In 1584 the premises of a printer, W. Carter, were searched and there were brought to light 'other naugthye papysticall bookes'. Accordingly, he was drawn along the ground from Newgate and hanged at Tyburn, London, on a charge of sedition for 'printing of lewde pamphlettes'. The Bishop of London described him as 'a very lewd fellow'.

The creation of the Company caused immediate conflicts with the royal printer, Christopher Barker, which were settled by agreement in 1578. But the printers' monopoly was not absolute. The king had granted the universities of Oxford and Cambridge printing monopolies as well. In 1629 the judges enforced these monopolies in favour of Cambridge university. The hardest thing for the Company to remember was that they were the creatures of the royal prerogative. In 1627 the Company challenged the king's commands. The Bishop of London, the official royal licensor, beseeched the King's Council 'to bring the stationers to better obedience; they are exceedingly bold in their printing.'[6]

Imports of books were banned but foreign works were smuggled in. Works approved by censors were re-written to admit uncensored passages. Public intelligence benefited

---

[5] *A Century of the English Book Trade 1457–1557*, E. Gordon Duff.
[6] *The Struggle for the Freedom of the Press*, W. Clyde p. 5

SLAVERY IN A LAND OF LIBERTY

from the black marketeers, smugglers and cheats who had helped a society falling victim to censors. Indeed, when governments sought to employ servants to uphold the rigour of their laws, they were often cheated by them.

The printing monopolies were attacked during the 1570s by a group of dissident printers led courageously by John Wolfe. He had learnt printing in Italy and Germany and, on his return to England, he petitioned the Privy Council for a patent of monopoly, in order to save himself the trouble of enduring an apprenticeship with a master of the Company. He was refused and set himself to print whatever 'pleased him best'. He printed a number of works covered by the monopoly of the Queen's Printer who, surprisingly, compromised with him and agreed to commission work from him in future, in order to discourage his trespasses. Wolfe then breached the copyright of other printers. When he was ordered to give bonds to cover his future good behaviour, he questioned the legality of the monopolies granted under royal prerogative and was gaoled. He had enlisted the support of a number of dissidents and from gaol he continued to organise a campaign directed against the monopolies. Upon his release, after two years in prison, the Court of Aldermen of the City of London recommended that the Stationers' Company keep him quiet by giving him sufficient work. By 1585 he owned more presses than all other printers, save the Queen's Printer. Having established himself against the monopolies he suffered an extraordinary conversion and allowed himself to become the bloodhound of the Company. He was able to expose a number of friends and fellow poachers who were endeavouring to follow his example. But fortunately his courageous campaign had laid the foundations of a revolt. A series of illegal puritan pamphlets appeared in 1572 attacking the Protestant Church government; it was alleged that its episcopal hierarchy resembled the institutions of romanism.

The demand for the free exchange of ideas on such matters as the marriage of the queen, the royal succession or the royal prerogatives, was taken up in February 1576 by Peter Wentworth, who argued for free speech in the House of Commons. Hitherto, the struggle had been maintained by printers and nonconformists. Now it was lifted from, so to speak, the street of daily life. It had become a matter of state. Five years earlier Strickland had introduced some ecclesiastical Bills and was asked by the council not to appear in Parliament again. It was rumoured, Wentworth ventured, that the queen's likes and dislikes affected debate. 'How', he asked, 'can Truth appear and conquer until falsehood and all subtleties that should shadow and darken it be found out?' She had, by her influence, 'committed a great band of dangerous faults to herself'. It was one thing to advance the liberties of the House in theory but to attack the sovereign was to alarm Members. Immediately a committee of Privy Councillors was formed to try Wentworth. He agreed to submit to their judgment only when they agreed that they were acting as members and not as Councillors. Wentworth conducted an intrepid defence but the House of Commons committed him to the Tower of London. After a month Elizabeth forgave him. In the next session the Chancellor, when confirming the new Speaker, warned that the House should not meddle with anything touching the queen's person, estate or Church government The House had the effrontery to appoint a day of fast on their own authority and the offence was expiated only by humble apology. In the session of 1587–8 a Member offered a Bill to sweep up all ecclesiastical laws. The Speaker prevented debate because it was contrary to the command of the queen. At the next meeting Wentworth demanded that some questions be read. Among them were:

> Whether this council was not a place for any member, freely and without control, by bill or speech, to utter any of the griefs of this commonwealth? . . . Whether there be any council that can make, add, or diminish from the laws of this realm, but only by this council of parliament?[7]

The Speaker did not read them, but instead showed them to a courtier, who had Wentworth committed to the Tower. It is not known how long he remained there. In 1593 again he incurred the grave displeasure of Elizabeth by requiring her to name a successor. Lord Burghley decided that such was the queen's displeasure that he must be committed again. It seems probable that he died there three years later.

After complete suppression of Catholicism, the main preoccupations of Elizabeth I was to contain the danger of invasion by Spain or France and she favoured either one or other, according to which of them held the strongest position in the Netherlands, the natural springboard for an invasion of England. She was prepared to use her hand in marriage as diplomacy required. Her wooing raised fears of marriage to a catholic prince and in 1579 a pamphlet appeared, entitled *The Discourse of a Gaping Gulf Whereinto England is like to be swallowed by another French Marriage; if the Lord forbid not the banes, by letting Her Majestie see the sin and punishment thereof*. The queen was incensed that a mere author and printer should pronounce on foreign policy and had them tried for felony. But the jury refused to convict for an offence which attracted capital punishment. They were tried again for sedition, found guilty and the author, John Stubbes, having suffered in the stillest silence the amputation of his right hand, lifted his hat with the left in salute to his Queen and with full voice.

Under the Tudors proceedings in Parliament were often secret in order to preserve a measure of independence from the Crown. There were moves, later in the sixteenth century, to bring debate out of the dark shadows of secrecy into the full light of the public glare. It was a move which Elizabeth strove to contain by royal proclamations, the Court of Star Chamber decrees, the Stationers' Company and by patents of monopoly.

The fight against the House of Commons: the seventeenth century

It should be remembered that in 1600 the Bible remained the major work of literature. Whilst Elizabeth had been able to smother public debate on religion and government

---

[7] *The Constitutional History of England*, H. Hallam [1872] vol i pp. 257–8.

by hiding affairs of state and, in particular foreign policy, behind her prerogative powers, James VI & I was unable to contain the explosion of debate on political affairs and ideas; he actually relished debate himself. He was articulate but, unfortunately for him, he was also conceited. He believed that he could establish the supremacy of the Crown on the ground that it was divinely appointed. The Tudors had been content and wiser to found their extensive powers on the prerogative attaching to the Crown. James attempted to remove argument from the field of reason altogether by asserting that the prerogative depended on the plenitude of the powers granted from God to the monarch. The real question, however, became not from whence the powers derived but what use was actually made of them in temporal government.

The first challenge to the Crown came from Parliament. In 1621 a Member of the Commons, Sandys, was committed to gaol and the king told Parliament that they enjoyed their privileges at his sufferance. Parliament drew up its Protestation in December 1621 declaring that their privileges were ancient and that it was the undoubted right of Englishmen that the Commons enjoy freedom of speech. The Protestation was entered in the Journals but James ordered them to be sent to him and he tore the Protestation out and forthwith dissolved Parliament. The issue of free speech in Parliament lived on but it never burst into the open during the reign of Charles 1. In 1629 Sir John Eliot, Holles, and Valentine were charged with sedition for words spoken in the Commons, The judges, hearing their application under habeas corpus held, after Charles 1 had privately asked them, that the enactment of 1512 concerned only Strode. In 1667 the two Houses of Parliament declared that Strode's Act of 1513 to be a general Act laying down ancient privileges.The House of Lords reversed the judgment of 1629, but only Holles, among the original three, was still alive then. However, Members of Parliament remained open to charges of sedition for speeches delivered and things said therein up to 1688.[8] But the Bill of Rights, 1689, ended that, by confirming the privilege of Parliament and since then words spoken in Parliament have not been questioned by bodies outside. Indeed, the freedom of speech in Parliament allows any Member immunity for anything said in Parliament, even when he knows his words to be untrue. In 1837 a case, *Hansard v Stockdale*, questioned the immunity of parliamentary papers. A report on prisons contained defamatory words about Stockdale who sued and was awarded £600. The sheriffs of Middlesex pursued the award. The Commons committed the sheriffs, along with Stockdale and his solicitor, to prison. On a writ of habeas corpus the prisoners sought their freedom. But the Commons replied that they were imprisoned on the warrant of the Speaker for contempt. The court held that had it no power to free the prisoners. To settle the matter an Act was passed removing the right to sue for defamation arising from material printed by order of the House.

Authors, printers and booksellers were haunted by the threat of proceedings for seditious libel, a looser offence than sedition itself, and by the knowledge that the

---

[8] 3 *State Trials*, p. 332.

judges, particularly those sitting in the Star Chamber, were ready to convict for the offence. In 1606 the Star Chamber decided in the *Case of Libellis Famiosis* that libel was a crime which survived the death of the person libelled and to which the defence that the libel was true was not available. The offence was committed by both the inventor and the publisher of the libel. The rules of evidence were loaded in favour of the prosecution.

The courageous stand in the previous century of Wolfe was matched later by Michael Sparke. He opposed printing monopolies and spent much time between 1621–31 in gaol as a result. Before the Ecclesiastical Commissioners in 1629 he disputed the authority of Star Chamber to regulate printing as a violation of rights enshrined in Magna Carta and other statutes.Sharpe availed himself of every device to overcome regulation printing in the name of authorised printers, altering text after approval by the licensors, printing before approval had been announced.

In 1630 the Court convicted Dr Alexander Leighton, a Scottish divine, for writing a pamphlet attacking the English clergy as 'anti-Christian and satanical'. They could not inflict a capital sentence, so they imposed the most severe in their power; he was fined £10,000, stripped of his ministry, to be pilloried and whipped, lose an ear, have his nose slit and his forehead branded first at Westminster and the same punishment was to be inflicted again at Cheapside, as soon as he had recovered sufficiently to absorb the unblunted pain a second time.

In 1632 the Court of Star Chamber tried William Prynne, a strict puritan, who was convicted with others of seditious libel in his book, *Histori-Mastix*, although it had been cleared by the censors before publication. In it he had attacked Romanism and such 'immoralities' as dancing, hunting, play-acting and public festivals. He attacked the Roman use of females on the stage, in such a way that suggested actresses were 'notorious whores'. He also attacked dancing and particularly dancing on the sabbath. The queen had performed in a masque with her ladies at court in *The Shepherd's Pastoral* by Walter Montague six weeks after publication. Archbishop Laud's chaplain, Dr Heylyn, charged with framing a case against Prynne, seized on this passage as evidence of sedition. No counsel was prepared to sign his answers to the charges, for Prynne was thought a rather obnoxious character. One of the judges said he was surprised the charge had not invoked a capital punishment, for the offence 'made his heart swell and the blood in his veins to boil'. He was sentenced to a fine of £5000, stripped of his degree, to the loss of his ears, to be pilloried and imprisoned for life. The licensor of Prynne's work pleaded that he had read only part and had been beguiled into applying his imprimatur. He was fined £50. In prison during 1637 Prynne was again charged with writing books against the hierarchy. Prynne complained that Archbishop Laud, whom he regarded as his adversary, happened to be sitting in judgment on him. The court usher was ordered to turn up the stubs of his ears so that the court could determine whether they had been cropped as closely as the law required. Again he was fined £5000 and imprisoned for life. The trial of Prynne, and those of Dr John Bastwick and Dr Henry Burton, publicised the execution of the sentence. Both aroused strong disapproval. In New Palace Yard at the public ceremony the crowd groaned as the ears of the accused were clipped. Burton addressed them, 'This day will never be forgotten . . . through these holes (poynting to the pillory) God can bring light to his Church.' A woman answered,'There are many hundreds which by God's assistance would willingly suffer for this day.'[9] Their departure from London was the occasion of shows of public sympathy.

The Church were engaged in the struggle to suppress opinions considered seditious. Religions uphold the fundamental relationship of man to his Creator and yet divide mankind on the trivial differences in beliefs, customs and the like, which are preserved and honoured as the hallmarks of particular religions. Thus the suppression of opinion seemed a natural function of a Church threatened by free thought. The Archbishop of Canterbury's duty to nominate the twenty or so master printers, on condition of their compliant behaviour, was the principal ecclesiastical power in the suppression of thought. The Church, by enlarging the jurisdiction of the Court of High Commission from matrimonial matters, church attendance and non-conformity to include libel and control of printing, added to the larger preventive power of the Archbishop a punitive power to its modest court.

In the early seventeenth century the growing interest in the affairs of the nation and the world created a demand for daily news. It was met at first from 1620 by news-sheets, or corontos, printed in Amsterdam. The English master printers did not tolerate free speech outside the control of the Company, nor were they willing to forgo either business or profits. In addition, James had no interest in reading about himself or his foreign policy in the Dutch news-sheets. Accordingly he reissued a proclamation in 1621 against the great liberty of discourse concerning matters of State. It had little effect and steps were soon taken to legalise news-sheets. Monopolies were granted to master printers to produce sheets covering particular topics of news. However, the experiment did not please the Crown and the licenses were withdrawn by Charles I twelve years later. The printers responded by printing ballads which alluded to events and news and rumour and circulated as keenly as news. In 1638 the king decided that a controlled printing press was better than no press and again granted monopolies of newsletters to trusted master printers who paid reasonable prices and gave undertakings that nothing derogatory to the interests of the Crown would be published by them.

John Selden drew attention to the want of legality in the exercise of control of printing by the Court of Star Chamber:

> There is no law to prevent the printing of any book but only a decree of the Star Chamber.Therefore, that any man should be fined, imprisoned, and his goods taken from him is a great invasion of the liberty of the subject and, therefore, I desire that a law be made on this.[10]

---

[9] *Early Stuarts*, G. Davies, 2nd edn, pp. 75–6.
[10] *History of England*, S. Gardiner, vol 7, p. 51.

In 1637 the Court of Star Chamber issued a further decree introduced a licensing system for unpublished material. The licensing system had broken down.The decree banned the printing of 'seditious, schismatical or offensive books or pamphlets to the scandal of Religion, or the Church or State' and appointed as censors the Lords Chief Justices, the Earl Marshall and assorted bishops, depending on the matter published. The royal prerogative was clipped back by Parliament. In 1641 the Court of Star Chamber was abolished along with the Court of High Commission. '[T]he destruction of the Star Chamber meant much more than the abolition of an unpopular tribunal; it meant the rooting up from its foundations of the whole administrative system which had been created by the Tudors and extended by the Tudors.'[11] Yet within two years the Long Parliament issued two orders, of March 1642 and June 1642, to effectively re-introduce what had been abolished.

In the uncertain times of civil war and censorship, a number of daily newspapers appeared and disappeared after an issue or two. At the time of the trial and execution of Charles I details of these most newsworthy events were blocked by the authorities, who were determined to purge the printing press of royalist and presbyterian sympathies. A new Treason Act made the offence of criticising or disparaging the Government a capital crime. It was, however, not these severe measures which disturbed the royalist press but the services of a middle-aged woman called 'Parliament Joan', who was described with precision as a fat woman about fifty. She was employed by Parliament to track down the royalist presses and was so successful that, within two months of her engagement, none remained.

The fall of Charles I also undermined the Stationers' Company which had been the creature of royal prerogative and the dependent of its protection. It was also split by the different interests of its members, some of whom wanted to retain their monopolies, others who wanted to increase them and some who wanted to do without them altogether. The unlicensed printers outside the Stationers' Company petitioned Parliament for the right to print without constraint. Its Puritan members remembered that they wanted to enjoy as free a printing press as possible; certainly they wanted an end to the regime enforced by the Court of Star Chamber. A report was presented to the Commons to consider what was to be done with the books seized by the High Commissioners. They proposed that certain innocent titles should be given back to booksellers, that less innocent titles, by for example by Thomas á Kempis, should be given to trusted noblemen, gentleman and scholars, but not to women, and that superstitious books should be burnt without delay. The Commons set up a Printing Committee to regulate the press. It was not their beneficent intention to accord freedom to papists, for example. Furthermore, the Stationers' Company complained at the activities of pirate printers who set up to evade the regulations. In 1643, however, the Long Parliament re-established the powers and the monopolies of the Company and declared that all books, pamphlets and papers had to be registered before publication with the Company.

---

[11] *The Law of the Constitution*, A. Dicey.

There had been many complaints in the past at the methods of control but none it seems against the principle of control. Until Henry Robinson demanded in 1644 freedom from censorship and free trade in commerce.

No man can have a natural monopoly of the truth, and the more freely each man exercises his own gifts in its pursuit, the more of truth will be discovered and possessed.[12]

John Milton also published his pamphlet *Aeropagitica* without licence in the same year:

[I]t is this liberty Lords and Commons which your own valorous and happy counsels have purchest us, liberty which is the nurse of all great wits; this is that which hath rarefied and enlightened our spirits like the influence of heaven; this which has enfranchised, enlarged and lifted up our apprehensions degrees above themselves. You cannot make us less capable, less knowing, less eagerly pursuing of truth, unless you first make yourselves, that made us so, less the lovers, less the founders of our true liberty.[13]

His essay ranks as one of the finest arguments for freedom from censorship. Yet it attracted little attention until it was re-published in 1738.'We read the noble apology on Milton for the freedom of the [printing] press with admiration,' wrote Hallam, 'but it had little influence on the parliament to whom it was addressed.'[14] Some years later, surprisingly perhaps, Milton acted as the censor of the news-sheets; his argument arrived before its time and was suited better for the digestion of later generations.

Lilburne had been arraigned before the Court of Star Chamber for unlicensed activities and the importation of 12,000 forbidden books and had come to regard the trials, not as processes of justice in which he might establish his innocence, but as excellent opportunities to draw attention to his ideas. In gaol he found the solitude to compose his thoughts and express them in writings against censorship. While the mass of mankind move, as T.S. Eliot described, with 'the cadence of consenting feet' in obedience to the conditions of life as they find them, those spirits like Lilburne follow an instinct to go their own way and, in so doing, render their own imprisonment and deprivation to the advantage of their fellow men. He was first charged in 1637 with the importation of books. The charge was not proved. But he refused to take the oath in the Court of Star Chamber. He was fined £500, and whipped through the streets of Westminster, to stand there in the pillory. It was estimated that he suffered five hundred blows from a three-thronged whip. He was too tall for the pillory and his

---

[12] *Tracts on Liberty in the Puritan Revolution*, W. Haller, vol i, p .69.
[13] *Aeropagitica*, E Arber (ed) p. 72.
[14] *The Constitutional History of England*, H. Hallam, vol iii, p. 3.

frame was uncomfortably contained. Yet in New Palace Yard the crowd talked to him. He spoke about the martyrs, like Prynne, and denounced the bishops, before a gag was crudely fastened to his bleeding mouth. The Court of Star Chamber were so incensed by his conduct under punishment, that they ordered him to endure solitary confinement in Fleet Prison. Despite being shackled and denied visits he wrote at least three pamphlets while in gaol.

In 1640 the parliamentarians, having released Prynne, Lilburne and other victims of the clerics from gaol, appointed a Committee to investigate the ecclesiastical tyranny. Lilburne had not been rendered docile by his imprisonment and attached a libel of Archbishop Laud on the Royal Exchange. It so inflamed spirits that an attack was made on the archbishop's house but he avoided death by threatening to use cannon and ammunition in his possession. In March 1641 the archbishop was, however, charged with high treason. Prynne spoke for the prosecution and accused him of 'miserable abuse of the Spiritual Keys, to shut up the Doors of Heaven, and to open the Gates of Hell'. The trial dragged on and the former victims of the notorious prelate, like Prynne, did not let slip the opportunity for procuring revenge. Laud was executed after a trial of four years at the age of seventy-two. He served as scapegoat for the Court of Star Chamber, whose judgments had only been occasionally concerned with the freedom of the printing press. Lilburne served briefly in the Parliamentarian Army and after leaving it in early 1645 he began to acquire a following.

An Ordinance of 1643 for the regulating of printing was introduced in traditional form. But from the outset it proved a failure. Two years afterwards Lilburne was referred to the House of Commons for publishing an unlicensed pamphlet in which he had challenged the opponents of free speech:

> For if you had not beene men that had been afraid of your cause, you would have been willing to have fought and contended with us on open grounds and equal terms, namely that the Presse might be open for us as you.

He published an anonymous pamphlet, while being held in Newgate Prison, entitled *England's Birthright*, attacking:

> that insufferable, unjust and tyrannical Monopoly of Printing whereby a great Company of the very same malignant fellows that Canterbury and his Malignant party engaged in their Arbitrary Designs against the Peoples' and Parliament's just Privileges; an Arbitrary Unlimited Power, even by a general Ordinance of Parliament, to print, divulge and disperse whatsoever Books, Pamphlets and Libells as they please, though they be full of Lyes, and tend to the poysoning of the Kingdome with unjust and Tyrannical Principles.[15]

---

[15] *Ibid.* vol. ii, p. 10.

He also claimed abolition of monopoly, toleration and the abolition of the excise and tithes.When he was released from Newgate, within six months he was apprehended by the Commons again in connection with a slander of a Member, Colonel King, and he published a letter refuting the charge. But in his refutation he had implicated the Earl of Manchester and within a few days he was apprehended by the House of Lords. He was not impressed with the legal powers of the Lords and published his criticism.The Lords confined him briefly to Newgate Prison for having published 'a scandalous and contemptuous paper'. On the review of his case by the Commons Lilburne questioned their legal authority and before the Lords. He was required by Black Rod to kneel and replied: 'I have better religion and manners than to kneel before any human or mortal power, however great, whom I have not offended.' For issuing unlicensed pamphlets and for his contempts the Lords charged him with High Crimes and Misdemeanours and put him in the Tower of London at their pleasure. In prison he became engaged in parliamentary battles with the Levellers and decided his campaign needed an appeal to the nation and the army, in which most were suffering from arrears of pay. He played an active part in supporting and encouraging the soldiers. Eventually he was released from the Tower in 1647 on bail.

A number of royalist printing presses flourished to the great displeasure of the Government. In one trial for libels issuing from these offending journals, the punishments outdid, it was said, the imagination of Aristophanes. One person against whom a libel was proved was condemned to be suspended at Tyburn and roasted slowly over a fire, while two people disguised as the Furies picked his inflamed flesh with two sharp daggers; the punishment was devised to give him a foretaste of hell. A co-accused was condemned to confinement in a high turret where his ambition might leave him, to be girt with a wooden sword and to be fed 'on the carcasses of Ravens as he had made such fatal music and was still croaking against his superiors'.[16]

Lilburne had joined the newly formed Levellers in presenting a petition to Parliament for a complete repeal of censorship. He drew up a petition demanding that Parliament use their powers to secure the liberties of the people. During the hearing of the petition the House of Commons refused to hear more and withdrew his bail. Once more Lilburne found himself in the Tower and his pamphlets continued to defy the restraint of the Stationers' Company. After five months he was released. But he was committed again for three months on suspicion of treason. Later he was charged with treason which Parliament had extended to cover seditious libels. During an address to the jury one of the judges, Lord Keble, warned Lilburne that 'if your intention had taken effect your plot was the greatest that ever England saw, for it struck at no less than the subversion of this Commonwealth'.[17] Lilburne appealed to the jury and they refused to convict and he was released. Four years later he escaped a possible sentence of death at the Old Bailey by the decision of a jury. He died in 1657.

---

[16] *Struggle For The Freedom of the Press*, W. Clyde, p. 123.
[17] *4 State Trials*, 1269, 1402.

During the Commonwealth of Cromwell Parliament granted the control of the printing trade in 1649 to itself in place of the Stationers' Company. It enforced the most brutal tyranny to suppress the newsbooks and pamphlets. The printing monopolies enjoyed by the master printers were not renewed. In 1655 Cromwell introduced new measures to control the news press and unleashed three commissioners to seek out and to prosecute unlicensed printers. He also prohibited all news-sheets except two licensed, official journals called *The Public Intelligence* and *Mercurius Publicus*. The Puritan Revolution had marked an easing of censorship by abolishing the Court of Star Chamber and the Court of High Commission. Yet the people seemed to draw back from claiming that to be freedom. In fact, Parliament could not suppress the royalist news press.

Following the restoration of the monarchy a Printing Act of 1662 restored censorship to what it had been in 1641, except that it did not revive the Court of Star Chamber In other words, Parliament became the controller of censorship. The Preamble states the mischief to be restrained as the 'general licentiouness' which had encouraged 'many evil disposed persons' to print 'heretical schismatical blasphemous seditious and treasonable' works. The Act was was created for 'settling the said Art of Mystery of Printing'. It was restricted to the master printers of the Stationers' Company and the official printers at Oxford and Cambridge universities. The Act determined that the number of master printers had to fall from fifty-nine to twenty before the 'Lord Arch Bishop' of Canterbury could consider further appointments. Master printers were restricted in their rights to employ apprentices. The Act provided for the employment of journeyman, or qualified apprentices, to ensure that they were fully employed and not tempted into unlicensed activities. The Act extended to importing and book selling. Only a shop licensed by the Stationers' Company was allowed to operate. Publications had to bear the name of the author and the printer, so they could be traced to the Stationers' register. The Act designated various holders of public office, the 'Lord Arch Bishop' of Canterbury and Secretaries of State for example, as the official censors. All publications had to be licensed by the official licensors before they could be printed. Books of law and history by the chancellor or chief-justices, of history and politics by the Secretary of State, of heraldry by the King-of-Arms, of divinity, physic or philosophy by the 'Lord Arch Bishop' of Canterbury or the 'Lord Bishop' of London. The monopolies, or copyrights as they were called, were preserved as before. The Act allowed the King's messengers, operating under a general warrant signed by one of the Secretaries of State, to search premises and seize documents in the investigation of treason and seditious libel. The powers of search, seizure and of arrest were based upon reasonable suspicion. They were frequently in use and the evasions of the licensing system were numerous, No printing was allowed outside London, except in York or the two universities. The business of licensing books was entrusted to the Surveyor of the Press, Sir Roger L'Estrange, a known scurrilous libeller on behalf, it was said, of popery and despotic power. He was succeeded by Edmund Bohun, a high Tory who pursued nonconformists vigorously.

Bohun was brought down by Charles Blount, who had long been hostile to the system of censorship. His writing came to notice in Bohun's term as the unknown author of *A Just Vindication of Learning*, a flagrant plagiarism of Milton's argument for free speech, *Aeropagitica*. The fine writing of Milton lifted the otherwise ordinary pamphlet to a higher plain. It was a success which Blount immediately followed with a bitter attack on the censor, again written anonymously, *A Just and True Character of Edmund Bohun*, which made the censor appear as dreadful as his predecessor. Not being licensed, the pamphlet passed from hand to hand. Simultaneously Blount sought permission for an anonymous autobiography, written by him, of Bohun. Bohun was so delighted to see his own thoughts as a high Tory and Churchman revealed so vividly and accurately, that he readily assented. He imagined rebellious Jacobins would be converted after reading this rich account of his thought. Blount was a skillful writer, but he was an ardent republican and strict atheist. The biography was entitled *King William and Mary Conquerors*. No sooner did the 'autobiography' become known than people became roused by the distasteful title, which misrepresented the well-known fact that the king and queen had been invited to the throne, and read no further. The House of Commons summoned Bohun as the licensor of this anonymous work. There he was assailed by condescension and laughter. After some questioning, in which he contradicted himself and became confused, the House resolved to burn the work in Palace Yard and put him in confinement.[18]

The newspapers, or newsbooks, did not thrive after the restoration and the circulation of news was spread more by informed conversation in coffee houses and by rumours in the street. The authorities feared these institutions so greatly that a proclamation ordering their suppression was issued in 1675. After a public outcry the coffee houses were re-opened and the proprietors were obliged to give undertakings to curb the manufacture of scandals and libels on their premises. Under the regime of licensing only the *London Gazette* was published, with a circulation of just 8000. It was edited by the Secretary of State. There were several periodicals. How many minister have dreamed of controlling a news monopoly! However, as will be explained, it did not endure beyond the Licensing Acts. Upon their cessation it took only weeks before London was flooded by newspapers.

In 1692 the House of Commons conducted a lively debate over the continuation of legislation to regulate printing. Petitions of printers and booksellers were studied and their arguments were entertained in Westminster. But, as no amendments to the 1662 legislation could be agreed upon, the regulations were continued. They expired two years later.

Without permission from those in authority and without the sanction of a constitutional enactment, the British people enjoy a large measure of freedom in thinking and expressing their thoughts. The origin of these freedoms is simply that they have been exercised and not that they have been granted by the Government or agreed

---

[18] *Commons' Journal*, 20 January 1693.

upon by popular consensus. In so far as any measure marked the demise of overt censorship, it was the refusal of the House of Commons in 1695 to renew the Licensing Act which had hitherto encumbered the written expression of ideas with a host of ridiculous restraints. On this occasion the Commons drew up a document listing eighteen reasons why they would refuse to renew the regulations. These reasons were technical and did not claim the freedom of the printing press. The document has been attributed to Locke.

The argument was put against the monopolies enforced by the Stationers' Company, against the vague and general regulations and it stressed the difficulties of prosecution. There was no general appeal for freedom from censorship. Parliament, which is wont to pretend to advance public welfare by increasing the burden, complexity and scope of legislation, demonstrated what great and lasting improvement came from undoing all that was done under the Printing Acts. The Commons were pressed in the next three sessions to introduce the Printing Acts, but on each occasion they deemed it unworkable. According to Macaulay, the legislators

> knew not what they were doing, what a revolution they were making, what power they were calling into existence. They pointed out concisely, clearly, forcibly, and sometimes with a grave irony which is not unbecoming, the absurdities and iniquities of the statute which was about to expire.[19]

Before beginning his historical work, Macaulay summed up the achievements of the British Revolution. He wrote:

> But of all the reforms produced by the Revolution, perhaps the most important was the full establishment of the liberty of unlicensed printing.The Censorship which, under some form or other existed, with rare and short intermissions, under every Government, monarchial and republican, from the time of Henry the Eighth downwards, expired, and has never since been reviewed.[20]

Proceedings in Parliament were granted immunity from outside prosecution by a provision in the Bill of Rights 1689.The Bill also outlawed 'Partial, Corrupt and Unqualified' jurors.

However, the king had commanded the judges several years previously to meet to determine that books scandalous to the Government or private persons or containing false news, even though not scandalous or seditious, were indictable.[21] In the same year it was also decided that to print a newspaper, even one which contained no falsity or

---

[19] *History of England*, T. Macaulay, ed Edinburgh [1896] vol iv, p. 125.
[20] *Ibid.* Penguin edn, pp. 552–3.
[21] *State Trials*, vol vii, 929.

scandal, was also illegal.[22] This was an advance on the judicial opinion at the close of the reign of Charles II, which had held that publication of political intelligence without permission of the king was a misdemeanour at common law.

The fight against the Crown and judiciary: the eighteenth century

The discontinuance of the Printing Acts in 1695 had not resulted in the cessation of censorship. An example of censorship to survive was the powers of the Lord Chamberlain to censor the theatre. His powers were given statutory force in Theatres Regulation Act 1843. The origin of this quaint superintendence was the attempt by Robert Walpole to silence the dramatists by obliging them to submit their plays to the Lord Chamberlain. In 1737, for example, Fielding's play, *The Historical Register*, had portrayed Walpole as the incompetent Quidam immersed in corruption. Finally in 1968 it was decided to supplant the opinion of the Lord Chamberlain with those of the theatre-going public, who, unlike the Lord Chamberlain, actually pay to see plays. Furthermore, they are not compelled to attend a play which contained scenes which they would describe as bestial.

Hand-in-hand with State censorship walked official propaganda. This was most evident in the news press. At the close of the seventeenth century there was only one official newspaper, the *London Gazette*, published in London. It covered court and foreign news. From a peak in its circulation of 5400 per day in 1704, when it was the largest paper, it declined to 2000 by 1717; its recipients comprised officials who were entitled to a free copy. Various editors from the private newspapers tried to make something of it but governments are dim proprietors and success never attended their journal.

The authorities did not welcome the appearance of commercial and scandalous newsletters and pamphlets. In 1702 Queen Anne ordered simply 'that the publication of false news' and scandalous books 'is to stop'. But the Commons had opened the door for the freedom of the printing press, largely because it had been undecided over an effective means to control it.

In 1712 the Government imposed a tax of a penny per page on newspapers to finance Marlborough's wars and to bridle the news press. This impost was accompanied by taxes on advertisements at one shilling per sheet and pamphlets at two shillings per sheet. A tax of a penny per copy of a whole sheet of paper and two shillings per sheet up to six sheets in octavo was imposed. Papers longer than six octavo sheets were exempt, provided that they were generally uncritical of the establishment. The taxes were clearly designed not to discourage the cheap news press, but to suppress it altogether. Taxes on newspapers continued at higher rates until 1855. As early as 1714 the statute was being flouted and very strictly interpreted as imposing a tax on the larger publications per edition, rather than per copy. The taxes repressed the growth

---

[22] *State Trials*, The Case of Carr, vol vi, 1126.

of national papers, made the publishing unprofitable and drove proprietors to accept subsidies from the State. Walpole perfected the fiscal oppression with the introduction of a new Stamp Act in 1724. Before its enactment there were eighty-two journals and newspapers; by 1726 the number fell to sixty-four. Taxes were imposed throughout the eighteenth century.

During the early part of the eighteenth century a large number of papers and writers received financial assistance from the Tory and Whig parties. Daniel Defoe was one of the most popular political writers prepared to write for any administration, provided 'they did not break in upon the constitution, and the laws and liberties of my country'. The Whig Government which came to power on the accession of George I in 1714 employed Defoe to infiltrate the Tory news press and mollify the attacks made on the Government. But he was also writing political pamphlets for the Tories. He became the principal writer for both the Tory *Journal* and the Whig *Post*. Neither side could afford to lose his services, even though they were aware of his engagements to the other party. Walpole, the Whig chief Minister, contributed an annual sum of around £10,000 for ten years of his administration to buy proprietors to favour his views. But after his fall in 1742 the public subsidy of the news press was discontinued. Jonathan Swift was persuaded to write for the Whigs, who urged him to write against the Occasional Conformity Bill. But Swift was a churchman of strong opinions and in 1711 he began writing as a political correspondent of the Tory *Examiner* and wrote a number of political pamphlets for them. Joseph Addison received gifts from the Whigs and Tories, but remained a Whig. Tobias Smollett and Henry Fielding flirted with politicians and enjoyed their favours. Even Samuel Johnson allowed himself to accept a pension of £300 per year, but at least he was honest; he admitted that he wanted the money.

In 1762 a weekly paper, the *Monitor*, was launched to attack George III's Tory Government. The Government responded by bringing out another, the *Briton*. Within a week an anonymous paper, the *New Briton*, actually published by John Wilkes, joined the attack alongside *the Monitor*. A week later the Government brought out the *Auditor*. But the 'official' papers made little impression. So the Government decided to shut down their opponents by prosecuting the writers and printers for seditious libel. The Attorney-General ruled that nine issues of the *New Briton* were seditious. Warrants were issued and forty-eight suspects were arrested, including Wilkes, who was released as he was protected as a Member of Parliament under parliamentary privilege. The persons arrested sued for unlawful arrest and search and seizure of papers under a general warrant and collected £100,000 in compensation from the State.

At the beginning of the eighteenth century no one was allowed to report proceedings in either Houses of Parliament. They were concerned with affairs of state, not with the lives of ordinary folk. It is plain from the complexities and the jargon employed that Parliament had little regard for the liberties of the individual. Edward Cave embarked on ending this constitutional secrecy. He published the *Gentleman's Magazine* in 1732, one of whose contributors. was Dr Johnson. Cave gained entry to the Commons by bribing the doormen. Political reporting was a noted feature in his magazine. By 1738 the Commons had had enough of this 'indignity' and resolved to proceed against reporters of their noble proceedings. Cave invented an imaginary legislature in Lilliput with two branches; the Houses of Hurpes and of Clinab. Walpole became Walelop, Halifax Haxilaf, Pultney Pulnub and so on. Dr Johnson wrote the political speeches between 1738–43. The magazine grew bolder until the Lords summoned Cave after a report of the trial of Lord Lovat for high treason. On his knees Cave begged their forgiveness and was reprimanded. He abolished the legislature in Lilliput. The test came in 1771 when the Commons forbad reporting and arrested one of six printers. The local magistrates set aside the proclamation, released the printer, who refused to appear before them, and imprisoned the messenger of the Commons who had made the arrest. The Commons responded by sending the Lord Mayor to the Tower. But the crowd which followed the Mayor made plain their opposition to the Commons. In the next session he was released and no further protest at parliamentary reporting was attempted. The Lords followed suit four years later. A number of journals appeared with reports of Parliament. Throughout the eighteenth century the Government sought to subsidise the news press from sources beyond the scrutiny of Parliament, like the secret service budget. Walpole was discovered to have spent over £50,000 in the last decade in office. A number of newspapers were given cash subsidies by the British and foreign governments, including *The Times* and the *Observer*. The Government bought circulations and distributed newspapers gratis, hired journalists, gave priority on intelligence to friendly editors, instructed newspapers.In short, it used its power in any way it could to control news. Members of the House of Commons were delegates of the people but in no sense did they admit up to the end of the seventeenth century, to their being responsible to the people. Therefore, they allowed no reports of their deliberations. In 1681 the Commons allowed the official publication of their votes after they had been censored by the Speaker. They forbade all unofficial publications of its votes and of its debates. Furthermore, they forbade this official report to be printed in newspapers.

By 1660 printing of seditions had been brought within the offences and the meaning of words became open to a great range of interpretations. In 1663 a printer, John Twyn, had been charged for treason for printing a seditious pamphlet in which he claimed that the king was accountable to the people and the people were entitled to revolt and govern themselves. He was convicted and drawn, hanged and quartered. In 1693 another printer, William Anderton, was put to death for printing a seditious pamphlet in the less spectacular manner on the scaffold. Both printers steadfastly refused to name their authors. In 1720 a printer's apprentice, John Matthews, was hanged for publishing a pamphlet supporting the claim of James the Pretender to the crown. These three prosecutions were the few that succeeded. But the offences of treason and sedition were difficult to prove before juries who were reluctant to convict. Consequently, treason went out of fashion for the offences of printing, publishing and thinking unwise ideas.

However, the offence of seditious libel, which did not involve the capital penalty, proved to be a more effective tool of censorship. In 1704 Chief Justice Holt declared:

To say that corrupt officers are appointed to administer affairs, is certainly a reflection on Government. If people should not be called to account for possessing the people with an ill opinion of the Government no Government can subsist. For it is very necessary for all Government that the people should have good opinion of it.[23]

Thus to bring Government into low opinion was to issue a libel.

In the Court of Star Chamber there had been no jury. But in the common law courts the jury created a number of problems for the authorities. They kept raising such tedious questions as whether words were seditious or not, when judges would have preferred them to concentrate on the facts at issue; namely, the straight-forward questions, did the accused write or publish the work? They were instructed to leave the question whether the words were seditious to the judge. Whether a seditious intent was present in the mind of the accused was a question which demanded a trained legal mind, rather than a random assessment of twelve laymen. The question of whether an assertion alleged to be a libel was actually true did not concern judges during the seventeenth century. If an accused sought to prove the truth of what he had uttered he was silenced. The *Case of the Seven Bishops* (1688) finally admitted the defence in a case of civil libel that a libellous statement could be true and, therefore, lawful.

The two Houses of Parliament also tried instances of seditious libels. If a committee, especially one appointed by them, found guilt proved then the offending publication was ordered to be burnt by the hangman and its author to be deterred according to their pleasure. While the Lords fastened particularly on libels directed against their members, the Commons devoted themselves with criticisms of their policies.

The trial which highlighted prosecution for seditious libel and brought it to public attention was the *Junius Case*.[24] Junius was the *nom de plume* of a critic of the Government. He advised the king to change his ministers and stay out of parliamentary affairs – advice quite as courageous as it was impertinent. Not being able to discover the identity of Junius, which remains unproven to this day, despite considerable research and speculation, the Attorney-General was obliged to prosecute the booksellers and printers. In one of these cases, Lord Mansfield directed the jury to consider only the question of publication and whether the material carried the sense alleged of it.[25] The jury convicted but in another action against the printer[26] they returned a verdict of 'Guilty' of publishing only. But parties in the case desired to know to which of them the verdict belonged. The court eventually ordered a new trial against the printer but it was not brought. In a third trial against a publisher[27] the jury returned a finding of 'Not Guilty'. These trials had attracted great interest and the

---

[23] 14 *State Trials*, R v Tutchin 1095.
[24] 19 *State Trials* 115.
[25] 20 *State Trials* 803.
[26] *Ibid.* 895.
[27] *Ibid.* 894.

public clearly favoured the accused. Lord Camden immediately tabled six questions about the role of the jury in cases involving seditious libel and Lord Mansfield answered them in a judgment thirteen years later. In the trial of the Dean of St Asaph, already discussed,[28] Lord Mansefield expressed the legal position when he held that, 'The liberty of the press consists in printing without any previous licence, subject to the consequences of the law.'[29] Erskine argued powerfully that the issue of whether the writing was seditious should be decided by the jury as a matter of fact rather than by the judge as a matter of law. Though Erskine lost the argument, Fox introduced his Libel Act in 1792 to establish that the jury had control over that crucial question. In the House of Lords it was opposed by judges as being contrary to common law. Thereafter, prosecutions for seditious libel seemed doomed.

After the French revolution in 1791 various restraints were imposed upon the communication of ideas; the news press were harried by prosecutions, the Treason Acts were given a wider scope and public meetings restricted and those sympathetic with France were broken up. Thomas Paine was indicted for publishing the second part of his *Rights of Man*, in which he criticised the monarchy, advocated public education, children's allowances and old-age pensions.This pamphlet sold more than one and a half million copies, which was a staggering total then. Erskine was then legal adviser to the Prince of Wales and a favourite for the position of Lord Chancellor and was advised to refuse the brief. Paine fled to Paris and was tried *in absentia*. In his defence Erskine formulated the right of a free press:

> The proposition which I wish to maintain as the basis of the liberty of the [printing] press, and without which it is an empty sound, is this: that every man, not intending to mislead, but seeking to enlighten others with his own reason and conscience, however erroneously, have dictated to him as truth, may address himself to the universal reason of a whole nation, either upon the subject of Government in general or that of our particular country.[30]

After Erskine's defence of the freedom of the press and before the Attorney-General's reply or the summing up by the judge, the jury, selected by the lawyers of the Crown, pronounced Paine guilty of publishing a seditious libel. He was sentenced to outlawry, which meant his property was forfeit and the gallows would be his welcome in England. Later Erskine wrote to Thomas Howell, the editor of *State Trials*, giving his reason for resisting the attempt to unhorse Paine, 'I took the liberty [in a letter to the king] to claim, as an invaluable part of [the] Constitution, the unquestionable right of the subjects to make his defence by any counsel of his free choice.'

---

[28] See p. 67.
[29] *R v Dean of St Asaph*, 3TR 431.
[30] *Thomas Erskine and Trial By Jury*, J. Hosteller, p. 97.

One judge in these trials uttered an ancient nostrum: 'No man had a right to speak of the Constitution unless he possessed landed property.'[31] He intended to infer that an unpropertied man was not motivated to defend society.

The Secretaries of State had been empowered since 1662 to issue general warrants for the arrest and search of suspects in cases of seditious libel; they inherited these powers from the defunct Stationers' Company. Lord Camden held in the case on *Entick v Carrington* (1765), which has been discussed above[32] that, despite the usage of a century, the Secretaries of State had no power under common law to issue general warrants.

In 1794 prosecutions were brought against the leaders of the Constitutional and Corresponding Societies for 'constructive treason'. Corresponding Societies became established in London in 1792, and in Edinburgh, Sheffield and Norwich. Their members were communicating the novel ideas of universal suffrage and annual parliaments. Their treason consisted of plotting to overthrow the Crown in order to replace it with a republic. In fact they were neither republicans, Jacobins or even against the Crown. Twelve members of these societies were arrested and in the panic the Habeas Corpus Act was suspended, allowing them to be held six months. In the first trial Erskine defended the secretary of the London Society, Thomas Hardy, and addressed the jury for seven consecutive days.

It is that, under the dominion of a barbarous state necessity, every protection of law is abrogated and destroyed; – it is that no man can say, under such a system of alarm and terror, that his life, his liberty, his reputation, or any one human blessing, is secure to him for a moment; it is that if accused of federalism, of moderatism, or incivism, or whatever else the changing fashions and factions of the day shall have lifted up into high treason against the State, he must see his friends, his family, and the light of heaven no more:- the accusation and the sentence being the same: following one another as thunder pursues the flash.[33]

The verdict of 'Not Guilty' was delivered by the foreman of the jury in a whisper and was received with public joy. The foreman then fainted. Next came the trial of John Hooke, returned as Member for Old Sarum, comprising a constituency of the landowner, an old woman and a pig. The jury pronounced a 'Not Guilty' verdict without even leaving the court. Lord Gordon who led the riots against Catholicism and Catholics was among those acquitted. 'I hate Lord Gordon', explained Dr Johnson, 'but I am glad he was not convicted of this constructive treason; for though I hate him, I love my country and myself.' The Government had to destroy about 800 arrest warrants, which would have been issued after conviction in these trials.

---

[31] *Richard Carlile*, G. Aldred, pp. 23–4.
[32] See pp. 46.
[33] 24 *State Trials* 878.

Parliament had power to summon, interrogate and punish printers, writers and publishers for writing libels against parliamentarians, for criticising Parliament or making 'a reflection on Government' and for the general offences of blasphemy and obscenity. It exercised these powers on the right to punish a breach of its privileges and to pursue anyone who wronged a parliamentarian. By the end of the eighteenth century, however, Parliament lost interest in conducting prosecutions and devoted its time to legislation and the affairs of State.

In May 1817 Lord Sidmouth wrote to the Lord-Lieutenants that persons selling libellous pamphlets could be held under the Hawkers and Pedlars Acts and confirming that magistrates had discretionary powers of arrest. *The Times* spoke out against this extra-judicial pronouncement:

We should prefer a censorship which, whatever its demerits, at least exempts authors and publishers from responsibility, to such a state of things. But we say that no writing is a libel till it is found such, and that the ultimate finders of a libel as found such are now declared by law to be the jury that has tried it.[34]

The suppression of opinion was directed both at individuals and the newspapers. Lord Chancellor Eldon declared in 1819 they were 'a most malignant and formidable enemy to the Constitution to which it owed its freedom'.[35] A duty of four pence per journal was imposed. Newsagents were prevented from 'lending' newspapers and during the Battle of the 'Unstamped' between 1830–35 there were 750 convictions for breach of this absurd duty. These duties were minimised to a great extent by reducing the print of papers and restricting the coverage of news. The cost of subscribing to a daily sheet of news was £10.

In 1820 the Constitutional Society was formed as a secular counterpart of the Society for the Suppression of Vice. They both failed when public opinion and, more importantly, juries turned against their private prosecutions. The fire of the attack on the radicals had gone out, key ministers, such as Lord Sidmouth, were replaced by the milder Robert Peel and in 1830 the Tory Government fell. Carlile had been present at the meeting on St Peter's Field, Manchester, in 1819 and afterwards reported the massacre fearlessly. He replied in open letters to the Regent and Home Secretary. He was arrested on bail for seditious libel and blasphemous libel arising out of publications made by him. He was offered immunity from the blasphemy charges on condition that he undertook to withdraw his accounts of the 'massacre of Peterloo'. But Carlile would give no such undertaking.

Repressive measures, contained in the Six Acts 1819, to suppress societies considered seditious, and to curtail freedom of speech were rushed through Parliament in the early decades of the nineteenth century. These measures gave the authorities effective control over the written and spoken word. The Six Acts represented the high-water mark of

---

[34] *The Times*, 14 May 1817.
[35] *The Struggle for the Freedom of the Press 1819–32*, W. Wickwar, p. 130.

the suppression of newspapers. The increase in Stamp Duty on newspapers was to restrain abuses arising from blasphemous and seditious libels. The effect of the increased stamp duty on newspapers, unsurprisingly, put an end to William Cobbett's *Weekly Political Register* and other radical papers.

> The cause of freedom of expression was served by the plain vigour of Cobbett and the invective of Junius but it was borne most courageously by Carlile who suffered and achieved more for the Liberty of the Press than any other Englishman of the nineteenth century.[36]

He was drawn into the struggle by publishing radical journals and pamphlets, Paine's books and selling others in London. He was fined £1500 and in 1819 sentenced for a term of three years in Dorchester Prison, having published Paine's *Age of Reason* and Palmer's *Principles of Nature*, which were both held to contain blasphemous libels. His bookshop in Fleet Street was closed and his stock of 70,000 books seized – which Carlile felt more painfully than the sentence of imprisonment. Like Lilburne, Carlile used his time in prison to read and write. He produced his journal, the *Republican*, and drew an audience of several thousand among artisans and factory workers, despite continual prosecutions of distributors and sellers for blasphemous and seditious libel. In 1825 Carlile was was released from gaol. He adopted an anti-Christian, anti-authority stance and he dabbled with some questions involving economic injustice. He believed in nature and reason. Soon he became the foremost champion of birth control, equality between the sexes and divorce through legal right, though he retained a Victorian moral code. Divorce was obtainable through a special Act of Parliament. Unfortunately, the circulation of the *Republican* dropped by 60 per cent to a weekly circulation of 2000 in 1826 and closed. He became what he called an 'atheist missionary' to purge Christianity of its corruption in order to restore its 'original purity and lustre.' He established a centre, the Rotunda, for this purpose in Blackfriars, London. He edited many journals, such as the *Prompter*, the *Union*, the *Gauntlet*, *A Scourge for the Littleness of 'Great' Me*.

In 1830 the Government moved against the Rotunda by charging Carlile on four counts of sedition. The jury acquitted him of two charges but he received a two-year sentence and a fine. Again his imprisonment was active but a further prosecution wrecked the *Rotunda*. While in prison he built up the *Gauntlet* to a respectable circulation of between 5000–10,000. After his release in 1835 Carlile spent his last eight years of life travelling and lecturing throughout Britain.

The end of prosecutions for seditious libel came when the Government realised that an accused either was allowed by the jury to win the case and achieve fame or he was convicted and became a martyr. The trial also granted publicity to the accused scribbler. In 1822 prosecutions were discontinued and so it remained until 1829 when

---

[36] *British History in the Nineteenth Century*, G. Trevelyan, p. 162.

two exceptional cases were brought. In 1832 the Attorney-General reiterated the policy[37] of not prosecuting libels. The end of criminal prosecutions for seditious and blasphemous libels was acknowledged by Lord Brougham, the Lord Chancellor. In 1832 he asked a Select Committee of the House of Commons enquiring into libel and slander:

> [If they] had ever considered the matter so as to shape a law that should draw the distinction between libels dangerous to the public or hurtful to individuals, and those which are harmless. That I have always found to perfectly impossible.[38]

At last reason had prevailed over oppression. The cessation of prosecutions of seditious libel was followed in 1843 by Lord Campbell's Act, which allowed the defence of the truth of matter, provided it was for the public benefit, to be pleaded in cases of criminal libel.

The freedom of expression is so natural a liberty of man, that its enjoyment comes to be regarded like breathing and it is easily forgotten that vigilance is be its only guardian. Yet the freedom can never be won for all time. As Burke warned: 'The price of liberty is eternal vigilance.'

One might imagine one of the prime duties of Government is to resolutely defend the freedom of speech, which for centuries it had so actively repressed. Since the beginning of the nineteenth century the people residing in Britain have enjoyed this freedom as a right. But in a recent example this great liberty was effectively surrendered. In February 1989 the Ayatollah Khomeini in Iran issued a death threat against Salman Rushdie, a British subject, for having dared to write a book attacking Muslim beliefs. Rushdie was guarded round the clock. He refused to bow to the death threats and became a hostage in his own country. The Foreign Office, through its Middle-East Department, re-established relations with Iran in September 1990 and in a letter to the author of this work, dated 5 June 1992, justified their move 'on the basis of mutual respect and non-interference in each other's affairs'. How can a country enjoying freedom of speech respect a foreign potentate who uses criminal incitement to attack this freedom in Britain? The Foreign Office are firmly committed to maintaining diplomacy, even with the devil himself, and it is not inferred that they should have upheld what the Government had decided not to defend. The Iranian authorities thought that they were being reasonable, for Britain her Government clearly held a poor opinion of Rushdie and because Britain regarded blasphemy as a criminal offence.

Blasphemy and blasphemous libel (written blasphemy) remains an offence at common law. The offence has been rarely brought. It should have been repealed instantly in order to preserve the liberty of an individual which is of greater intrinsic

---

[37] Parl. Deb 3rd series vol xiii col 1141.
[38] *The Struggle for the Freedom of the Press 1819-32*, W. Wickwar, p. 308-9.

importance than the power of the Church of England. The Iranians complained that the offence of blasphemy did not cover their religion. It was their strong point. The opportunity to abolish the offence and so introduce equality between sects and religions was missed because heed was paid to the opinion of bishops in the Church of England.

The fact was that Prime Minister Thatcher ignored the serious public aspect of the crisis: that a foreign government had violated the British freedom of speech by an incitement to murder. An attack an individual's freedom is an attack against freedom of speech in Britain. How contemptible is the sight of Rusdie scuttling around Britain, the bastion of the freedom of speech, like a hunted animal. His weakness mirrored the weakness of Thatcher's Government in dealing with a most important public issue.

In 1993 Douglas Hogg, minister at the Foreign Office, called in the Iranian Chargé d'Affaires and expressed the anger of the British Government at a repetition of the illegal *fatwa* against Rushdie. It was reported a week later in Iran that the mullahs were astonished at the conduct of the British Government, whom they imagined shared their distaste of Rushdie. Indeed, that had been patently evident.

Rushdie is the latest in a line of rare individuals who have considered freedom of expression as a fundamental human right more important than their individual liberty. By such intrepid individuals has the British liberty of the printing press been won from the Crown, Parliament and judiciary.

7

Freedom of Conscience

It is no business of the authorities to concern themselves with the thoughts, beliefs or ideas of individuals, unless they are suspected to be criminal. It matters not that an individual is filled with ideas that the authorities or the established order of society believe to be revolutionary. It is of no concern that an individual may disrespect the Crown, political, religious or legal leaders.

Yet it is the tendency of the authorities to encourage the formation of an orthodoxy of ideas around their thinking. The history of the struggle over religious conscience waged between individual and State serves as a reminder of that inclination. It may take any form but religion brings out the folly and comedy most sharply.

It irked Henry VIII greatly that his countrymen should acknowledge the Pope as their spiritual head and pay him taxes; both practices were insulting to His Majesty. He was determined to found his Empire on a strong state in England. The birth of a male heir was particularly important to that grand design. But he lacked this essential prop of kingship. That it was in the power on earth to deny him a further opportunity of procreation was preposterous.

He had the motive and will to assert himself as king. Thomas Cromwell supplied the means. He effected the breach with the pontiff and with the substance and practices of Romanism. He terrorised the nation into submission, so that it could take the royal impression with that quietude and docility which terror inspires. He accomplished, later, the subjugation of Ireland.

First, Henry VIII had to subdue the clergy. There were a traditional group and they liked to maintain their beliefs and way of doing things. They were rich, magnificently so. The decisive quarrel concerned the fall of Cromwell's illustrious predecessor. Cardinal Wolsey had been convicted but the judges implicated the whole people in his guilt. Cromwell gave a general pardon to the people, but not to the clergy. He was prepared to grant them the same pardon in exchange for a handsome fine, now amounting to several millions, and submission to the king as the temporal and spiritual 'Protector'. They paid without demur and submitted to this fantastic oath after the terms had been widened fractionally. The Archbishop of Canterbury – in effect a head of department in government – put the matter to the 1531 Convocation of the clergy and deemed that silence, which was uniform among his flock, could be taken as agreement to Cromwell's terms.

In 1532 Parliament quashed legal appeals to Rome and granted power to the king to suspend payment of first fruits, due out of a bishop's first year of office to Rome.Two years later by the Act of Supremacy Henry was made 'supreme head on earth' of the Church of England and months afterwards Thomas Cromwell became its Vicar-General. The selection of bishops, previously within the power of Rome, was restored to the chapters of cathedrals. They were freed to elect, provided they elected the nomination of the Crown; failure to do so risked the receipt of a writ. What had been issued to Rome had been usurped by the Crown.

Having emasculated the episcopacy, Henry turned to the monasteries and Houses of Religion. Most were rich, many dissolute and all were independent of the Crown. That last attribute angered Cromwell. Four hundred of the thousand monastic establishments in England and Wales were dissolved in 1536. The spoils were so great that the king was able to do without taxation again in his reign.The pulpit was then an important public platform and, by directing the clergy on what was to be preached, the Vicar-General made the pulpit a seat of propaganda directed against Rome.

The marriage to Anne Boleyn was enforced by the Vicar-General's Act of Succession in 1534 which obliged everyone to swear that the marriage to Catherine had been contrary to Scripture and invalid from the beginning and that the king was supreme head of the new Church. Sir Thomas More preferred execution to compliance. Silence was no defence to treason: instead it was taken as open denial.

After three years of marriage Anne was condemned of having been adulterous and was beheaded. Jane Seymour, who became queen in her place, died in 1537 while giving birth to Edward VI, who succeeded Henry but was to expire of consumption at the age of sixteen – more the runt of the litter, than a glorious heir for which Henry had given himself so selflessly to a miscellany of wives.

It was not sufficient only to reduce the clergy to outer obedience. Henry was persuaded to formulate some of the doctrines of their faith though the Act of Six Articles in 1539, which covered doctrines of transubstantiation, clerical celibacy, private masses and confessions. He did not want to allow departures or heresies from the new paths which he had laid down.

Cromwell ventured into foreign affairs. One of his initial steps was to procure the marriage of Henry to the sister-in-law of the Elector of Saxony, Anne of Cleves. The elector was a Lutheran and Cromwell wanted to forge an alliance with the German princes. But Henry found Anne coarse and unwieldy. Yet he could not get out of the marriage which Cromwell had procured. Although Cromwell was granted the earldom of Essex, all was not well between the two men. The king made no attempt to save him from the gallows to which the pent up fury of the nobles bid him in July 1540. When he was arrested Cromwell had exclaimed in utter disbelief, 'On your consciences, I ask you, am I a traitor?' Such has been the posture of many State servants: mindful of the needs of the Crown or ruling power and shamelessly neglectful of the liberties of the people.

Under Cromwell religion had been administered according to the Puritan mind. Superstitions and traditional rituals were discarded, priests' surplices were left off and public officials, be they soldiers, magistrates or priests, were guided by Christian piety. Theatres were closed, Sunday sport forbidden, Christmas passed without being adorned by junketing, mummers or mince pies, racing, bull-baiting or cock-fighting. This world of sparkling righteousness and insufferable priggishness passed swiftly after the death of Thomas Cromwell. Yet Puritanism was to rise in the following century in a less extreme form as a force in religion and thought.

Under Edward VI religion was steered down a Protestant aisle. In 1548 the Book of Common Prayer translated from the universal Latin tongue into English and was imposed on the Church by the Act of Uniformity in 1559. The Latin Mass was replaced by the Communion service. In 1552 the Thirty-Nine Articles of Faith were introduced as the doctrinal markers of Protestantism.

Under Mary there was a Catholic reaction. It was a violent reaction of cruel killings and persecutions. Many showed great courage and character as they perished at the stake. In their last moments their spirits gleamed with their inner strength. Flames could not burn their souls or ideas. Some were clerics but many were ordinary folk.

Elizabeth, the daughter of Anne Boleyn, found the country sunk to its lowest ebb; helpless without army, navy or ally, save Spain; bankrupt; riven with discontent and misgovernment; and divided by religion. She favoured neither Puritans nor Catholics, but was drawn to a middle path. She declared that she had no wish to meddle with people's consciences. Burnings ceased and prisoners were set free. In 1559 she restored the Book of Common Prayer. She broke links with Rome but steadfastly refused to incline further towards Protestantism. She preferred what might seem, from a Government view, a picture of chaos in religion; as individuals followed their own feelings. She was not drawn to an enforced uniformity. She evidenced a rare insight into State power and individual liberty. Yet foreign pressure to win England back for the Pope led her to enact the Test Act in 1563, as a move to stifle the foreign threat. The Act obliged all holders of office to swear an oath of allegiance to the Queen and to abjure the temporal authority of the pontiff. Effectively Catholics were excluded from all public employment. It also set up a Commission to enforce the Act of Uniformity and the Thirty-Nine Articles of Faith were enacted by the Convocation of the clergy. However, the foreign threat evaporated. There were problems with Mary Queen of Scots who determined to restore the papacy in England, but she was deserted in 1567 and the threat from Scotland passed away, only to be replaced by open conflict with Rome, now under Pius V, who favoured war with England. His agents failed either to mount an invasion or foment a domestic revolution, which was defeated with much ferocity. In 1570 Pius issued a Bull of Excommunication and Deposition against Elizabeth. It purported to release her subjects from the religious oaths which they had given and forbade her nobles and people to obey her on pain of excommunication. However, Pius had allowed his policy to outrun his jurisdiction and his attempt to unseat Elizabeth failed.

She was able to maintain her policy of preserving religious peace. She restrained the public excitement of religious fervour and resisted the Puritan pressures. Gradually the threat of Catholicism passed away; it remained strong only in the extreme West, which was poorly populated. A new generation accepted the dual policy without demur of maintaining resolute enmity to Rome together with religious moderation.

But in 1579 the papacy began its next strike against Elizabeth, by using the new resolve of Philip of Spain to end the peace with England. A force failed to excite the Irish into revolt. A group of Jesuit missionaries, who had hoped to fire Catholic leaders throughout England were tracked down, imprisoned or put to flight. The plan to use King James of Scotland failed too, after he had concluded an alliance in 1586 with Elizabeth, for which he hoped the English Crown would be his at her death. Yet the Spanish had been successful in re-conquering the Netherlands. The enmity of Rome stiffened the resistance of the English and it could be said that the offensive rendered the nation Protestant. Its religious zeal was mingled with, it appears, a greater love of its liberty.

Meanwhile at home the drift among the clergy to greater Puritanism and Nonconformism angered Elizabeth and she strengthened the powers of the Ecclesiastical Commission. All matters touching the Acts of Supremacy and Uniformity fell within its concern and it was armed with the power to deprive clergies of their living. Religious meetings in private houses were forbidden.

In the autumn of 1587 Sir Francis Drake raided the Spanish Armada, gathering in Cadiz, and in his own words it was an operation for 'singeing of the Spanish king's beard'. In July of the following year the Armada was sighted off the Lizard. The Spanish brought 22,000 soldiers in 132 warships, armed with 2500 cannon and they had another 17,000 in the Netherlands. However, the Dutch fleet imposed a blockade to prevent them crossing the Channel. The English fleet numbered eighty and only four equalled the tonnage of the smallest Spanish galleon. The Armada suffered many losses but managed to weigh anchor at Calais. But the English fell on them at night and in terror the Spanish fled, to be dispersed by the currents and broken by the storms around Orkney. Only fifty vessels returned to Corunna. The naval supremacy of Spain had been wrecked and the papacy had been firmly rebuffed.

Indeed the reign of Elizabeth had been a time of Renaissance and England had awoken from the oppressive tyranny of Henry VIII and withstood its enemies within Europe and the British Isles. England had broken free of feudal traditions and lost the thirst for religious strife. Elizabeth hated Calvinism but she could arrest its progress in a world whose main learning was the translated Bible and the conviction that sin and good, heaven and hell, life and death were personal matters rather than the possessions of churches.

James VI & I was known as 'the wisest fool in Christendom'. He allowed the Convocation of the clergy in 1604 to insist on the full compliance of clerics with the Thirty-Nine Articles of Faith. Since 1571 the Church had demanded observance of only those touching faith and the sacraments; those concerning discipline and ritual were allowed to go unheeded. This allowed the Church to be kept as 'broad' as possible. In 1605 300 Puritan clergy were expelled from their livings. James allowed the fines for recusancy, failure to attend Church, to be remitted. This had the effect of increasing the number of Catholics and this emboldened a number to plan an elaborate papist plot of which the Gunpowder Plot was to have been the trigger. Otherwise James left religious matters and busied himself with quarrelling with his judges and with Parliament.

The Puritans watched the advance of Catholicism in France and Germany with dread. At home they feared the leadership of the Church under Archbishop Laud inclining more to Rome, in matters of ceremony and doctrine, and becoming more dependent on the Crown. They thought they had glimpsed the hand of treachery delivering them to the Church of Babylon. Laud believed episcopal succession was the essential fabric of a Church. Yet both Luther and Calvin saw no need for bishops. Therefore, as Laud drew back from Protestants in Europe, he moved, necessarily, closer to Rome. He believed the Anglican Church should be affiliated to Rome. However, his jurisdiction was confined to his bishopric in London, which, although it afforded him access to the crown, nonetheless was small. In 1633 he became Archbishop of Canterbury and was able to employ his High Commission to harry Puritan ministers, dismiss them or curtail their right to preach. His energies were directed to lay conformity in matters of Bible-reading, sport on the sabbath and the like. His own chapel at Lambeth was furnished with an altar instead of a plain table and was pervaded by a High Church air. So severe was this rule from above that many looked for a freedom which had been taken from them in the Old World to the New World of America. Laud was unseated from office in December 1640 and, after a long trial, hanged for treason.

The House of Commons sought to return religion to what it had been with Elizabeth. Commissioners were sent round churches to strip them of 'images, altars, or tables turned altarwise, crucifixes, superstitious pictures, monuments, and reliques of idolatry'. The House also voted to exclude bishops from the House of Lords, where they had acted as a curb on freedom.

A number of congregations, who rejected a National Church, began forming in Elizabeth's reign. Many fled to Holland where they could develop their independence. They questioned many of the prevailing views, but on account of their opposition to the need of adult baptism, they became known as Baptists, or Independents or Congregationalists. It is from a congregation of such spirits that the Pilgrim Fathers were formed. When a number of them returned from New England in 1640 their movement began to attract public attention. Their growth was encouraged and both Houses of Parliament accepted the Presbyterian form of Church Government. No one imagined that an individual should be free to think and practise his religious thoughts, yet under the looser control of religion after the Civil War dissidence grew apace.

Charles II promised from Breda to protect a measure of liberty of conscience. He issued on his own authority his first Declaration of Indulgence in 1662, which granted full equality to Christians. Parliament, however, did nor share his beneficence towards Catholics. Nor did they like the Declaration suspending their laws. They forced Charles to withdraw it. The Church wanted a prelacy and service format and toleration was granted to Catholics but not to independents or Nonconformists. Edward Clarendon, his chief minister, sought to destroy the growth of the Nonconformists by enacting the Test and Corporation Acts in 1673, which required every person entering municipal office to take Communion according to Anglican rites and to declare that he abjured treason against the king. It was strict in the letter but, in practice, it was treated with contempt.

A more effective measure was the Act of Uniformity which demanded the assent of every priest to the Prayer Book and clothed only those orders conferred by bishops with legality. About 2000 vicars failed to comply with the Act and were dismissed as Nonconformists. The Act broke with all Protestant religions on the Continent by legalising only episcopal orders. The greatest effect of the Act is that Nonconformists, who had been always warring, became welded together by a common cause.

Many clergy fled London at the emergence of the plague in London and their places were filled by others who had been expelled by the harsh Acts. For fear of civil unrest they passed the Five Mile Act in 1695 which enforced an oath on the clergy to renounce taking arms against the king or, on a failure to swear, an exile from their normal residence for a five-mile distance.

James VII & II determined to reassert Catholicism. He suspended the harsh Acts and appointed judges who would champion his prerogative power to override statute law. The way was open for Catholics to enter public employment. He stirred up great discontent and after the birth of his son, William of Orange was invited to take his throne.

Writing *A Letter Concerning Toleration* in 1685 Locke says:

> The toleration of those that differ from others in matters of religion is so agreeable to the Gospel of Jesus Christ, and to the genuine reason of mankind, that it seems monstrous for men to be so blind, as not to perceive the necessity and advantage of it in so clear a light . . . the care of souls cannot belong to the civil magistrate, because his power consists in outward force.[1]

Locke's article appeared in the year when Henry IV's Edict of Nantes, granting toleration towards Protestants, was brutally set aside by Louis XIV. Many Protestants fled France to Holland where Locke was then living. Locke wrote anonymously and did not write as a member of any Church. The fact that he wrote at a key moment in the history of religious toleration does not suggest that he himself played any role in what was to unfold in Britain. Indeed, Locke was intolerant of Catholics, for their wont to obey a foreign leader, and of atheists.

---

[1] *Political Writings*, J. Locke, Penguin edn, p. 393, 396.

The Toleration Act 1688 accorded the freedom of worship and ended the political manipulation of the religious conscience of the people. Of this Act Macaulay wrote:

> We question whether in the whole of that vast mass of legislation, from the Great Charter downwards, there be a single law has so diminished the sum of human suffering, which has done so much to allay public passions, which has put an end to some much petty tyranny and vexation, which has bought gladness, peace, and a sense of security to so many private dwellings.[2]

Disabilities, notably exclusion from Parliament were removed in the Roman Catholics Relief Acts (1791) the Religious Disabilities Act (1829) and (1846).

Blasphemy was an offence at common law. In 1676 Lord Chief Justice Matthew Hale held in a trial of an accused who, had claimed that Jesus Christ was a bastard and a whore-master, that blasphemous words were an offence against God and religion and constituted a crime. But in 1832 Lord Brougham, the Lord Chancellor, spoke against retention of the offence of blasphemy.

> I am of the opinion that the Law [of blasphemy] is totally useless: it does not prevent a single person from blaspheming. I believe a man who has this disposition is not a rational being . . . and no fear of punishment will prevent him indulging his senseless propensity.[3]

Since 1920 there have only been two prosecutions. In the first in 1922[4] blasphemy was held to occur when indecent and offensive attacks were made on Christianity. In the case of *R v Lemon*[5] it was held that *Gay News*, having published a homosexual poem, offensive to Christians, could be guilty of blasphemy, even though the intention to blaspheme was not proved. The Law Commission[6] doubted whether the offence protected any Christian religion apart from the Church of England. In *ex p Choudray*[7], which involved an appeal by Muslims to prosecute Rushdie over his book, *The Satanic Verses* (1988), it was held that blasphemy did not extend beyond the established religion of England. The Law Commission of 1985 recommended with a majority of three to two to abolish the offence for the simple reason that 'religion' was impossible to define[8] and by the Williams Committeee's Report on Obscenity and Film Censorship.

At a time when the mixture of religions, faiths, spiritual paths varies among the population of Britain, the establishment of the Church of England seems inappropri-

---

[2] *The History of England*, T. H. Macaulay, Penguin edn 1983, p. 647.
[3] *Struggle for the Freedom of the Press 1819–32*, W. Wicklaw, p. 309.
[4] *R v Gott* (1922) 16 Cr App Rep 87.
[5] [1979] AC 617.
[6] Working Paper No 79 at p.82.
[7] [1991] 1 QB 429.
[8] Working Paper 79 at p. 546.

ate. It is estimated that its congregations are declining to about 2 per cent of the population. There are two consequences of this establishment which have no basis in reason. The first is that the Prime Minister should have any involvement in the choice of bishops. He has a superfluity of powers to appoint, remunerate and honour and the sooner they are diminished the more he will be focused on the prime concern of political administration. The second is that leading bishops sit in the Second Chamber. Why are not similar *ex officio* appointments available to academics, generals, scientists or even leaders of industry?

Although Britain enjoys religious toleration, the relationship between Church and State is not finally worked out. Government is concerned with the material aspect of human life and Church concerns faith and belief. It is desirable to keep the two activities separate by removing the Church of England from the political stage altogether. British history reveals the dangers of mixing religion with government.

The nature of man and the nature of society are essentially spiritual and contain the essence of beliefs in every sincere religion and spiritual teaching. Man the world over is conceived in one humanity and the Creator and Nature would settle for an aspiration of man to live in harmony with the Creation.

One reason for disestablishing the Church of England as matter of priority is to keep British politics free of religion and sects. For when one is favoured other sects or religions, which may grow larger, will demand similar official status and in order to preserve tradition British politics will become a patchwork of religions and sects, some of whom have traditions of unrest and militancy. Locke never intended toleration to weaken the nation.

To continue a state of affairs which no longer reflect realities is too dangerous to continue purely out of tradition. In fact, it survives as a consequence of lethargy which benefits no-one. The statement of Dr Priestly in the 1760s – 'The toleration in England, notwithstanding our boasted liberty, is far from being completed'[9] – is still true at the turn of the millennium.

---

[9] *An Essay on the First Principles of Government*, J. Priestly, p. 117.

8

Individual Freedom and Public Order

Almost the first duty of government is to preserve individual liberties at the same time as maintaining the Queen's Peace. That concept of the peace of society dates from Anglo-Saxon times, when the monarch ensured peace. It may often appear to be simple to achieve the overriding duty of maintaining the peace of society by suspending individual liberties altogether. Peace can be understood as an absence of open conflict in society and, similarly, the duty of government can be set at providing adequate resources to break up disorder. But the development of a peaceful society is a more creative work, its goals are higher and its foundations reach into the most fundamental issues of political thought. The peace of the graveyard may be suitable for the dead and may suit authority well. Ministers responsible for order breathe a sigh of relief if their period of office passes without a major disturbance.

A dynamic peace of society depends upon the enjoyment of both civil and economic liberties. Parliament, however, persists in the belief that the police are the defence of the peace of this nation, while refusing to acknowledge that the underlying seedbed of crime and disorder is poverty. The eradication of this condition of poverty constitutes the the most profound measure that government effect to preserve order in society. That connection between poverty and disorder is not admitted because, it is said, there are no statistics to prove that connection. When Parliament replaces diagnosis by statistics, it abandons reason. Instead of concentrating solely on the actions of criminals, regard should be to the economic background of society. High levels of unemployment and of inflation are certain to promote disorder. When millions are unemployed or money is losing its value through periods of inflation, these ills are indicating that the economic order of society is rotten. Crime is a natural environment of disorder, in the same way that static rubbish provides an inviting habitat for rats. Parliament is invariably concerned with regulating outward conduct and rarely with taking into consideration the causation of economic injustice.

During peace at times of emergencies wide executive powers are granted to the authorities, who might have to act suddenly, under prerogative powers of the Crown, which do not require immediate approval by Parliament. But governments in the twentieth century have derived their emergency legislative powers from Parliament.

Under the Emergency Powers Act 1920, as amended in 1964, a state of emergency can be declared by Proclamation, if it appears to the Crown that events have happened, or are about to happen, which threaten to deprive the essentials of life through interference in the supply of food, water, fuel, light or means of locomotion. Parliament must be informed immediately or summoned, if in recess, within five days and if it does not prolong the state of emergency then the state lapses after one month. Since the Second World War eight states of emergency have been declared and five were experienced between 1970 and 1974, when opposition to industrial relations legislation caused strikes in the coal mines, the docks and the electricity supply stations.

If, at any time, the police chiefs feel unable to contain disorder they can seek the aid of the armed forces through the Home Secretary, who will confer with the Minister of Defence. The armed forces would appear to act in these circumstances under the power conferred by Section 3 of the Criminal Law Act 1967, which provides that, 'a person may use such force as is reasonable in the circumstances in the prevention of crime'. The armed forces acting in civil affairs remain personally liable for any excesses of force. Troops were called in to act in civil disturbances regularly before the creation of police forces in the 1830s. Since that time, however, their deployment has become more infrequent. Their last civil intervention occurred during the Featherstone riots, over a dispute by Yorkshire miners, in 1893. They did keep essential services in being during the strike which crippled the fire service during the winter of 1977–8 and during the prison officers' strike during 1980, but they were not employed during the miner's strike in 1984/5.

If government is unable to contain disorders with the assistance of the police and the armed forces then it can hand over government to the chiefs of the forces. In these dire circumstances the commander of the armed forces becomes an absolute ruler and martial law displaces the jurisdiction of the courts. The return to civilian government is a step which then lies in his discretion.

The security services – MI5, MI6, GCHQ – were placed under the control of the Home Secretary. The Security Service Act 1989 exercises some measure of statutory control outside their operational matters. For these they have only to report annually to the Home Secretary and Prime Minister.

When war has been declared the Government passes an Emergency Powers Act. In 1939 powers were taken to issue regulations by Order in Council, to impose charges, to conscript and to direct labour.

During the recent decades there have been laws on terrorism which apply to Northern Ireland. In the Queen's Speech of 1999 it was announced that laws on terrorism would be extended to outlaw groups such as animal rights and religious cults who use or threaten serious violence. A new Terrorist Bill will include powers of banning, confiscation and prolonged detention.

Domestic public order has been maintained by many historical usages. Conservators of the Peace were first appointed in 1195 by Richard I in every county and became a permanent feature, from 1361 as justices of the peace, in the next century. In 1285 the Statute of Winchester re-established the hundred as the cell of the King's Peace. and adopted the 'hue and cry' as the compulsory pursuit of criminals. However this statute did not apply to the City of London. A separate measure divided the City into twenty-four wards and introduced the 'marching ward' as a keeper of the peace. That Statute was designed to preserve peace in the City of London, in which 73 per cent of London's population lived in 1560. The powers were extended in 1585, 1737 and 1771. Committees, assisted by constables, first emerged in the statute of Winchester 1285 and one was appointed in each hundred. Powers of arrest were conferred in 1316, and in 1352 powers to punish. Their functions were to preserve the peace, inquire of wrongdoing and determine cases of trespass, homicide and felonies. From the fifteenth century they were appointed by the Chancellor after consulting the Lord Lieutenant of the county and there were required in 1775 to hold premises of a rateable value of £100 per annum. In the nineteenth century most of their functions were taken over by the newly formed county councils.

Since the Norman Conquest England has suffered two civil wars: the War of the Roses in the late fifteenth century and the civil wars under Charles I in the seventeenth. But civil wars have not been a regular feature of the history of England. An eighteenth-century view was stated thus: 'English history will inform us that the people have always borne extreme oppression for a long time before there has appeared any danger of insurrection against the government.'[1] In 1381 there was the Peasants' Revolt; in 1450 Cade's Rebellion, which complained, uncharacteristically, about corrupt government and high taxation; the religious risings, called the Pilgrimage of Grace in 1536; the Rebellion in the West in 1549; and Wyatt's Rebellion in 1554 in Kent against the marriage of Mary to Philip of Spain. After her accession in 1553 two hundred were executed for religious behaviour. Lastly, there was the Northern Rebellion in 1569 in support of Mary Queen of Scots. All were put down and, during the next two centuries, were replaced by local riots, unlawful assemblies, tumultuous marches, public brawls and the erratic wandering of vagabonds.

The common law developed offences, which may be charged in order to restrain such mindless interferences with the peace and quiet of the community. There were five offences at common law. First, unlawful assembly when three or more persons meet for a common purpose in such manner as a breach of peace may reasonably apprehended, in the mind of reasonable people. Second, rout occurs when an unlawful assembly proceeds from its meeting place, or in other words is en route. Third, riot occurs when the common purpose is carried out. In addition to the common law offence, riot became a statutory offence with the Riot Act 1714. This Act was passed to repress disorder following the accession to the throne of the House of Hanover. A mayor, sheriff or justice of the peace orders rioters to disperse. If anyone remained after one hour they became guilty of a felony or serious crime and liable to penal

---

[1] *Ibid* p. 33.

servitude for life. Fourth, affray when two or more persons fight in public and cause reasonable people to become frightened. Fifth, forcible entry when lands or tenements are entered and retained.

But the fears in Britain raised by the French Revolution in 1791 and the Napoleonic War took hold from 1793 to about 1830. A veil of darkness, tyranny and magisterial power fell over Britain. The Habeas Corpus Act was suspended, sermons were indicted as seditious. Following the mutiny on the Nore in 1797 The Incitement to Mutiny Act 1797 made it a grave crime to seduce members of the armed forces. This Act was re-enacted in 1934 in relation to the armed forces and in 1996 in relation to the police.

The last phase in the struggle for the freedom of speech took place during the early 1820s during the troubles which preceded the Reform Bill. The struggle was led by Cobbett who published the *Weekly Political Register* and by the oratory of Henry Hunt. This campaign occurred towards the end of the dark period which followed the French Revolution. British authorities suspected meetings, ideas and even celebrations and feared that these would undermine peace and order.

Large meetings took place in Manchester, Nottingham and Wolverhampton and one in Spa Fields, London, broke up in a riotous procession though Clerkenwell. After the end of the Napoleonic War there was a great deal of unrest, due to the large numbers of unemployed and depression. In early 1817 the Prince Regent rode to Parliament through empty streets and a window of his carriage were damaged on his return. The Government was alarmed by this incident and there was talk of plots to the seize the Bank of England and the Tower of London.[2] An Act suspending Habeas Corpus 1817 for a period of six months in respect of anyone suspected of treason was followed by the Seditious Meetings Act 1817, which re-enacted the 1795 Act and added features such as banning meetings within a mile of Westminster. Samuel Coleridge described the measures as being 'conceived and laid in the dunghill of despotism among yet unhatched eggs of the old serpent. In due time and in fit opportunity they crawled into light.'[3] Measures to suppress societies 'dangerous to the peace and the tranquility of this Kingdom' were rushed through both Houses of Parliament within a week. This Act imposed control of public meetings, whether held in a pub or reading room, to magistrates. In May 1817 Lord Sidmouth wrote, 'I am quite assured that the general opinion of the mass of the people is sound, and that the disaffected are few in numbers, and contemptible in description and consideration.' But he thought the 'spark of disaffection in the embers of sedition' was imagined. A good harvest in 1817 and the revival of trade quietened disturbances.

Two years later disorder broke out. By the summer of 1819 there seemed sufficient tranquillity for a General Election. Large meetings demanding the reform of Parliament were held in Birmingham and Manchester. At a second meeting the magistrates ordered the arrest of Hunt. But it was unable to be put into effect, thus

---

[2] *English Historical Documents*, vol xi, p. 328.
[3] *A Radical Reader*, Penguin edn, C. Hampton (ed.), p. 378.

compelling magistrates to order troops to break up the meeting. A crowd of about 60,000 the mass of whom had no vote, had gathered on the warm afternoon of 16 August 1819 in St Peter's Field to demand parliamentary reform, universal suffrage, education and repeal of the Corn Laws. The magistrates did not like it but allowed it to proceed as a family outing, but they ordered scavengers to remove stones from the site in order to render the people harmless. They included women, children and a band playing 'God Save the Queen' and everyone was dressed in their best clothes on Sunday. The demand for reform was underwritten by the fact that Manchester returned no Members of Parliament, whereas a mound called Old Sarum in Salisbury returned two. As Hunt began to speak the local yeomanry and Dragoons cavalry appeared brandishing swords. Hunt bade the crowd cheer at their arrival. Then the cavalry arrested Hunt and seized the flags in the crowd. When the magistrates ordered them to charge, the cavalry proceeded to cut down the crowd with sabres and with clubs. Within ten minutes the living fled the field, leaving behind eleven dead, including two women and a child, and over four hundred injured, including 113 women. The incident became known as the Peterloo 'massacre'. The wounded were to frightened to seek medical assistance or poor relief. These people did not seem to belong to society and the law existed to repress their protests. Hunt, who had offered to surrender to the authorities on the previous evening, was imprisoned for two and a half years.

The Prince Regent, acting on advice tendered by the Cabinet, wrote thanking the magistrates, one of whom was a clergyman, for ordering the cavalry to charge, and soldiers and police in Manchester for preserving public tranquillity. Carlile, who had been present at the meeting, replied in open letters to the Prince Regent and Home Secretary. He was arrested on bail for seditious libel and blasphemy arising out of publications made by him. He was offered immunity from the blasphemy charges on condition that he undertook to withdraw his accounts of the 'massacre' in Manchester. But Carlile would give no such undertaking. He was fined £1500 and imprisoned for a term of two years.

The Tory Government included Lord Eldon, Lord Chancellor, Lord Sidmouth, Home Secretary, and Viscount Castlereagh, Leader in the Commons, and this troika of reaction detested democracy. Lord Byron immortalised Castlereagh in the title of a poem calling him an 'intellectual eunuch'. Unsurprisingly, the Government introduced the Six Acts 1819, which prohibited military training with arms, suppressing seditious meetings, extending the newspaper stamp to all publications and powers to search and seize material thought seditious, all of which were added to reinforce the Combination Acts 1799 and 1800 which had banned industrial meetings. The call for a revolution became a movement for reform and public order was restored.

Public order is threatened by processions, marches and protests, which, even when they are intended to promote a peaceful aim or idea, are marred by outbreaks of violence. It is desirable in a democracy that people should be free to associate and demonstrate for a cause or to give expression to their opposition to authority; it is an exercise of free speech. But these rights are not absolute rights in law, for they cannot be exercised beyond the point at which they injure the rights of others. The authorities have to ensure that the peace of society is preserved and that the life of the community continues without serious disruption. In doing this they are drawing a line between the enjoyment of rights and their abuse and it is not a simple matter to weigh the risks of disorder against the rights of association and the freedom of speech before a public event takes place.

The current law regulating public events has been developed over the last hundred years. In 1882 the Salvation Army planned to march through the streets of Weston-super-Mare and their enemies, the Skeleton Army, planned to disrupt the march, as they had done on previous occasions. The magistrates ordered that the march be cancelled but the Salvationists defied the ban. The Skeletons carried out their threat. The police charged the leaders of the march with holding an unlawful assembly. The court held in *Beatty v Gillbank* that the leaders could not be convicted, as they had committed nothing unlawful, even though they had known that violence would result.The decision left the authorities powerless and the community unprotected when a lawful march provoked violent reactions.

During the 1930s the dangers were exposed by the violent reactions to the Fascist marches. The Fascists emerged in the great depression, against the background of political movements in Germany and Italy and in response to the deranged programme of Sir Oswald Mosley.

Entering the House of Commons in 1918 as a Conservative at the age of twenty-two, Mosley believed passionately in patriotism, the British Empire, a national housing scheme, and, before anything, he had an unbounded belief in himself. He left the Conservatives, drifted through the Liberal ranks and in 1924 came to rest on the Labour benches. Mosley concentrated on economic policies and in 1925 he issued his own unauthorised programme of State intervention with growing arrogance and conviction. He urged that economic problems required the application of the best brains and a complete free hand to implement their advice. In 1929 Mosley hoped to become Foreign Secretary but was offered only the Duchy of Lancaster. In Cabinet he clashed with Philip Snowden, the Chancellor of the Exchequer. He put his programme to the Labour Party and they rejected it in 1930. He started the New Party with a gift of £50,000 from Sir William Morris [later Lord Nuffield], with the intellectual abilities of Harold Nicolson and with the combative skills of welter-weight boxing champion, Kid Lewis, who trained the party's 'stewards'. The 1931 election returned the worst of all democratic creatures, a coalition Government, but no candidate of the New Party was returned. Mosley visited Benito Mussolini and was attracted by Fascism. On his return he wrote about his impressions of *Il Duce*, as Mussolini was known, in Rothermere's sympathetic *Daily Mail*. 'The great Italian represents the first emergence of the modern man to power; it is an interesting and instructive phenomenon. Englishmen who have long suffered from statesmanship in skirts can pay him no more tribute, than to say, "Here at least is a man." ' Mosley put himself at the head of the British Union of Fascists, which was to number about 20,000 at its height. He set himself to mirror the 'man'. His followers were uniformed in black shirts, in order, as Mosley put it, to display 'the outward and visible sign of an inward spiritual grace'. The first clash between Fascists and their opponents occurred at a public meeting in Manchester, after a 'steward' attacked a persistent questioner who had been probing the anti-semitic sentiment of the Fascists. In 1934 a crowd attacked 400 'stewards' in Bristol and, after a meeting in Worthing, Mosley and a number of others were charged with riotous assembly and acquitted. Mosley maintained that the Communist agitators attacked and his 'stewards' defended his supporters and that what was at stake was freedom of speech. In June 13,000 attended a meeting in Earls Court, London, and there were a number of interruptions as 'stewards' ejected hecklers. There was a rough meeting in Oxford and several academic witnesses believed that Mosley had incited the violence from the platform. Towards the end of 1934 the Fascists began staging provocative marches through the East End of London and the large Jewish population were provoked. In 1936 there was a pitched battle in Cable Street in London; 83 arrests were made and 100 were injured.

The Government decided to act. The authorities were hindered by the ruling in *Beatty v Gillbank*[4] and could not ban the Fascist marches. In *Duncan v Jones*[5] it was established that a street orator could be moved on by the police, when they feared on good grounds that a public disturbance would have occurred. This case has gave rise to controversy, but it damaged the principle of common law laid down in the case of *Beatty v Gillbank*.

A Public Order Act was rushed through Parliament in a month and reached the statute book in December 1936. During its Second Reading speaker after speaker paid tribute to the Home Secretary, John Simon, for the skill of his measures and the excellence of his speech. Andrew MacLaren, the Member for Burslem, Stoke-on -Trent, was one of the few to speak critically:

If the House is determined to keep democracy and liberty flourishing in this country – and it is the only country in the world that is giving men hope that there may be some revival of democracy throughout the world – if this House cherishes democracy and liberty, I beg it not to make, by a device of this kind, perhaps the mistake which will put a strait-jacket on democracy, but rather to get back to the root problems that create the necessity for this superficial bill.[6]

He felt that exposure of the sources of finance would destroy Mosley. He was seeking the deeper causes of violence which throw up the Mosleys and their blinkered followers from time to time, whereas the majority was concentrating on defeating the menace of Fascism. Fascism in Britain was on the wane before the passing of the Act and it dwindled after it.

---

[4] Supra
[5] [1936] 1KB 218.
[6] House of Commons, 16 November 1936, col 1443

The Public Order Act 1936 banned the wearing of military uniforms and the training or controlling an association of persons for the purpose of usurping the function of the police or armed forces or for the use or display of force in promoting political objects. It allowed the police to impose such directions on marches, if they have reasonable grounds for apprehending serious public disorder or impose bans for periods of up to three months with the consent of the local authority and of the Home Secretary. The Act also made an offence conduct which is threatening or insulting with intent to cause a breach of the peace.

There is good reason for allowing bodies of people to train and drill openly, provided they do not impersonate the police or armed forces. It is better that such bodies excite the reaction of society than be suppressed by the censure of the State, for it is not possible to protect a society from itself. But the important provisions in the Act were the power to control and to ban processions. The police have made sparing use of their power to divert marches from the route which its organisers would wish to take.

The offence of unlawful assembly, however, was adapted by the courts to cover assemblies which became unlawful if their conduct gave reasonable fear for a breach of the peace. As such it was charged in *R v Caird* against members of a mob, numbering about 400 protesters against the former army *régime* in Greece, who stormed the Garden House Hotel, Cambridge, in 1969 where a number of diners were celebrating during a 'Greek week' of festivities. The mob were addressed by megaphone from a tutor's window and eventually broke through a police cordon around the hotel, threw bricks through windows, wrecked the dining room and stamped on its weak roof; all this put the guests, who were enclosed by the violence, in considerable fear. A group of offenders, plucked out of the mob, were convicted of unlawful assembly. The new offence of violent disorder involves three or more people using or threatening to use force and their conduct makes persons of reasonable firmness fear for their safety. The maximum sentence is fixed at five years imprisonment.

In criminal prosecutions concerning public order the intention of the offender to use violence or his awareness that his conduct may be violent or may threaten violence must be proved. The person of reasonable firmness denotes a fictional character, like the man on the top of the Clapham omnibus, and introduces an objective standard of normality, which would rule out the reaction of an abnormally sensitive or timid person who may recoil at any show of robustness. The Act also extended the commission of these offences to private land or premises, on which they were not chargeable under the common law offences.

In 1979 a march organised by the Hackney Trade Council was re-routed to prevent it passing the headquarters of the National Front Party and a march organised by the anti-vivisectionists was re-routed away from the premises of Biorex Laboratories in Islington. Two marches in Leicester organised by the National Front were re-directed to avoid crossing marches organised by the Racial Solidarity Group and another was prevented passing through an immigrant section of the city. The National Front all but perished as a political party after its disastrous performance in the General Election of 1979.

The power to ban marches lies initially with the police. They must request a ban from the local council who seek the approval of the Home Secretary and in London the Commissioner of Police makes a direct approach to the Home Secretary. Up to the end of 1980 from the inception of the power in 1936 a total of banning orders had reached seventy-five. In recent years a great deal of public attention has been attracted by the violence which has attended marches and demonstrations. Much of the violence has been launched against the police and it is a simple matter, once disorder has broken out, to accuse the police of provocation and violent repression and equally difficult for the police to maintain order by non-violent conduct.

The most serious violence in Britain has occurred in a number of riots over recent years. They have occurred against a background of rising unemployment, which has reached levels the highest levels since the 1930's. The rioters have usually involved large numbers of black male youths. During the riots a large number of criminal activities from looting to murder have been committed.

From 1900 to 1975 there was a downward trend in the number of violent disorders. But a number of disorders then occurred and the worst year for civil disturbance since the Second World War was in 1981. Riots broke out in London (Brixton), Liverpool (Toxteth), Bristol (St Paul's), Manchester, Birmingham and in several other cities throughout Britain. There was a strong racial and youth elements in the riots, which seemed to have been spontaneous protests against the harsh regime of policing. But in fact these areas were poor and Lord Scarmam reported on the riots in Brixton and concluded that the law on stop and search should be repealed, for the police had used their powers against ethnic youths. Large immigration had certainly created tensions, which have been kept mostly under control by the efforts of both police and immigrants.

In 1984 the coal miners' strike took a heavy toll on police and countless policemen were injured in demonstrations at Mansfield and Orgreave. It was the longest and bitterest dispute in Britain. Over 9800 arrests were made, over 10,000 offences charged and about 75 per cent were proved.

Against this background of disturbance and the tensions of the cold war a new Public Order Act was introduced in 1986. The Act retains the power to ban marches on the same terms as the earlier Act but it imposes upon leaders an obligation to notify the police of the details of any procession. An appeal lies to the courts for the imposition of a banning order. But the court will not decide on the rightness of a decision reached by a police chief, a local authority or the Home Secretary; unless there is an allegation of an improper motive influencing the decision. The important new measure in the Act is the obligation placed on the organisers of processions and marches to notify the police six working days before an event, or as soon as is practical in cases when that length of notice cannot be given. The only exceptions are reserved for traditional events such as carnivals and for funeral processions. In fact there was a requirement to give notice in a third of the Local Government areas before the Act came into effect and it was estimated that notice was given voluntarily in about 80 per cent of such events. The overwhelming number of marches proceed as smoothly as the flow of water in a stream, but the few that have caused or provoked violence are, it seems, a sufficient reason why all should be burdened with an obligation to which penalties for non-compliance have been attached.

The Act created the offence of trespassery assembly held on land to which there exists no public right of access. In 1995 a peaceful demonstration was held at Stonehenge in defiance of an order banning demonstrations. The demonstrators refused to disperse when so ordered by police. The case turned on whether the public had a right to use the highway for the purposes of a trespassery assembly. On appeal the High Court held in *DPP v Jones*[7] that a demonstration on the highway, even if it was peaceful and did not disturb traffic, exceeded the right of the public to pass and repass.

Against this procedure is that the decision to give directions over the route and conduct should be given on grounds of public order without political considerations. Furthermore, the police have not only the experience of anticipating problems and making appropriate contingency plans but also the responsibility for dealing with them, if they are unable to prevent them. Holding these responsibilities it is surely quite unreasonable that the police should not have advance notice of public events, which, even if peaceful, may involve considerable disruption to public highways and urban centres.

The new offence of riot in the 1986 Act has been reserved for serious offences involving twelve or more persons who threaten or use violence for a common purpose and the effect is to cause a person of reasonable firmness to fear for his own safety. The offence can only be charged with the consent of the Director of Public Prosecutions and the maximum sentence is life imprisonment. The offence of rout, similar to riot has been abolished.

The offence of affray is retained in the 1986 Act to cover the use or threat of use of violence against anyone and his conduct is such as would cause a person of reasonable firmness to fear for his safety. The maximum sentence is three years imprisonment. The Act introduces two new offences in this category: that of using words or behaviour with intent to cause fear of immediate violence and that comprising acts of hooliganism which cause harassment, alarm and distress to old or vulnerable people. It includes provisions to outlaw public incitement of racial hatred. It widens the existing scope of serious public disorder, which is the test the police must apply when seeking a banning order or when making directions, to include serious damage to property, serious disruption of the life of the community and intimidation of other persons. A large section of the Act creates offences of violent provocation, harassment, alarm and distress. It deals with a number of current problems. It includes powers to exclude

---

[7] [1997] 2 All ER 119.

persons from football grounds, creates an offence of contaminating goods for public sale and enables police to evict groups of squatters who have caused damage and brought twelve or more vehicles on land which they refuse to leave.

In the White Paper[8] reviewing public order the Government considered the arguments for charging the cost of policing demonstrations and processions to the people taking part. They estimated that the cost of policing events which involved 100 or more police in London amounted to £6 million in 1984. The inhabitants of the capital will endure a certain amount of inconvenience and disruption as part of the price of living there, in order that others may exercise their right to demonstrate and let off steam. But there is little reason why they should automatically bear the great part of the cost, particularly when it is possible to recoup the costs from those taking part. The Government, however, decided to leave the position unaltered because it would not be clear which events would be charged to participants or not, because it might be difficult to collect the charge and because it might involved leaders of protests with police. These arguments may be sufficient to prevent Government from involving itself in charging and collecting the amounts due, but have less force in regard to providing local authorities with a discretion to do so.

In 1990 the people defied the sovereignty of Parliament and the rule of law to register their contempt for the unjust poll tax. To argue that the people must observe every law which cascades from the manufactory in Westminster, imagines that the people are unthinking simpletons. Rather than criticising lawbreakers on this issue, Parliament should remind itself of the limits imposed on the sovereignty of Parliament[9] when enacting such an unjust tax, whose operation would have the effect of increasing the liability of tenants while reducing those of freeholders.

The maintenance of peace depends to a large extent upon the police preserving the fine balance between unlawful behaviour and the right of individuals to protest, or as Locke put the right 'to appeal to heaven'. But it is essential that the police are not allowed to become the baton of the state.

One of the consuming ideals of Government is to provide a condition of full-employment and thereby ensure that everyone is busy in a job, earning a living. However, it is possible for government to promote a just foundation which will allow independent livelihoods, rather than employment, to arise.

---

[8] Cmnd 9510.
[9] See p. 20.

9

Bill of Rights

At a time when Parliament is engaged in continual legislative activity and when that is having little effect on the deep-seated problems of society, there is an understandable desire to preserve liberty by some constitutional safeguard which stands above the hugger-mugger of party politics. When the constitution is undermined by the economic disorders, modifications are proposed in order to persuade the people to remain quiescent.

Britain was, until 1998, the only leading democratic society in the world which enjoyed neither a written constitution nor a Bill of Rights. The British Parliament can enact any law and repeal any law by majority of one on any day. No international treaty has effect in Britain until enacted by Parliament. Yet her protection of civil rights and constitutional stability has been as effective as those of any nation in modern history.

After the Revolution of 1688 Parliament introduced the Bill, or Claim, of Rights in agreement with the Crown. It was a measure, first, to restrain the prerogative powers of the monarch, no longer appropriate to a constitutional monarchy, and, second, to assert some rights of Parliament. Its similarity with a modern Bill of Rights, which seeks to declare the inalienable rights of the individual, lies only in its title.

Since the Second World War international charters of individual liberties have become fashionable; the United Nations produced the Universal Declaration of Human Rights in 1948, the Council of Europe produced, with the full participation of British lawyers, the European Convention for the Protection of Human Rights and Fundamental Freedoms (ECHR) in 1949 and other countries, particularly those gaining their independence from imperial control, adopted written constitutions. The British Government ratified the European Convention in 1951, incurring international obligations under it, but did not incorporate it into domestic law as other signatories have done. In 1966 access to the European Court of Human Rights in Strasburg was granted to British subjects who could show that they had no remedy available under British law. The ECHR is not part of the law of the EU.

To give an idea of this Convention the leading articles are:

Article 2 *Everyone's right to life shall be protected by law. No one shall be deprived of life intentionally save in the execution of a sentence of a court following the conviction of a crime for which the penalty is provided by law.*

Article 3 *No one shall be subjected to torture and inhuman and degrading treatment.*

Article 4 *No one shall be held in slavery and forced labour.*

Article 5 *Everyone has the right to liberty and security of person. No one shall be deprived of his liberty save in the following cases and in accordance with a procedure prescribed by law.*

Article 6 *Everyone is entitled to a fair and public hearing . . . Judgment shall be pronounced publicly.*
2. Everyone charged with a criminal offence shall be presumed innocent until proved guilty according to law.

Article 7 *No one shall be held guilty of any act . . ., which does not constitute a criminal offence under national . . . law.*

Article 8 *Everyone has the right to respect for his private and family life and his home and his correspondence.*

Article 9 *Everyone has the right to freedom of thought, conscience and religion.*

Article 10 *Everyone has the right to freedom of expression. This right shall include freedom to hold opinions and to receive and impart information and ideas without interference by public authority . . .*
2. The exercise of these freedoms . . . may be subject to such as formalities, conditions, restrictions or penalties as are prescribed by law and are necessary in a democratic society, in the interests of national security, territorial integrity or public safety, for the prevention of disorder or crime, for the protection of health and morals, for the protection of reputation or rights of others, for preventing the disclosure of information received in confidence, or for maintaining the authority and impartiality of the judiciary.

Article 11 *Everyone has the right to freedom of peaceful assembly and to freedom of association with others.*
2. No restrictions shall be placed on the exercise of these rights other than such as are prescribed by law and are necessary in a democratic society in the interests of national security or public safety, for the prevention of disorder or crime, for the protection of health and morals or the protection of the rights and freedoms of others.

Article 12 *Men and women of marriageable age have the right to marry and found a family.*

This summary is sufficient to indicate that English law protects similar rights and allows similar exceptions as those outlined above. The principal difference between the European Convention and English law are that the Convention declares positive rights of the individual – such as the right to life – whereas English law presumes fundamental rights of individuals – as a consequence of existence – and concentrates on remedies. ECHR was drafted in 1949 to apply a minimum standard of liberties for use where society and law had been devastated, whereas English law governing civil liberties has evolved over centuries. Between 1970 and 1990 thirty cases were heard against the UK by the European Court and a third were dismissed. Up to 1995 Britain was found guilty of thirty-five violations.

There is an argument that judges and lawyers have failed to meet the challenge of social, environmental and industrial affairs by confining themselves within the limits of the common law. Consequently, the Government has been left to extend statute law in these spheres and in the process have eroded fundamental liberties. The law created by Parliament and the law declared by judges sometimes overlap but they are different spheres of law which exist to perform different functions in society.

A Select Committee of the House of Lords summarised the advantages and disadvantages of a Bill of Rights in 1978. Among the former were listed advantages of little weight or merit: for example, that under a Bill the individual 'might be better off, and could not be worse off'; that positive declarations of rights are preferable to the negative definition of common law curbs on such rights, that it is desirable that British law be developed on European lines, that if the European Convention was reduced to law it would have a greater impact on law and government and would 'freshen up the principles of common law.' The advantages of a more substantial nature include the fact that the under the Bill the UK courts could exercise the jurisdiction of the European Court in Strasburg and that the Convention would confer certain rights in favour of the individual, which do not exist in English law. The disadvantages included the fact that the Convention would graft onto English and Scots law an incompatible system of law, which would alter the relationship of Parliament and the courts and give back to the courts legislative policy in race relations, freedom of speech, the law on privacy and education. The judges would be required to play a more political role by having to decide matters of contention which are better reserved for the rougher theatre of Parliament, where public opinion has greater weight and respect. In a court of law the case proceeds by argument and counter argument under very strict supervision and rules.

The Select Committee could not decide that a Bill of Rights was necessary but, if it was, they chose to adopt the ECHR. The Bill, therefore, did not pass beyond its Second Reading. In 1985, however, the House of Lords passed the Human Rights and Fundamental Freedoms Bill which incorporated the ECHR. Lord Scarman supported the Bill on the grounds that it would accord British subjects an immediate right to go to British courts on the matters covered by the Convention, that the experience of British courts in becoming involved with the Convention would be valuable and that the unremarkable Convention itself would acquire a power to influence and educate opinion in Britain on civil rights.

Lord Elwyn-Jones also spoke against the Bill.

The administration of justice depends on the respect which all people . . . feel for the judges, and in my view that respect depends very much on keeping judges out of politics. To pass this Bill of Rights cannot but have the tendency to bring judges more and more into politics.[1]

Lord Denning concentrated on Section 4 of the Bill which attempts to entrench the Convention.

When I read clause 4 of this Bill, it offends all our constitutional principles. What it says is that any statute already made by both Houses can be examined by the courts of law, and the court can say that statute is invalid because it offends against the constitution. That is so in regard to past Acts. In regard to future Acts, it says, again, that anyone can ask for a declaration in the courts to say that Acts of this Parliament are invalid because they offend against the convention. This is such a fundamental principle of our constitution that I remind Your Lordships of what Lord Reid said in *Pinchin v British Railways Board*.[2] The idea that a court is entitled to disregard a provision of an Act of Parliament on any ground must seem strange and startling to anyone with a knowledge of the history and law of our constitution.[3]

In 1983 Lord Denning let it be known that he was in favour of incorporation of the Convention.[4]

Despite this strength of opposition, clause 4 was allowed to pass though the committee stage without argument, owing to pressure of business. The danger of formulating rights in general terms is, as Lord Diplock warned, that:

it will be open to every fanatic, every crackpot to challenge any law they disagree with and which they think ... little or anything at all from the absolute right conferred by the first sentence in each article.[5]

He cited the example of Germany which introduced a constitution with entrenched provision. Between 1952–78 no less than 40,000 cases were brought under a similar code in the German constitution, in the opinion of Lord Diplock, only about four were 'really important.'

The Committee of the Lords agreed that if there was a Bill, it should be the ECHR. A Bill of Rights, whether modelled on the ECHR or not, may fill a few gaps in civil liberties but society is suffering from the greater ills of poverty, unemployment, debt, both public and private, and inflation. Upon these more serious questions a Bill of Rights has no protection. In the session of 1985–6 the House of Lords passed a Bill of Rights but it was not taken up by the Commons. In 1987 Sir Edward Gardiner, a

---

[1] *Hansard* Lords, vol 369, col 190.
[2] [1974] AC 765 at 782.
[3] *Hansard* Lords, vol. 36, 9 col. 171.
[4] *A Bill of Rights?*, M. Zander, p. 18.
[5] *Hansard* Lords, vol. 369, cols. 1366–67.

Conservative Member of Parliament, introduced a Private Member's Bill, but without eventual success. Lord Lester, a Liberal Democrat peer, attempted to incorporate the ECHR in 1994 and 1996 and both attempts failed.

There the matter stood until the election of Labour in 1997 with an election promise to incorporate the ECHR, which was done by the Human Rights Act 1998. The Home Secretary has nominated that its provisions will come into effect on 2 October 2000. In introducing the ECHR at Second Reading the Home Secretary made it plain that the introduction was a political measure, rather than a matter of legal necessity. He said:

> Nothing in this Bill will take away the freedoms that our citizens already enjoy. However, those freedoms alone are not enough: they need to be complimented by positive rights that individuals can assert when they believe that they been treated unfairly by the state . . . The Bill . . . is a key component of our drive to modernise our society and refresh our democracy.[6]

It is difficult to argue that a code of human rights drawn up in the aftermath of the Second World War for use by States without an effective legal system will either modernise or refresh Britain. A main justification for the ECHR was that the individual in Britain could pursue rights against the State in British courts without the need of going to the European Court of Human Rights in Strasburg. The cases brought successfully before the European Court, though they matter greatly to the individuals involved, do not greatly enlarge liberty.

The White Paper, *Rights Bought Home*, which introduces the Human Rights Act 1998 attempts to cover the point made by Lord Denning. At para 2.7 it describes that legislation, both past and future, shall be interpreted as far as possible with the Convention and that courts 'will be required to interpret to uphold the Convention', unless the legislation is clearly incompatible with it. It describes this as a 'rule of construction'.

An interesting intervention during the Second Reading was made by Douglas Hogg:

> Is not the real change in that the Bill is achieving that in, in the past, the House had always laid out statutory provisions with great particularity, stating very clearly what the House wishes to provide by way of rights or obligations? This Bill, by incorporating the convention, is stating rights in very general terms, leaving the application of particular facts to each case and thus the enlargement of particular rights to judges.[7]

The danger is that people will be deceived by the range of the ECHR and become either complacent that such a piece of paper exists or they will become disillusioned by

---

[6] *Hansard* Commons, vol 306, Cols 76–81.
[7] *Ibid* col 85

its limited nature. A code could become a trivialisation of human existence in a democratic nation. At moments of dire need an individual may require the protection of a lawyer or politician but to rely on them for earthly existence would be uncertain and expensive folly.

There seemed to be two powerful reasons for not exaggerating the importance of the ECHR. First, the civil and economic rights of an individual arise from Nature as birthrights.They do not arise from scraps of paper in the form of declarations, codes or Acts. These are at best approximations of civil liberties. Civil rights on their own are undermined by economic injustice. Second, codes of human rights are drafted by lawyers and approved by Parliament, who have more often been the destroyers of the liberty of the individual than its supporter. Members often seem have little understanding of the natural liberty of the individual, which arises of itself and believe that their enactments will have exactly the effects which their provisions or election manifestos declare.

In 1999 the Court of Human Rights in Strasbourg ruled that the young boys convicted of the murder of James Bulger had not received a fair trial. This constituted interference in the administration of justice in Britain. The ruling did not, however, alter the sentence. The British trial was conducted by a judge and it cannot be reasonably impugned in a legal sense that the judge is incapable of conducting a fair trial of a young offender. The Court comprise sixteen judges from States which are not famed for their administration of justice. In another ruling in 2000 the Court declaring the smacking of children unlawful. When the rearing of children is a matter for judges reviewing the conduct of responsible parents the law is trivialized. Human rights threaten to become political rather than legal and that change will not help liberty but will spread a picnic for lawyers.

10

Civil Slavery

Slavery is inhuman. The fact that one human can have property in the person and the property of another denotes today a low state of civilisation and a high state of injustice. Locke considered slavery as the relic of a condition before society had been formed. He considered 'the natural liberty of Man is to be free from any Superior Power on Earth, and to have only the Law of Nature as his Rule.' In 1661 he wrote:

> I have no less a love of liberty, without which a man shall find himself less happy than a beast. Slavery being a condition which robs us of all the benefits of life, and embitters the greatest blessings, reason itself in slaves (which is the grand privilege of other men) increasing the weight of their chains and joining with their oppressors to torment them.[1]

British traders became involved in the slave trade by trading manufactured goods with African slave hunters in return for slaves, who were shipped to the New World and sold there for sugar. Traders congregated in Bristol, which not only provided them with an excellent port but also a collection point near the sites of metal workings around the city but also from Shropshire, where the Industrial Revolution is said to have begun in Britain. The Africans traded manufactured products at the beginning of the industrial age in Britain throughout the first half of the eighteenth century. They were willing to round up slaves or stir up war, in which they could capture prisoners and deliver them to the Portuguese and Spanish from 1443 and British traders after 1550 on the western coast of Africa. From the beginning of th eighteenth century Liverpool overtook Bristol in the slave trade. In the late eighteenth century a slave costing £20–£25 in Africa could be sold in the New World at double that price. It was estimated bout twelve million were transported in 50,000 voyages by the Europeans to the West Indies and America between the last decades of the sixteenth century and the eighteenth century. By 1768 the English were estimated to be carrying half the slaves

---

[1] *Political Writings*, J. Locke, Penguin edn, p. 148.

transported. Plantation owners brought slaves from the traders with sugar, coffee and tobacco, which became popular in Europe.

The abolition of slavery in Britain towards the end of the eighteenth century was prompted by a young clerk, Granville Sharp, who worked in the Ordnance Office, at the Tower of London. One day in 1765 he was leaving the surgery of his brother, William, nearby in Mincing Lane. The surgery opened every morning to relieve the sickness of the poor. As he left, Granville passed an individual, Jonathan Strong, who was waiting outside in the queue and evidently in a poor state, as though he was ready to drop to the ground. He had been beaten over the body and head with a pistol so often that he could hardly walk and was about to lose his sight. Apparently his master was a British lawyer, David Lisle, practicing in Barbados. The heat there acted on Lisle's liver which gave rise to outbursts of rage. After one such fit he had abandoned Strong in the street. William arranged for his admission to St Bartholomew's Hospital and after four months he was restored to health. The Sharp brothers supported and clothed him until he could earn his living by working for Mr Brown, an apothecary, in Fenchurch Street. Two years later he was spotted by Lisle in the street who, having noted Strong's improved health, followed his carriage back to the apothecary's shop. Days later he sold him to a planter from Jamaica at the discounted price of £30 (the market price was £50, or about £4500 at current values) and had him incarcerated in Poultry Counter Prison, where the gaoler would keep him until a ship was leaving for the West Indies. Realising the implications of his return, Strong sent a note to the Sharps, who at first did not remember his name. The gaoler denied to the brothers that he was holding such a person. They were suspicious and went to the gaol. They charged the gaoler not to deliver Strong to any person before he had been brought before the Lord Mayor. After hearing arguments from the planter's lawyer, the Lord Mayor declared that Strong had done no offence and could walk free. Thereupon the sea captain seized Strong by the arm, saying that he was taking him as the property of the buyer. The city coroner whispered in Sharp's ear, 'Charge him.' In an angry voice Sharp stated powerfully, 'Sir, I charge you for an assault.' Thereupon, the sea captain loosed his grip and the parties left the court freely, without a word.

The process began to become more complicated, when Sharp was sued for £200 in damages for depriving the planter of his alleged property. He relied on the statement of the law officers of the Crown, dated 14 January 1729, who had written: 'We are of the opinion that a slave coming from the West Indies to Great Britain . . . does not become free . . . [and] that the Master may legally compel him to return again.' Sharp refused to accept the advice of his lawyer that such an opinion had upheld at least by Lord Mansfield, saying: 'he could not believe the law of England was really so injurious to natural rights as so many great lawyers for political reasons had been pleased to assert.'[2] To add to the legal challenge, Lisle called on Sharp for 'gentlemanlike satisfaction' – a duel – and Sharp replied that a student of law would want no satisfaction other than the law would allow.

---

[2] *Granville Sharp and the Freedom of Slaves in England*, E. Lascelles p. 22.

He decided to research the legal position himself. He discovered that the law officers' opinion was at variance with dicta uttered more than twenty years earlier by Chief Justice Holt in the case of *Smith v Browne*.[3] He had held: 'As soon as a negro comes to England he is free; one may be a villein but not a slave' and in another in 1707 'By common law no man can have a property in another.'[4]

Sharp himself prepared his legal position. Early in his researches he lit upon this passage in the first edition of Dr Blackstone's *Commentaries* published in 1765:

> And this spirit of liberty is so deeply implanted in our constitution, and rooted in our very soil, that a slave, or negro, the moment he lands in England, falls under the protection of law, and with regard to all natural rights becomes at that moment a freeman.[5]

Yet Blackstone was writing a eulogy on the law for the instruction of gentlemen and some had considerable investments in slaves, so later in the chapter he modified this statement, no doubt to accommodate their interests. He wrote: 'a negro the instant he lands in England, becomes a free man, that is the law will protect him, his life, his liberty, and his property . Yet contractual rights will remain exactly in the same state as before.'[6] In the second edition of his *Commentaries*, however, immediately after the first passage, cited above, he added a sentence 'though a master's right to his services may probably (or possibly) continue.' He implies that a slave can make binding contracts during slavery which will still take legal effect after his slavery has ended. Such an opinion savours more of politics than law. Smith was writing his *Wealth of Nations* at about this time in praise of the Government of Britain in a book destined for the gentlemen in much the same spirit as Blackstone. Similarly Smith sought to please both free traders and protected interests.

When Sharp had submitted a memorandum, entitled *The Injustice of Tolerating Slavery In England*, to the Commentator. He was pleased that Blackstone did not disagree with his argument, despite him remarking that 'it will be uphill work in the King's Bench'.[7] Sharp even engaged him for his defence of the writ, until Sharp discovered in a conference that he changed his ideas, and opposed him. The Solicitor-General arrived later and supported Blackstone. In 1769 Sharp sent his tract to the planter. He did not reply to Sharp's argument and the action died.

At this time another case concerned an African, Hylas, and his wife Mary, who had been shipped back to the West Indies as a slave. He had been emancipated and, armed with a memorandum by Sharp, he brought a case for her return. It was held by Lord Justice Wilmot that being married to a free man, she was freed by her marriage.

---

[3] 1701 Holt, KB 495.
[4] 2 Salkeld 666.
[5] *Commentaries*, W. Blackstone, vol i, p. 123.
[6] Ibid, p. 413.
[7] *Lord Mansfield*, E. Heward p. 142.

In July 1770 Sharp was told by a Mrs Bankes that her household had been roused in the night by the cries of Thomas Lewis, who had been seized by a Mr Stapylton, who had been his former owner. He had been taken aboard a vessel bound for Jamaica. Sharp immediately applied for a writ of habeas corpus, but the ship had left Gravesend. However, it docked at Spithead to avoid contrary winds and the writ was served. Lewis was 'chained to the masthead, bathed in tears, and casting a last mournful look at the land of his freedom.'[8] The case came before Lord Mansfield in February 1771. Counsel for the slave produced Sharp's tract with the submission that 'no man can be legally detained as a slave in this country.' Mansfield was relieved to avoid that issue when it was found that Stapylton could not produce evidence of even his nominal title to Lewis. Afterwards he told the defence counsel:

> There are a great many opinions given upon it [slavery]; I am aware of many of them; but perhaps it is much better it should never be finally discussed or settled. I don't know what the consequence may be, if the masters were to lose their property by accidentally bringing their slaves to England. I hope it will never finally be discussed, for I would have all masters think them free, and all negroes think they were not, because then they would both behave better.[9]

Next year another slave, James Somersett, was rescued from irons on a vessel. He had been brought from America by his owner, Charles Stewart, in 1769. While in England he had absconded. Later he was recaptured and put on the *Anne and Mary* which was bound for Jamaica. Somersett appealed for advice to Sharp, who arranged his defence. This time an earlier case was cited,[10] in which it had been held that the air of England was too pure for a slave to breathe. The argument of the traders was that the transaction was the subject of a contract, recognisable under English law. Twice Lord Mansfield adjourned the case. He 'strongly recommended' the parties to settle and twice advised the slave-owner to free Somersett. For at that time it was estimated that there were about 14,000 slaves in England and, at a price of £50 a head, their owners would lose £700,000 (about £61 million at current values), if Sharp won his action. Courts in Scotland and France had outlawed slavery. The slave-owner pressed on and Mansfield finally had to face the issue. He freed the slave six months after the trial opened. Sharp noted in his diary: 'James Somersett came to tell me that judgment was to-day given in his favour.' The effect of the judgment was to achieve one milestone on a long road.

Sharp was besieged for help by former slaves desiring employment or support. Obtaining employment was difficult and those who did not continue in the employ of their masters, lived on the Poor Law or were helped by charity. Four years later Sharp

---

[8] *Granville Sharp and the Freedom of Slaves in England*, E. Lascelles p. 26.
[9] *Memoirs of Granville Sharp*, P. Hoare, p. 91.
[10] *Cartwright's Case* 11 Eliz. Rushworth 2, 468.

devoted himself to abolishing slavery. He wrote tracts and brought the question to leaders in England, America and France. In 1785 Thomas Clarkson wrote his prize essay and shortly afterwards met and enlisted the support of William Wilberforce at a dinner party. Sharp became chairman in 1787 of the *Society to Abolish Slavery* which he formed with Wilberforce and Clarkson. Wilberforce took the issue up in Parliament and the campaign ended when the Act of Abolition was eventually passed by Parliament in 1807. It prohibited British subjects engaging in the slave trade. But it was finally brought to an end thirty years later.

The general idea was that the judiciary and then Parliament were sufficiently moved to effect the abolition of slavery. It was Sharp, however, who took the first steps as a private individual. His motivation began as personal conscience at seeing the distressing condition of Jonathan Strong.

ECONOMIC LIBERTIES

Introduction

In Britain the abolition of civil slavery did not mean the dawn of liberty. Rather it was an important step towards it. Just as a bird needs two wings in order to fly freely in the sky, so an individual needs both civil and economic freedom before he can realise the liberty which is a birthright bequeathed by Nature.

Economic freedom includes the freedom of the individual to trade freely during peacetime without interference of the State in the form of taxation of his labour, profits or expenditure, without tariffs, subsidies, control of interest or exchange rates.

Parliamentarans have abandoned the nineteenth century tradition of free trade and imposed State control, termed protectionism, with the consequences which were predicted accurately and extensively in the 1830s and 40s and again in the first decade of the twentieth century. The apotheosis of protectionism in modern times is the European Union. What is so objectional is not Europe – Britain has been a European nation for almost two millennia and will remain one as a matter of culture and geography – but the protectionism which rules it, and has ruled the German States, Germany and France since the Middle Ages. The political belief that Britain will diminish protectionism by being involved in the EU can only be mounted by people who ignore the experience of free trade in Britain.

Before the individual can be free, society needs to eradicate the cause of general poverty and introduce a just distribution of wealth which would allow him from his livelihood to look after himself and family. For it is manifestly unreasonable that he should be taxed to enable the State to discharge responsibilities that are evidentally private.

Parliamentarians have also lacked both courage and vision to face the cause of poverty or introduce a just distribution of wealth. These failures inflict general poverty on the mass of society and prevent them from looking after private responsibilities. Instead they have attempted to mitigate poverty over the last four centuries by providing the poor law and then the welfare state. The services provided are as inadequate as the political thinking behind them. It reduces Parliament to the level of pantomime and make-belief when Ministers talk about health or education.

The political thinking behind the State intervention and State mitigation is like that which the Tudors applied to government in the sixteenth century. It is out of touch with the technology of the day.

The mass of British society labour for a wage fixed at a subsistence level by the unemployed man. They do not reap the reward of their labour and cannot even look after themselves. Yet through their expenditure – the weight of income tax, indirect taxes and corporation tax is passed ultimately into the price system – they provide the taxation required by government to look after them. A subsistence wage subject to the main weight of taxation is denoted in this book by the phrase wage slavery.

It will be argued in the following chapters that the EU and the welfare state along with the general poverty which they attempt to mitigate are unnecessary evils. Until wage slavery is abolished in Britain this land nor its people can be considered just, prosperous or even democratic. If justice replaced State control the potential prosperity and democracy of the British people would be unbounded.

11

Free Trade

The concept of free trade is based on principles based on self-evident grounds of human nature. It is not a concept built by political parties. The concept is not as important as the distribution of wealth but at a time when government have generally assumed more control of economic matters it has become an important element of political thought. Of all nations Britain has just claim to be reckoned a leading example of free trade, not because the concept was invented in Britain but because they were the only nation to put it into effect.

An objective understanding of free trade in concept and in history is a key element in the education of both a voter and a politician in a democracy. It is essential to political thought in the same way that grammar is a necessity in literature. It renders a great deal of politician's rhetoric on trade laughable for its superficiality and dangerous for its unnecessary complexity.

Politicians have a habit of pretending to determine the national interest. In war the national interest in survival overides individual liberty and property. During peace the national interest of a democratic individual consists in the protection of the indiviual's liberty and property. When government pretend that a national interest can exist which damages the individual its thinking is unhinged from reality.

People and commercial bodies trade but nations do not. The activity of trade across a street or across national frontiers operates on similar principles as human breathing. The inward breath, or import, sustains life, and the outward breath, or export, creates capacity for the next inhalation. Thus the true relationship of import and export is that one is the counterpart of the other. People consume imports and pay for them in exports. To suppose that a people live by exporting is like imagining they live by exhaling, instead of breathing in and then out.

The perennial interest of every people consists during conditions of peace in the maintenance of the individual's liberty to trade. That interest is at the same time the interest of mankind. Trade is an activity that endures without the aid of the State, rather like the digestive system of humans does not require the manual assistance of the diner. The important principle of international trade is that the import precede and creates the demand for the export. A people may adopt free trade without international agreement.

There is no example of free trade being introduced to mankind by an international committee such as that meeting under the auspices of General Agreement on Tariffs and Trade. Free trade is moulded into the natural order and will arise whenever a country lifts its own domestic restrictions on imports. Once a nation has introduced free imports, it will attract to itself the exports of the world. If the rest of the world shut the free import country out of their markets, there would be no trade.The exporters of the world would force their governments to cease their blockade. The idea that a nation, however small, cannot introduce immediate free trade is a puny notion.

FREE TRADE IN BRITAIN

In France during the seventeenth century the interference in trade and commerce gave rise to the cry of *laissez-faire* [let things go as they will], as merchants tired of detailed State regulation. Jan de Wit in Holland, Sir Josiah Child in England and Vincent Gournay in France, among many others, began in the seventeenth and eighteenth centuries to formulate similar demands for the State to allow free trade to arise by the elimination of protectionist regulation. The concept of free trade was included in the study of the new economic science around 1750 by the French *économistes*. It seemed to fit naturally with their ideas on property and taxation. Several economistes wrote about free trade. The piece which Turgot wrote about the protection of iron masters in France in 1773 contained a devastating exposure of protectionism. He described it an illusory system supported by sophistry. While Turgot was *Contrôleur-Général*, between 1774–6, he introduced free trade in grain. However, after he fell from power, his reforms was reversed and France resumed the protectionist course which Colbert had set down for her. In the following century Britain became the home of free trade and France remained the bastille of protection.

The introduction of free trade in Britain in the mid nineteenth century is a dramatic example of a democracy awakening to a political idea and forcing a new economic order upon government.Such examples are rare. It contains universal principles as pertinent to the twenty-first century and these emerge from a brief sketch of British economic history since the early nineteenth century.

The population in Britain had swelled from about 10 million in 1750 to about 25 million by 1815. In view of the growth of an urban population, corn had to be imported to feed about three million urban dwellers.The grain trade had attracted protection in various forms since a statute of 1436 to regulate its export.Twenty years of war had encouraged domestic production of grain. After the conclusion of the Napoleonic Wars, in 1815, Parliament, then dominated by rural landowners, passed the Corn Laws, which prohibited imports of wheat below a price of 80 shillings per quarter. The Act was replaced in 1828 with a regime of sliding scales; the price at which wheat could be imported rose and fell in step with the home price up to a price of 72 shillings a quarter.But the margin between the two prices ensured a considerable premium for home producers over the international market and prevented the consumer enjoying both the foreign corn and the foreign trade which would pay for it.

During the 1830s industrialists and businessmen began to realise that the corn laws operated to increase wages and costs, reduce profits and deny them markets. In 1838, after an appalling harvest, a number of businessmen in the Lancashire cotton trade formed the Anti-Corn Law Association. They held meetings to explain the commercial case against the corn laws in Manchester and other industrial centres. In January 1839 the Association, later to be called the League, held a public dinner for 800. A fortnightly paper, the *Anti-Corn Law Circular*, was published in April 1839 and reached a circulation of 15,000 within six weeks. Propaganda was turned out in tracts, posters and handbills of every size and fit for every conceivable purpose. Meetings were gathered at tea parties, dinners and public places. Although the northern towns were alive to the issue of the high price of corn, Lord Melbourne's Government was deaf to the plight of the unemployed or to the distress of textile factory owners.

One of the most energetic leaders of the League was Richard Cobden, of whom it was said that 'when he spoke, so mild was his voice, so unassuming his style of giving an opinion, so clearly was the opinion given, that I saw at once the source of so much of that importance that he has acquired'.[1]

Cobden was returned as Member for Stockport in June 1841. He brought with him a keen sense of political principles, a sharper insight into the economic condition of the people than that held by the rural Members. He saw that the landowners were in control of Parliament and that they used their power for their own advantage. He was not deflected by stepping, as it were, into public fame. The Commons did not make a show of their welcome; they resented northern tradesmen who asked questions. Cobden was seen as a troublemaker, whom the spirit of the Reform movement had brought into political life, and his case was regarded as specious sophistry.

In September 1841 he enlisted the active support of John Bright, who recalled years later the circumstances of the pact between them, thus:

I was in the depths of despair, for the light and sunshine of my house had been extinguished, all that was left on earth of my young wife . . . was lying stiff and cold in the chamber above us . . . Mr Cobden called me as his friend, and addressed me with words of condolence. After a time he looked up and said, 'There are thousands of houses in England at this moment where wives, mothers, and children are dying of hunger. Now,' he said, 'when the first paroxysm of your grief is past, I would advise you to come with me, and we will never rest until the Corn Law is repealed.' I accepted his invitation. I knew that the description he had given of the homes of thousands was not an exaggerated description . . . the sufferings of the country were fearful . . . I felt in my conscience that there was a work which someone must do . . . and from that time forward we never ceased to labour hard on the resolution which we had made.[2]

[1] *Whistler at the Plough, and Free Trade*, A. Somerville, p. 82.
[2] *Life of Cobden*, J. Morley, p. 190.

By the end of 1842, after four years of arguing for freedom, Sir Robert Peel, the Prime Minister, was coldly unsympathetic. Cobden was wearied after four years of toil; trade was beginning to revive and the price of corn fell. They planned to take their cause during 1843 to rural towns and to the farmers. The meetings were long; the farmers brought their self-interested arguments and prejudice, the speakers used their oratory to induce them to look beyond them and endeavoured to instil, if not conviction, at least doubt over their role in society. At Bedford, for example, a large crowd assembled at 3 p.m. and continued listening and questioning for six hours, despite being drenched by heavy showers.Yet after a tour of England with meetings almost every week, the position of the Corn Laws still seemed secure; the weather was mild, the harvest reasonable, trade was reviving and the Budget was balanced.

Nonetheless during this rural campaign Cobden came to appreciate the agricultural dimension of the question more fully and to realise that the Corn Laws operated only in favour of the rural landowners, as distinct from farmers, whom Cobden described as tenant farmers. Though a man might own the land which he farmed, from an economic viewpoint his income was derived in part from landholding and in part from farming, as if he was farming as his own tenant. Tenant farmers gained nothing from high prices, for their rent rose commensurately with the price of corn. The agricultural worker's earnings were actually diminished by high prices. He shocked the Commons with several speeches by describing the wretched condition of farm workers and tenant farmers. In particular Cobden troubled the conscience of Peel by such examples as that the value of exports to Brazil in 1844 exceeded the annual consumption of goods by farmworkers and their families in Britain. He quoted from a Poor Commissioner's report that rural conditions in Wiltshire, Somerset, Dorset, the county of reformer Lord Ashley, were miserable indeed. After one such speech Peel crumpled his notes and turned to Sidney Herbert to say, 'You must answer this, for I cannot.' Though there was little evident sign for Cobden's optimism and conviction, he wrote in the summer of 1845:

> They [the Government] are going to repeal it [the Corn Law], as I told you, mark my words, at a season of distress. The distress may come; aye, three weeks of showery weather when the wheat is in bloom or ripening would repeal these corn laws.[3]

The first weeks in August 1845 were cold and wet and a potato disease struck in the ground and in store. It was particularly severe in Ireland, where the potato had become the last resort in a diet that included neither meat nor grain The only *pis aller* beneath a potato diet was starvation. The reason why the potato had become the stable diet in Ireland is an example in a fertile country of unjust and unnecessary poverty The corn rotted in fields, unharvested, north of the Trent. Repeal of the Corn Laws had become

[3] *Ibid* p. 325.

142

inevitable. On 28 October Cobden attacked Peel before an audience of 8000 in Manchester; Peel would be a poltroon and a criminal, warned Cobden, if he did not open the ports to foreign wheat. As Cobden remarked, it was sad and ironic that an argument for abundance and plenty came upon its hour at a moment of dire distress. Peel was no reformer. He was able, however, to accept that he had no alternative but to repeal the Corn Laws, which was accomplished over a period of three years. The measure was carried on the Third Reading in the Commons by a majority of ninety-eight. Two-thirds of his party voted against their leader. Within days the protectionists in the Tory Party, led by Disraeli, who had been stalking Peel for sometime, combined with the Whigs on the Irish Coercion Bill and voted Peel out of office. The Tories are by tradition quick to ditch a leader, whom they no longer trust.

In his resignation speech Peel commended Cobden, whom, he said, 'has been acting from pure and disinterested motives, has with untiring energy, made appeals to our reason, and has enforced those appeals with an eloquence the more to be admired because it was unaffected and unadorned'.[4]

The Anti-Corn League had fulfilled its object. There had been moments of success and intervals of dreary disappointment, but, finally, fortune, or in reality misfortune, had crowned their labours. The League was wound up.

One of the keenest observers of the Corn Law question in the Commons was Count Camillo Cavour, the great Italian statesman, who became a free-trader and who had predicted the repeal of the corn laws in 1843:

> When an economic system is seen as being contrary to reason, justice and equity, when its best defenders are reduced to using arguments of convenience and opportunities, such a system is sapped at its base; the least unforeseen circumstance will overturn the whole edifice.[5]

A friend warned him, 'Those are very fine principles for such as are knocking at the doors of office; but once the doors open ... they are principles which you throw out of the window.' Cavour replied, 'I will make my principles triumph or I will resign.'[6]

He became Minister of Commerce in Piedmont and was determined to introduce free trade but protectionism was too strong for him to do so by outright reform. He chose instead to introduce it by means of commercial treaties with other governments.

Proposing one such treaty in 1852 to the House of Deputies in Turin he commended the measure thus:

> I believe these arguments to be just, unexceptional, and evident ... I think I have proved that duties which are protective of the soil have the effect of inflicting a

---

[4] *Hansard* LXXXVII col 1054.
[5] *The Early Life and Letters of Cavour*, A. Whyte, p. 298.
[6] *Reminiscences of the Life and Character of Count Cavour*, W. de la Rive pp. 196–7.

tax upon the consumers to the benefit of the growers, and especially, I will even say exclusively, to the benefit of the proprietors of the soil. This, gentlemen, is a crying injustice, which is impossible to justify by the light of reason. Property to be respected, must not enjoy any favours, which are not the necessary and legitimate consequences of the economical arrangements of the country ... I believe that property is the groundwork and the foundation of the social order; but it is precisely because I wish to see the principle founded on a solid basis, and because I wish it may be able to resist the attacks of Utopists and demagogues, that I wish to see it rest upon the solid foundations of justice and equity and not upon the quicksand of privilege and monopoly.[7]

He soon became Prime Minister of Piedmont and then one of the leaders of the *Risorgimento* and had to address himself to the formation of Italy.

In 1859 William Gladstone, the Chancellor of the Exchequer, won the grudging approval of Lord Palmerston to send Cobden, who was planning to spend the winter there, to Paris in order to negotiate a commercial treaty. Though Cobden had little enthusiasm for commercial treaties, he was willing to attempt to convert the French Government to free trade in France, after the economist, M. Chevalier, had come to London to assure Cobden that a commercial treaty was the only method of reducing protection in France. The idea that Cobden saw commercial treaties as a way of introducing free trade is without foundation. A nation had only to look to repealing its own import duties: what it might negotiate with other nations was merely cosmetic arrangements.

He met Emperor Louis Napoleon, who entertained the hope of emulating Peel's reform but who admitted that France was more taken by revolutions than reforms and was in the grip of the protectionists, none more extreme than M. Magne, the Finance Minister, whom Cobden described as 'that furious ... that canon-ball ... protectionist'.[8] During one meeting with the Emperor, Cobden startled him by estimating that men in France were working 20 per cent longer, for 20 per cent less wages and had to pay 10 per cent more for clothing than in England. The Emperor seized a pen and recorded the figures, saying 'what an answer to those people'.[9] The Emperor's ministers, demanded an inquiry into the suspension of protectionism. The Emperor granted the inquiry, but limited its duration to two days. The Treaty was signed and Cobden attended the arduous meetings to agree its details. The negotiations were completed after eleven months. Cobden described his impression of these meetings:

The iron masters are the landed interest of France. They constitute the Praetorian guard of monopoly. Bankers, courtiers, authors, bishops and priests are to be

---

[7] *Cavour in Parliamento.*
[8] *Life Of Cobden*, J. Morley, pp. 723 & 727.
[9] Ibid p. 724.

found in the ranks of the iron masters. The French witnesses, of course, tell the old story of alarm and ruin, and discourse most feelingly of the misery which their work people will suffer if their protection is withdrawn . . . I am transported back 20 years.'[10]

The Commercial Treaty with France advanced the cause of free trade hardly one inch and Cobden became aware of the impassive power of the French protectionists.

The repeal of the Corn Laws in Britain was such a remarkable episode that it is well to pause and ponder some of the principles which it established. It was more than a succession of fortunate events. The issue fastened on imports. The removal of tariffs and quotas levied upon imports lies within the sovereignty of national Government.

The only proviso to the introduction of free trade is that government stops interfering with currency values, either by manipulation of fixed parities or with interest rates. Commercial banks are quite able to set interest rates of their own. Locke wrote an essay for Lord Ashley in 1671 which argued against control of interest rates by the State. Such meddling invariably gives rise to trade imbalances. An economy with a floating rate and market rates of interest need have no fears of balance of payments. When a currency is maintained at an artificial level as a component of a financial level then that policy is certainly flawed.

The repeal of the Corn Laws ended the manipulation of the economy by politicians and restored trading markets to the democratic control of the people. The intelligence of a worldwide market is incomparably greater than an economy controlled by a state. As Turgot described, it is quite beyond the means of a State to amass the economic forces and details which impel each individual in a multiplicity of daily transactions. Indeed the advent of computers and satellites does not bring this to pass. Even were it conceivable to collect this mass of data on time, all the time, then government would only ensure things would go exactly as they would have gone without them acting at all.

The repeal of the Corn Laws in 1846–9 marked the introduction of free trade in Britain. It was described decades later by Disraeli as a law of political gravity in the nineteenth century. There was a return to the tradition of protection in the Conservative Party, which was deluded by the empty argument about tariff reform later deployed by Joseph Chamberlain from 1903. Chamberlain tried to dress protectionism with an intellectual argument. In reality protection derives from the inclination to injustice and self-interest. This attempt was decisively rebuffed by the landslide victory of the Liberals in 1906.

THE DEMISE OF FREE TRADE IN BRITAIN

Free trade has one feature which makes it unpopular among politicians: it can be accomplished almost without them. They are so insecure of their role that they cannot

---

[10] *Ibid* p. 758.

admit that trade would run better without their interference. Free trade prevailed up to the First World War but became one of its casualties. Asquith imposed duties on motor cars, as a wartime measure. That was a surprising measure from one who had upheld free trade so keenly. In 1917 the Corn Production Act demanded pasture to be ploughed up and guaranteed cereal prices to encourage home production. That measure was repealed after the war. But it served as a precedent for government intervention in the Second War. These measures were repealed after the war, but they had been evidence of a new wave of protectionism which was to break on political thinking.

When the air is full of warlike patriotism it is easy to justify protectionist moves, but the justification is as hollow in war, as in peace. Tariffs are an ineffective source of revenue and they engender protectionist clamour from one industry after another. No industry exists which would not attempt to win an advantage or subsidy from government. But industry stands second to agriculture in the queue for state hand-outs. To encourage home production in agriculture artificially is to diminish overseas trade. The effect is to reduce trade and, thus, merchant shipping. This has the effect in wartime of making a merchant fleet, reduced by protectionism, more vulnerable to enemy navies.

In 1925 protectionism was derided by Stanley Baldwin, the Prime Minister, who introduced several Industry Safeguarding Acts.. However, these enactments were protectionist in everything but name. They had the effect of shielding industries from international competition, which might render them healthy and profitable. The Commons was addressed by batteries of lawyers arguing that the foreign competitors of their British clients employed sweated labour and received unfair subsidisation. Their arguments were put to committee members as if they were disinterested arbitrators, intent on administering justice. That mantle of impartial dignity was maintained by giving the members public titles. But the mantle was transparent when an industry happened to be situated in a member's constituency or when a member had been seduced by a protectionist lobby and had acted to protect 'British' industry. These proceedings became a farce, a parliamentary pantomime.

In 1931 there was a gold scare. Ramsay MacDonald headed a National Government, containing Conservative and Liberal Ministers. Pretending to strike a pose of national survival, hallowed by solemn music and embellished by false gravity, his Government revealed itself to be timid and ineffective.

The Government imposed widespread tariffs against international trade at the Ottawa Conference. It was sanctioned as an appropriate measure by Maynard Keynes, who, in 1926, had brushed aside the system of *laissez-faire*, without reasonable argument.

As the twentieth century unfolded protectionism was extended beyond import duties and trade to include State control of the economy. It came to include protection of agriculture, the fixing of interest and currency rates by Government, fiscal policy and deficit finance.

Britain has had no more eloquent champions of free trade than Cobden and Churchill. Speaking in Manchester during 1904 Churchill declared:

[I]t was Cobden's work to lay a mighty stone. I say it was Cobden's work not because he did it himself . . . but somehow Cobden's name seemed to inherit the odium, and so he ought to have all the glory too. Other stones have been laid on the stone that Cobden laid; and even now there is plenty of work for the stone masons and master builders. But we believe that the work which Cobden did was done forever; that the stone he laid shall never be translated; that the stone shall never been transplanted; that the heights he he gained shall never be abandoned.[11]

Cobden wrote in a letter from Russia during 1848:

How much unnecessary solicitude and alarm England devotes to the affairs of foreign countries; with how little knowledge we enter upon the task of regulating the concerns of other people; and how much better we might employ our energies in improving matters at home.[12]

Great though the introduction of free trade had been, Cobden realised it was not an entire answer to the distribution of wealth. He stated at Rochdale in 1864:

If you apply free trade to land and labour too, then . . . the men who do that will have done for England probably more than we have done by making free trade in corn.[13]

Free trade is an enduring principle of political thought. British experience attests to two indisputable facts. First, free trade arises when a nation opens itself to world trade by lifting import restrictions. Second, Britain's trading strength arises for its large need for imports. Such a desirable condition as free free trade arises of itself and consists in the absence of interference by Government. Free trade is a democratic condition. It will achieve more, so much more, than the protectionism, which is the lying justification of state interference. Listening to Ministers justifying protectionism is like listening to a conjuror who once claimed to have heard a dog laugh.

---

[11] *Chartwell Papers* 9/20/75, vol i.
[12] Letter to Bright 18 September 1846.
[13] *Speeches by Richard Cobden*, ed J. Bright jnr. & J. Thorold Rogers, p. 493.

12

An Example of Protectionism – The European Union

[I]f the servants of the people, forgetting their masters and their masters interests, should pursue a separate one of their own; if, instead of considering that they made for the people, they should consider the people are made for them; if . . . the risk . . . of revolution would be . . . less than these [ills] which were actually suffered; then in the name of God, I ask, what principles are those which ought to restrain an injured and insulted people from asserting the natural rights . . . or even punishing their governors, that is their servants,who had abused their trust?

J Priestly

Rather than follow her own example of free trade Britain has slipped slowly since the 1920s into state control and protectionism. Vanished is the concept of the freedom of the individual which has been replaced by the counterfeit of state control. Politicians of this belief should have studied the concept and the history of free trade in order to comprehend that the individual can benefit many time more from state inaction than from the endless state activity.

Protectionism is the word to designate State control of the economy. It may take many forms: subsidies, currency schemes, interest rates and even details of taxation. In the vocabulary of political correctness it has been discarded as a dirty word and replaced by the nicer-sounding pragmatism, which judges every situation on its merits and appearance. In fact, the pragmatist, by treating every issue separately lacks profundity, which comes from seeing individual problems as linked to a whole. In France State control is called *dirigisme*.

The European Union (EU) is a leading example of pragmatic protectionism. It is protectionist in its foundation, in its intent, in its operation and in its want of vision. So much is evident from the fact that if State control was removed the entire edifice would collapse. The EU has been developed without critical examination of their people within its boundaries. Its outworn protectionism, its failings, its foolery, its corruption have been tolerated and ignored.

European leaders have only to state an aim, which seems popular and plausible at first sight, for the people of Europe to go and accept without further question that its ends will be accomplished. While they turn a blind eye to failure and waste, politicians invest themselves and their bureaucrats with increasing powers. The camouflage employed by the protectionist is in stating aims that seem reasonable and then retreating behind an impenetrable cover of detail, expert waffle and an air of restless activity. While political leaders and bureaucrats eat their jam today, the people of EU have to wait for unspecified benefits tomorrow.

THE FOUNDATION OF THE EUROPEAN UNION

It would not do justice to the EU or to the European consumer/taxpayer to begin an account of its foundation with preliminary talks in the 1920s and 1930s or after the Second War or at the signature of the Treaty of Rome in 1957. Such beginnings would be too short a time to comprehend the forces which gave rise to its foundation. The EU is a product of political thinking which had roots in history, both ancient and modern.

The foundation of the EU rests on the protectionist tradition which has ruled in France and Germany for centuries. In France the champion of protectionism was Jean Colbert, the seventeenth-century statesman. He was determined to improve French industry and craft by rigorous State control of every commercial detail. He was also amassing taxes for the State, while gathering a handsome fortune for himself. Colbertism became the model of protectionism in Europe. It consisted in devising as many controls over manufacture, skills, education, markets, prices, duties, transport, and a host of connected matters, as could be imagined.

Colbert did not confine his efforts to domestic matters. He

believed that international trade was a form of warfare; that the triumph of one country must be at the expense of another; that wealth was measured by bullion; that tariffs, aggression and conquest are the best means of accumulating and monopolising bullion and are, therefore, the weapons by which national greatness is achieved.[1]

The Constituent Assembly of 1790 abolished internal tariffs and tolls and a year later imposed an external tariff against foreign trade. The rate varied from 5 to 20 per cent on manufactured goods. Raw materials and foodstuffs were admitted free. It proved impossible to prevent imports from Britain. Heavy penalties were designated for traders of British products, then large quantities of goods were classed as being of British origin and the police were given powers of search but still the smuggling continued unabated. A decree in 1806 banned trade with Britain with the intention of blockading her. A result of that embargo was to halt and reverse the upward rise in French trade. If one arm of trade – British exports – was reduced then the other – British imports – suffers equally, for they would include French exports. After the

---

[1] *Louis XIV*, D. Ogg, Chp. 3.

Napoleonic Wars iron, textiles and agriculture remained heavily protected and enjoyed effective monopolies in the French market. Even while imports were declining, duties on steel were increased.

Corn was protected by the creation of three zones within France, which were badly arranged and caused price differentials. Imports of corn were prohibited. There was talk of repeal to allow imports, but friends and foes alike had come to regard the grain duties as the cornerstone of the whole protective system. It was not until the 1840s that protection was challenged in France. Frederic Bastiat wrote about the repeal of the Corn Laws and similar agitation was set afoot in France. But the protectionists were sufficiently entrenched to hold off wild notions of free trade. However the new Emperor, Napoleon III, admired the conversion of Britain to free trade, and abolished prohibition of imports and reduced tariffs.In 1860 he concluded a treaty with Britain. Similar treaties extended the concessions of either side under 'the most favoured nation' to Germany, Italy, Switzerland, Spain, the Netherlands, Norway and Sweden. Duties were reduced, navigational restrictions were lifted. But a financial crisis in 1870 turned the tide back to the ancient tradition of protection and in 1877 the balance was further tilted by a constitutional crisis. How often national disorder blocks liberating reform. Back came agricultural protection under the guise that France had many peasant farmers needing it. Both across industries and agriculture a new tariff bill passed the Chamber of Deputies in 1909. France returned to protection like a lover giving up a flirtation to return to an old mistress.

Napoleon played as central a role in German history as in that of France. For twenty years he ruled the Rhineland. Prussia stood apart and, when the Napoleonic Wars ended in 1815, became the engine of the unification of the German states. It began by abolishing sixty domestic tariffs levied on 2800 classes of goods. In their place tariffs were imposed in 1819 against manufactured goods at 1 per cent, and 'colonial produce' and wine at 30 per cent; only raw materials were imported free of tariffs.The intention was to create a large home market from which the foreigner was effectively excluded. This system was extended to small states surrounded by Prussia. The Prussian Union spread by the assimilation of Bavaria, Württemberg and Saxony into the customs union, the *Zollverein*, which came into existence from January 1834. Under this system raw materials were imported free of duty but imports of manufactured goods were subject to a 10 per cent tariff. In 1841 Friedrich List published his book, *System of National Economy*, the main theme of which he expressed thus, 'without a common tariff system . . . political nationality is robbed of its most solid foundation'. He had linked the two elements which endanger international peace: protectionism and nationalism. List advocated protection for as long as infant industries were unable to stand alone. Thereafter, the pressures for greater protection came first from the iron and textile producers and then wool, gloves, silver and leather followed. In 1853 Austria bound itself by treaty to join the *Zollverein* later but that never came to pass. The treaty of 1860 between Britain and France spelt danger for the *Zollverein* because that treaty brought into existence the 'most favoured

Henry Broughman

Thomas Erskine

COLONEL JOHN LILBURNE.

From a Print prefixed to his Trial 1649

PUBLISHED BY CHARLES & HENRY BALDWIN, NEWGATE STREET.

John Lilburne

William Prynne

William Cobbett

Richard Carlile

Glanville Sharp

Richard Cobden

Winston Churchill

nation' clause, under which the benefits negotiated by a nation were passed on automatically to that nation's future treaty partners. Thus if Prussia secured a treaty with France, that would dictate in a large measure a treaty she might have with another country.Thus by lowering duties with France she would be bound to hand the same terms to Austria with whom she had a treaty. Special terms, therefore, with the *Zollverein* would disappear. The 'most favoured nation' clause was designed to spread free trade. Germany was for the next twenty years proceeding down the path to greater free trade. Upon the conclusion of the treaty between the North German Confederation and the South German States in 1871, the duties were assumed by the newly formed German nation. But in 1878 Bismarck declared that free trade did not suit Germany and the *Zollverein* was revived. Protectionist forces rallied and a new tariff was introduced in 1902 and was superseded by another in 1906. Upon the eve of the First World War Germany's trade was predominantly with the rest of Europe – about 55 per cent of imports and 75 per cent of exports.[2]

It is upon these two pillars of protectionism, or State control, as France and Germany have followed in modern history, that the EU has been built. It is natural for their political leaders to negotiate for the supposed advantage of their respective nations, which can only be at the expense of each other. They understand such political manoeuvring.

The Napoleonic Wars had the effect of preventing imports of foreign corn into England. Landowners enjoyed high rents during the years of the blockade. But in 1815 the wars were terminated and the blockade was lifted.The rural landowners, who feared foreign imports would reduce rent, controlled the House of Commons with the same mastery that a cat holds over a mouse. Accordingly the Corn Laws were enacted, to impose such a high tariff against imports of foreign corn, that the domestic price of corn could be held at the high prices it had reached in the Napoleonic War.

In short, State control has ruled France and Germany for a long time. The alternative system of free trade ruled Britain for about seventy years.[3] It was briefly introduced by Cavour into Piedmont. The foundation, therefore, of the EEC has always been sunk in petrified protectionism.

The dynamic of their modern relationship was formulated by De Gaulle, in brutal but concrete terms: 'The EEC is a horse and carriage; Germany is the horse and France is the coachman'.[4] Bernard Connolly, the chief of monetary affairs for six years from 1989 at the European Commission, gives a more precise definition of French protectionism: ' The [British] idea of politics is, literally, foreign to French technocrats.What they are interested in is power – first imposing *their* will on France and then imposing their conception of France's will on everyone else.'[5] Former French Prime Minister and European Commissioner, Raymond Barre, dismissed democracy, saying

---

[2] *Modern Tariff History*, P. Ashley, p. 125.
[3] See Ch 13.
[4] *The Rotten Heart of Europe*, B. Connolly, p. 7.
[5] *Ibid* p. 390.

'I never have understood why public opinion about European ideas should be taken into account.'[6] Under the *ancien régime* it had been an élite of self-interested bodies: the court, the nobles, the clerics, the farmers-general and the magistrates. In the twentieth century it is an élite of schooled bureaucrats, who possess infinite regulatory imagination but little interest in individual freedom.

The ethic of negotiating a national advantage at the expense of so-called allies is political fantasy. Listening to politicians arriving home to claim an all-night session in Brussels has been for their advantage is a ridiculous spectacle. This fake philosophy was formulated by M. Chirac, who was quoted by Henry Kissinger as saying, 'We are in a system of nations in Europe where each nation defends its interest.'[7] It is a strange notion that an association is formed in order to enable a member to protect interests against other members. In plain language, France regards foreign relations as a game of selfishness and her interest will always prevail over those of mankind.

Britain did not participate in the creation of that union. Her different tradition lay with the world more than with a part of Europe. In 1938 Churchill wrote of Britain, 'We are with Europe but not of it. We are linked but not compromised. We are interested and associated, but not absorbed.'[8] Our tradition is to restrain the State and free the individual. The tradition in France and Germany is the opposite.

Two contrasting views about liberty were expressed by Edmund Burke, the eighteenth century statesman, and Peter Mandelson, an architect of New Labour. Burke said, 'The people never give up their liberties but under some delusion.' Mandelson told an audience in Florence, 'Loss of sovereignty only concerns people if they think we are giving it up to no good purpose.'[9]

THE CREATION OF THE EUROPEAN ECONOMIC COMMUNITY [EEC]

In Europe the public mood after the Second World War was in search of something new and striking and there was a general desire to bury hatchets and to renew the ties of humanity by creating unity among former enemies. The mistakes of Versailles after the First World War were not repeated. But instead of talking as sovereign nations, France and Germany hastened to realise pre-war hopes[10] to become unified. The terms of that union were settled by excited bureaucrats.

In 1949 Churchill described in a talk at Zurich

wide areas [of] a vast quivering mass of tormented, hungry, careworn and bewildered human beings [who] gape at the ruins of their cities and homes, and scan the dark horizons for the approach of some new peril, tyranny or terror.

---

[6] *Eurofacts*, 5 December 1997.
[7] *Daily Telegraph*, 7 May 1998.
[8] *The Times*, M. Gilbert Oct 1996.
[9] *Eurofacts*, 8 May 1998.
[10] For an account of these see *Britain Held Hostage*, L. Jenkins.

Among the victors there is a babel of jarring voices; among the vanquished a sullen silence of despair.' [He pleaded]Let there be justice, mercy and freedom.[11]

He called on France and Germany to create the United States of Europe, while Britain acted as a sponsor and a link with the English-speaking world. But neither he nor his Labour opponents were drawn into the centrifugal pull of the Continent. The EEC was created from thousands of regulations and thousands of negotiating sessions. Its scaffolding consists of endless directives in several languages. Jean Monnet, head of the French Commissariat du Plan, was a founding father. The Commissariat was an understandable institution in France. Arriving after the war at a railway station a traveller to France was confronted by the sign ordering '*Allez au Control*'. The French tradition of government over the centuries has been to control.

Monnet left a diary. He was close to the centre of the European Movement. One reads about Monnet's delight at negotiating sessions and friendship with important political personages. Everything seemed negotiable to him. Nations could be treated like counters, institutions could be invented according to his bureaucratic imagination. He loved putting his knees under an international table. There is no evidence in the diary of vision. There is hardly a hint of humour. But once he chided a fellow bureaucrat, who was working in Luxemburg, when he complained of the lack of distractions in the capital. Monnet replied, 'Europe will not be made in night clubs.' Monnet's talents consisted of making plans and convincing people to accept them with an uncritical enthusiasm. He made politicians believe he was creating a new Europe and they swallowed his idea with equal glee.

Five years after the war relations between Britain, France and Germany over the future of Europe became becalmed. Monnet produced a plan to integrate the steel industry, which had been the anvil of the Second War. He handed it to Robert Schuman, the French Foreign Minister, who was departing Paris by train for a weekend. Upon his return, he adopted Monnet's idea and immediately produced the Schuman Plan to pool the sovereignty of European states under a 'High Authority'. Within three weeks Germany, Italy, Belgium, the Netherlands and Luxemburg accepted the invitation of France to negotiate the matter. Britain declined to take a seat.The Conservative Government which came to power in 1951 had no interest in becoming involved in the European plan, which he had supported while in Opposition. Churchill told Jock Colville, his secretary, that his policy was simple: houses and meat and not getting scuppered. The United States favoured the European Movement as evidence that it was beginning to become responsible for itself at last.

Within a year the participants founded the European Coal and Steel Community [ECSC], which was set up to operate as a cartel with the purpose of holding up steel prices. Like almost everything to follow in the EEC the ECSC favoured high prices for producers at the expense of both the taxpayer and consumer. It was a fitting institution

---

[11] *The Speeches of Winston Churchill*, D. Cannadine (ed.) p. 310.

to foreshadow other protectionist bodies. It was intended to create a common market in coal, iron ore and steel, which were identified as the main products in post-war economies. Above the 'High Authority' was a Special Council of Ministers representing member governments .In five years trade in coal and steel soared. That was understandable after a destructive war. 'The High Authority', under Monnet, felt emboldened.Monnet was planning to launch a more ambitious community than that dealing with iron and steel. That was only the first stage.

Troops from the People's Democratic Republic of North Korea invaded South Korea on 25 June 1950. War immediately raised the question of European participation and that of Germany in particular.The problem demanded a similar European community with another Council of Ministers, a 'High Authority', a Court of Justice and an Assembly. The Korean War provided Monnet the route towards political unity. The six participants initialled the treaty establishing the European Defence Community. Churchill dismissed moves to form it as 'tomfoolery'[12] and he remonstrated:

European army! European Army! It won't be an army. It'll be a sludgy amalgam. What soldiers want to sing are their own marching songs.[13]

However, appointments by the French Government of a number of Gaullists changed the attitude of France. De Gaulle himself described Monnet as 'the Inspirer' of 'supranational monstrosities'. France did not want to pool its 'victorious' army with Germany's non-existent one. Schuman had departed office as French Foreign Minister. Having extracted France from Indo-China, Pierre Mendès France, the French Prime Minister, wanted to pursue a conservative military role. When the French National Assembly voted to reject the Defence Community, the majority triumphantly sang *La Marseillaise*. Britain was opposed and the idea failed.The idea of an EU defence force has been suggested many times. In October 1955 Monnet formed the 'Action Committee for the United States of Europe'. Its members were the political parties and trade unions in the six participant countries, excepting the Communist and extreme right-wing parties in Europe. It quickly begot a 'Community' for nuclear energy. However, Monnet was thinking about the creation of a common market.

In the following summer foreign ministers of the six member nations met at Messina in Italy and a number of papers on similar lines were read. A committee was established to give effect to their wishes and Paul-Henri Spaak, the Foreign Minister of Belgium and former Secretary-General of the United Nations, was elected its chairman. He commissioned the Spaak report from an Inter-Governmental Committee, which outlined proposals for the nuclear energy community and for the EEC. At one point the national representatives were haggling over the enduring issue of duties on bananas. Spaak gave them two hours to resolve the matter after which time he

---

[12] *The First Statesman of Independence: Jean Monnet*, F. Duchênem p. 245.
[13] *This Blessed Plot*, H. Young, p. 76.

would announce at a Press conference that European Community would not be built because it could not agree on banana duties. Resolution was achieved and the EEC was launched. The High Authority was replaced by the Commission.

On 25 March 1957 ministers representing the six participating countries signed the Treaty of Rome which has been ever since the bulb of everything which has developed in the EU. The Treaty contained 248 articles. After reading a few the smugness of the drafters becomes apparent. Every clause is tied with a ribbon, but human life is too intelligent to be contained in a plan and too spontaneous for bureaucrats to predict even in a million clauses.

In 1960 Austria, Britain, Denmark, Finland, Norway, and Switzerland formed the European Free Trade Area. But Britain applied to join the EEC in 1961, attracted by the rate of growth among members which was about double the rate in Britain. Harold Macmillan, the British Prime Minister, thought it would give Britain a cold shower to wake them up, but the request was rebuffed by de Gaulle in 1963 and a second attempt in 1967 received the same response. But the General resigned and the next application was placed in the hands of Edward Heath. The Conservatives promised to negotiate: no less no more. But Heath did not warn the British people that 91 per cent of the EEC's Budget was being poured down the throats of rural landowners, gave them no warning about the dangers of protectionism, which had been thoroughly exposed during the nineteenth century in Britain, nor heeded the written advice[14] of Lord Kilmuir, the Lord Chancellor, in December 1960 that joining would involve serious surrenders of sovereignty, which he felt needed to be brought out in the open. In other words, Heath did not face the issues which would affect the liberties of the British people. Many people in Britain were deluded over the nature of the EEC. For example, Enoch Powell admitted: 'I said to myself [the EEC] that's going for free trade. I am in favour of free trade.'[15] In 1973 Britain joined the EEC. In 1973 the British Parliament acceded to the Treaty of Rome. After 1973 the growth of EEC members declined. In its wake Ireland and Denmark joined (Norway applied but withdrew its application). In 1975 Britain held a Referendum and 67.2 per cent of the votes cast voted in favour of remaining in.In 1981 Greece joined and was followed five years later by Spain and Portugal. In 1995 the members were brought up to fifteen by the accession of Finland, Sweden, and Austria. The population of the EU is about 370 million.

Such is a brief description of the steps after the Second World War by which the EEC was founded. There is a vague perception in Britain that talking protectionist business with Germany and France avoids war. In fact Cobden warned that precisely the opposite would occur: 'tariffs are the breeding ground of bayonets'. Alain Juppé, the former French Prime Minister, did not share this vague hope when he emphatically stated that, 'Only nuclear deterrence has been able to bring a half century of peace.'[16]

---

[14] *Eurofacts*, 20 Nov 1998.
[15] *This Blessed Plot*, H. Young, p. 242.
[16] *Eurofacts*, 20 October 1995.

It is hoped that political union can be scrambled together from a mass of directives on the shape of bananas and bureaucratic conclaves. This deluge of regulation was ridiculed by a card in a Welsh bookshop, which stated,

> There 56 words in the Lord's prayer, 297 in the Ten Commandments, 300 in the American Declaration of Independence and 29,911 in the EEC directive on the export of eggs.[17]

The EU has been driven more by brute political force than by visions of humanity, justice, liberty and wisdom.Its development has been hidden from robust scrutiny by the complexity of its regulations and by the perversity of its *raison d'être*.

The development from a community of tariffs to a common market was set down in the Single European Act 1986. It allowed a large areas of social and economic policy to be be enacted by the Commission and, if approved by the Council of Ministers, to pass automatically into the domestic law of members without ratification by their Parliaments. Effectively it has killed the English common law principle that ignorance of the law is no excuse. For how can people possibly understand the stream of directives pouring out of Brussels? The Act also introduced majority voting in the Council of Ministers for everything except fiscal harmonisation and destroyed the Luxemburg compromise, which allowed a nation to veto European proposals which it did not like. No member can be forced to accept standards in matter such as health, safety or the environment if these are set by the EU at lower standards than those already in force. The Single European Act also introduced a community without frontiers and border controls. Britain opted to stay outside the Schengen Agreement to abolish border controls.

The Treaty of Rome was amended by the Maastricht Treaty, signed in February 1992, was concerned primarily with allowing for the enlargement of the Community in the post-cold war world and for the introduction of European Monetary Union [EMU].The treaty's essential political purpose was to 'give France greater control and leverage over Germany, particularly in the crucial realm of monetary policy. For Germany . . . [it] was a means of assuaging the fears of its European neighbours about German power and independence'.[18] To symbolise these aims Germany had to give up the D-Mark.This would be a large step and Germany had to be sure that financial controls were as tight as their own – particularly when a number of members would be economically weaker.

Further amendments to the founding treaties were made by the Treaty of Amsterdam in 1997 to cover movement of persons, employment, the environment and miscellaneous practical and administrative matters.The Treaty of Rome had set up a common market and the Treaties of Maastricht and Amsterdam set the EU on course to political union.

---

[17] *Ibid*, 11 April 1997.
[18] *Imperfect Union*, M. J. Baun, p. 5.

THE COMMON AGRICULTURAL POLICY

The protection of agriculture traditionally reflected the dominance of landed interests. Protection of agriculture can be wrapped in patriotism and in France patriotism and food are each highly prized. Patriotism and economic nationalism are buttresses of protection but the central pillar is often the injustice enjoyed by the landed at the expense of the landless.

The CAP was the means by which France wanted to offset the gain of the industrial market for Germany. French protectionism is fortified by two beliefs observed at the Treaty of Versailles after the First World War by Keynes, the British economist. He wrote that Clemenceau, the French Prime Minister, 'was possessed by one illusion – France – and one delusion – mankind'. That attitude lies behind the idea that France has special need of the CAP. While it is excusable for Germany, with a similar protectionist tradition, to condone this corrupt policy, it is lamentable to observe British politicians allowing the extortion of their people to satisfy this protectionist agreement.

Agriculture is a world-wide activity. Left to itself during peace, it can feed mankind. When free trade reigned in Britain from 1849 to the 1920s agriculture prospered and even in years of depression the British people were not short of food as a result of free trade. The globe enjoys differences in climate and fertility.Technology can aid production and transport to bring to a small country such as Britain the corn-growing plains and ranches of the world.

It is politically correct to ignore the CAP and dwell on a less contentious area of EU activity. The CAP is regarded as an unmentionable dinosaur. Yet it merits detailed consideration because it, together with the expense of fish policy, takes about 55 per cent of the total Budget. It used to be 91 per cent in 1973 and continued through the 1970s and early 1980s at 70 per cent. At present its drop to 55 per cent reflects greater expenditure in other directions.

The EEC came into existence to protect agriculture and steel. Germany was expected to gain from trade in Europe. France feared the industrial power of Germany, but hoped to harness it by using the EEC to advance French agriculture. The Treaty of Rome set out ten paragraphs on agriculture which indicate the base of the policy. The Treaty set five aims for agriculture: the production of agriculture within the EEC be increased by promoting its 'rational development'; the earnings of those engaged in agriculture be increased; agriculture markets be stabilised; food supplies be assured; and that the prices of agricultural produce be reasonable.

These aims seem sensible objects, but they were to be brought about by State intervention, instead of agriculture. Like so much to follow in policy drafts the ends were more important than the means.

Germany in the 1950s wanted to continue importing food at low prices from the world while leaving its own farmers to benefit from the high level of protection awarded to its farmers. France wished both to deny the consumers of the EEC access to the low-cost farmers of the world and eliminate competition from farmers within the EEC by keeping agricultural prices below the German level.Producers outside were excluded by a high tariff around the EEC. The compromise devised by Sicco Mansholt, the first Commissioner of Agriculture, was the variable import levy which would have to be paid on imports into the EEC of agricultural products produced outside.The levy would vary with the difference between the protected price, which would be set by the EEC and the world price. Germany was attracted by the prospect of the industrial gain and in January 1962 accepted the variable levy, which effectively ended their cheap imports of food produced outside the EEC. The import levies were the first pillar of the CAP. The levies excluded world agricultural trade. The second pillar was the protected system prices which the CAP would impose within the EEC.

De Gaulle determined to promote the interests of France in 1964 by threatening to leave the EEC if the agricultural price level was not fixed. In fact, the price of wheat – a key agricultural price since it formed a large cost of feeding animals – was fixed at a much higher level than France desired. When EEC market prices fell below the protected prices, the CAP would intervene and buy the EEC farmer's production at the protected prices. The CAP would then store the produce taken off the market.

In the 1930s British protectionism had been increased in agriculture by the creation of such public bodies as the Milk Marketing Board. During the Second World War Britain introduced a regime of guaranteed prices on the model of the Corn Production Act 1917. The wartime measures were enshrined, as a permanent feature of the protection of British agriculture during peacetime, in the Agriculture Act 1947. This Act introduced guaranteed prices through a system of deficiency prices, by which it appeared consumers obtained their food at world price levels, whereas as taxpayers they subsidised prices.The ability of politicians to ignore the burdens of taxation is endless. The more modest subsidies awarded by the British Government reflected the weaker political strength of British farmers over those on the Continent.

The protection awarded under the CAP was a belt-and-braces form of protection. The EEC farmer was assured of a good price for everything he produced. That end was assured without taking account of consumer desires. The CAP was promising to buy as much as the producers could make at a price considerably above the world price level. The European farmer would think at this point, 'so far so good, but having bought our surplus production this year at the taxpayer's expense, the CAP will only bring the surplus back on the EEC market next year to obtain value for the EEC taxpayer'. The CAP would merely remove the surplus, store it and dispose of it outside the EEC, thereby creating more space in its warehouses, refrigerators, and stores for future surpluses.

The point needs reiterating that protection is awarded to producers with no thought of the consumer. First, the external tariff excluded competition from farmers throughout the world. In addition, the consumer has to provide the cost of purchasing the surplus, storing it and selling it. It is a simple truth that consumers throughout the

EEC are not persuaded that the CAP was devised for their protection. In the negotiations which led to Britain's entry in 1973 Heath chose not to mention the nature and injustice of the CAP to British consumers. Rather than be branded a liar for talking about them, he decided to be a coward for not even mentioning them.

The outside world began to protest at the scale of exports from the EEC. They protested at having lost a free market in the EEC, which was largely that of Britain.Then they faced the greater injury of losing other export markets because the EEC was off-loading surpluses at subsidised prices. However, the EEC having shut out world prices by the external tariff and instituted a higher protected price within, could not recover their costs by selling at world prices, which in the case of wheat was about half the amount which the farmer within the EEC had been paid. Their answer was to forget the taxpayers' expense in acquiring the surplus and their expense in storing the produce and use more taxpayers' funds to subsidise the export to bring prices down again to world levels. Between 1975 and 1984 agricultural exports grew by 256 per cent, while imports grew by only 14 per cent. The great problem was to operate the CAP from year to year, so that next year there would be capacity to store future surpluses. The best solution was to lose cargoes afloat and make the fishes the ultimate beneficiaries of the EEC consumers' generous gullibility. The next best solution was the massive destruction of surpluses on land. The expenditure on the destruction of crops, mainly fruit in the year 1994 was £439 million.World agriculture stood aghast at such bad faith. The taxpayers of the EEC did not complain. Mountains of unwanted meat and butter, lakes of milk and wine presented a contrast to starvation and misery breaking out in the Third World.

The blank cheque had to be limited in order to stop the CAP devouring the entire Budget. In 1982 quotas were applied to sugar and two years later to milk. The administrative paperwork involved in establishing quotas and the policing of them are beyond even imagination. In 1988 restraints on other products were called stabilisers. They operated in the same way as quotas which allowed production to be supported only up to a point. The other brilliant reform to limit production introduced the fusion of regulation and magic. Farmers were paid for setting aside (holding land out of production) one-fifth of their arable land for five years. The policy of paying for everything farmers produced had failed and at a stroke was succeeded by the reverse policy of paying them to do nothing. In 1992 Ray MacSharry, the Commissioner for Agriculture, limited the export subsidies and moved the CAP towards the substitution of subsidies for guaranteed prices.

The CAP has proved to be stream of regulations which pour out of Brussels with the ease of diarrhoea from a donkey. Grants are claimed for paper buildings, unmanifest carcasses, imaginary olives, for itinerant butter and other objects of a traffic in fraud and crime.The Treaty of Rome was amended in 1975 to create a Court of Auditors to ensure expenditure was 'sound'.

The corruption begins with the Treaty of Rome, the Council of Ministers, the President and members of the Commission. Why bother about the greengrocer who sells unauthorised bananas, while allowing the Council of Ministers and the European Commissioners off the more serious charge of having conspired to create and sustain fraud on a large scale?

The CAP was operated by reference to prices of agricultural produce. As they were expressed in different foreign currencies, the policy was fractured by the monetary system. In 1969 the D-Mark was revalued and to preserve the German farmers from a loss of income a device to compensate for currency movements was employed. It involved supposing fictional currency rates for agriculture and protecting farmer from foreign exchange fluctuations by means of currency adjustments, known as monetary compensation amounts. These became border taxes or subsidies. Though introduced as temporary measures they will endure until a common currency embraces the whole EU. Whether it works is another speculation.

Throughout the 1970s and 1980s the Common External Tariffs on agricultural produce were on average 70 per cent over world prices. It was estimated that an average family in Britain spent in 1994 £50.43p per week on food. The National Consumer Council estimated that the cost to an average family in Britain of the high prices due to the CAP amounted to £20 per week. Christopher Booker, a journalist and writer, estimated in 1994 that the costs of the CAP amounted to £28 per week for every British family. An official put the cost to a family of four at £13.64 per week.[19] He drew attention to the losses incurred as monies paid to Brussels are due in pounds and paid out to British farmers in ecus. So that when the pound exchange rate is high, the farmers lose out by as much as about 50 per cent.[20]

One of the effects of the CAP has been to encourage farmers to produce as much as possible. A typical example was the cultivation of rape which increased in Britain over seventy times up to 1995 since joining the CAP. The application of nitrates and pesticides was greatly increased. These unwholesome ingredients were measured as excessive in the water of several areas of rural England. Sir Leon Brittan, a British Commissioner, threatened to prosecute a water supplier in Norfolk for failing to deliver water of a standard acceptable to EU standards! He along with the other members of the Commission, who administer the CAP, should have been prosecuted for the foreseeable results of pursuing a policy which has encouraged the excessive use of nitrates and pesticides, which constitute the main pollutants of water, according to tests of the Water Drinking Authority.

One favourite sleight of hand employed by protectionists is to identify a person likely to arouse public sympathy, such as the hill farmer in Wales, or simple peasant in a remote region. He, says the protectionist, needs special protection from the State. For his sake they introduce the protection of agriculture. However, they are not interested in benefiting him but in enriching the wealthy farmer in the Paris Basin or in the East Midlands of England. Many smaller farmers derive small benefits either because they

[19] *Ibid* 10 Nov 1995.
[20] *Ibid* 7 Nov 1997.

breed pigs or keep chickens which are not protected or because they are too small to count under the CAP.

To expose the lie behind the CAP, it is necessary to return to one of Cobden's arguments which he began to deploy in Britain during 1843.[21] He denied that the protection of agriculture resulted in the protection of agriculture at all. For the purposes of his argument he split what is meant by agriculture into two distinct economic interests. By farmer he meant the producer of food, who tenanted the land. By landowner he meant the freehold owner of land. If a farmer owned the land on which he farmed he was both tenant farmer, deemed to rent his land and landowner as well. Cobden distinguished between these two capacities by showing that he might be enriched either as a farmer engaged in agriculture or as a landowner engaged in collecting rent. It was like, said Cobden, distinguishing between sailors and ship-owners. With that distinction in mind, it is possible to see that all the aid which is heaped supposedly on agriculture under any scheme of State interference and the CAP – the external tariffs, guaranteed prices, the intervention, subsidies, grants, loans, compensation – is, in fact, taken from the tenant farmer when his rent is reviewed in the form of an increase in his rent. It does not need statistics to prove that – just reason and a sense of justice. But a similar exercise was taken by Sir Richard Body, one of the few free-traders in the House of Commons. He showed that the amount of government intervention in Britain after the Agriculture Act 1947 until 1973 augmented the value of agricultural land by an equivalent amount.[22] The CAP, concerned with enrichment of landowners, certainly does not favour the consumers/ taxpayers of the EU, it does not constitute a continuing benefit to agriculture.

The consequences of the State interference in agriculture are catalogued in Harvey's cogently argued book *The Killing of the Countryside*.[23] It recounts the damage to arable and dairy small holdings, uplands, downlands, moorlands, chalklands, meadows, pasture, grasses, soil fertility, rivers, water supplies, hedgerows, wild flowers, butter-flies, insects, and birds through government intervention which has encouraged the use of artificial fertiliser and pesticides. To be sure these materials are used not to secure the health or pleasure of the consumer, but to boost the landowner's rent.

The effect of the CAP would have been achieved far more efficiently if the paymasters, i.e. the consumers of the EEC, wrote cheques to rural landowners without bothering to enquire about the reason. They are paying a fine imposed under protectionism and as long as they tolerate protectionism they have no reason to complain about its price.

The consumer has surrendered the freedom to buy food freely in the world and to enjoy the best and cheapest available in the world. This freedom became important with the discovery of refrigeration at the beginning of this century and improvement

---

[21] See pp. 138–43.
[22] *The Triumph and Shame*, R. Body.
[23] *The Killing of the Countryside*, G. Harvey.

in transport. The British housewife could buy Canadian salmon, Argentinean beef, New Zealand lamb and dairy products and meat from North America, or Australia and so on.The door has been closed against the course of natural commerce in the empty expectation of some benefit in the EU. To cede rights to the State is the most dangerous delegation. Gradually liberty taken from the individual becomes power acquired by the State. The idea of a 'people's EU' is an attempt not to enhance the liberty of individuals but to win their allegiance after the takeover.

There was a promise of reform during Britain's presidency. Tony Blair, the British Prime Minister, stated in The Hague in January 1998 that, 'The CAP needs modernising . . . Governments will have to spend money to keep people in rural areas . . . the present system is an absurdity . . . it is time to grasp fully the nettle of reform.'[24] However, in May 1998 Dr Cunningham, his agricultural minister, was lunching and entertaining the EU farm ministers at the rural estate of the 12th Duke of Northumberland, who must have been benefiting as a landowner from the CAP. Politicians seem blind to universal truth: 'There is no such thing as a free lunch.' Until politicians appreciate that landowners and farmers are distinct beings, even though they may be united in one person, there is no prospect of reform. In February 1999 an attempt to introduce reform ended with the blockade of motorways around Strasburg and Brussels as thousands of farmers from France formed over 800 convoys.

In short, there are just three beneficiaries of the CAP: the pensioned-bureaucrat, the crook and the landowners.

COMMON FISHERIES POLICY

Fish have been caught for centuries off Aldeburgh in Suffolk and the trade was immortalised in the opera *Peter Grimes* by Benjamin Britten. Suddenly in August 1994 the fishermen were ordered by Brussels to stop fishing sole in their 10-ft open boats for that year. The fishermen watched the short horizon in amazement.There were two factory fishing vessels from Belgium equipped to vacuum the seabed. Political correctness was thrown aside and the most conservative figures signed a protest leaflet, for clearly here was a case of manifest injustice. How did this situation arise? The European Commission fix annual quotas for different-length fishing vessels and for types of fish. The 10-ft boats had completed their quotas and the bigger vessels had not. The actual impact of the quotas on fishing ground off Aldeburgh are disastrous. A 10-ft boat traverses the fishing grounds within five miles of the coast twice per fishing trip, whereas a larger trawler fish horizontally off the coast and, after they have been fished, the fish breeding grounds remain exhausted for weeks.

There was no provision in the Treaty of Rome to cover fish in the sea; Article 38 of the Treaty applied only to fish products. Article 235 gave authority to legislate on matters not strictly relevant to any object of the Treaty of Rome. It was a weak foundation. Eventually in Article 3 of the Maastricht Treaty 1992 the Common Fisheries Policy (CFP) received official legitimacy.

---

[24] *Eurofacts* 3 July 1998.

In 1970 four nations – Britain, Denmark, Ireland and Norway – applied for membership and each had extensive fishing waters. Britain owned fishing rights for 12 miles out. The CFP was concocted in a hurry and ready on 30 June 1970, just before Britain, Norway and others delivered their application to join the EEC. The hurry was due to the importance of Britain's and Norway's territorial waters which were extended in 1976 to 200 miles. Between these two a massive monopoly of fish would be admitted to the hallowed precincts of Brussels. The EEC provided by regulation that member states could fish each other's ponds.

Heath was determined to take Britain into the EEC and he chose to forget the fishermen but his right-hand minister pretended in the House of Commons that he had done no such thing. Geoffrey Rippon assured the House that the fishing arrangements were temporary and would lapse. Heath had also not warned the British people of the dangers of the CAP and perhaps he thought fishing of minor import. Heath tried to persuade Norway to surrender her fishing grounds. Britain signed up in January 1972 and Norway decided stay out. In a referendum her people shrank from membership principally on account of fishing grounds. Rippon lied to the House on 13 December 1971 by pretending that the fishing arrangements made for Britain were not

not just transitional arrangements which automatically lapse at the end of a fixed period.

This was not only dishonesty in Parliament but a toe-in-the-door for much political dishonesty to follow. Britain had obtained a ten-year period, at the end of which she applied for an extension for exclusive rights over 45 per cent her fishing rights. She was accorded 37 per cent, although she contributed about 70 per cent of the fishing grounds of the EEC. When the ten-year period ended on 6 January 1983 a Danish fisherman tested the law by fishing within Britain's 12- mile limit. He was convicted of illegal fishing and fined £30,000, but, on appeal to the European Court of Justice, the British verdict and sentence were overturned. The grounds were that Britain's period of derogation had expired and the new permission from the EEC to Britain to fish within the twelve mile limit was not confirmed until 27 January 1983.When this period runs out in 2002 and thereafter there will be no 12- mile limit.

In 1982 Brussels drew up a quota system for each variety of fish. It might sound sensible to conserve fish but in practice it becomes ridiculous. In order to comply with the quota system backed by criminal law, fisherman had to throw dead fish back in the sea in vast quantities. Returning dead fish, reckoned as much as 40 per cent of the live catch,[25] to the sea had more to do with with the pretence that there was any substance in the CFP, apart from piracy.

The next disaster to befall British fishing was the accession in 1986 of Spain, whose fishing fleet amounted to three quarters of the entire Community fleet. It had fished

---

[25] *Ibid* 13 September 1996.

out much of its own territorial waters.The Community compromised by excluding Spain from the CFP for sixteen years. In order to gain immediate access, Spanish boats flew the British flag, purchased the British quotas to fish, a practice which became known as 'quota hopping'. Parliament terminated the practice but the European Court of Justice overthrew in 1991 the statute on the ground that the British statute illegally discriminated against another member of the Community. In 1996 Norway was included in the applicants for entry and Spanish fishing interests could not pass up the opportunity to share in her abundant fishing grounds until 2003.In order to avoid Spain vetoing the four new entries into the EU in 1996, they were admitted to the CFP. But in a Referendum the Norwegians voted narrowly and wisely to stay out. They followed the example of Greenland, who left the Community in 1986 as a result of the CFP.

In 1992 the EU began a conservation programme which would limit landed tonnages. Britain was required to cut its fishing fleet by a fifth and Spain by only four per cent.The British Government disingenuously presented two policies to achieve this end as being a 'good deal for Britain'. First, a relatively modest sum of £25 million was set aside to compensate British fishermen who destroyed their boats and in 1996 this sum was doubled. This was the counterpart of paying farmers to set land aside. Second, in order to meet the EU standard without having to pay out so much in compensation, was the measure to prevent fishermen fishing for more than so many days a year. This was the measure that caused much protest in Aldeburgh.

To add insult to injury Britain replied to Canadian protests about Spanish fishermen acting illegally that the Canadians were 'liars' and 'pirates'. In 1995 the EU were compensating the Spanish and for loss of fishing rights in Moroccan waters and in 1996 it was revealed that the EU was paying almost £900 million to African states to enable Spanish and Portuguese to fish their waters. It also spent hundreds of millions on modernising the Spanish fleet.

The complex rules of the CFP are generally observed by northern Europeans and flouted by Spain. Britain has lost its fishing grounds and blame must be laid not at the dishonesty of our EU partners but at British politicians who lacked the integrity and courage to stand against this daylight appropriation. Most of the blame must be laid upon Heath, who deserves the derision of his nation for judging 'only 22,000 British fishermen' as 'politically insignificant'.[26]

Such a notion strikes at the foundation of democracy. Rippon must bear the dishonour of having lied to the House of Commons. Heath describes the blame laid on him as 'absurd and insulting'.[27]

The Labour Party manifesto at the 1997 General Election struck a new note in the fishing fiasco: they 'will seek a thorough overhaul of the CFP to conserve our fish stocks in the long-term interests of the UK fishing industry'. But as the British

---

[26] *The Castle of Lies*, C. Booker & R. North, p. 80.
[27] *The Course of My Life*, Sir E. Heath, p. 700.

Government indicated in both Houses of Parliament that it had no such intention; the note proved imaginary.[28]

Finally, in 1998 the Conservative Opposition expressed their intention to repatriate control over fisheries by, presumably, repealing the CFP. That would go a small way to purge the dishonesty of the Conservative ministers who took Britain into the EEC and a means of securing the 12-mile limit which runs out in 2002.

EUROMONEY

Before describing the failure of the attempts to control money values, it is worth giving an outline of how international monetary values are fixed by the free money markets of the financial centres of the globe. The peace and confidence of mankind is continually disturbed by the occurrence of volcanoes, floods, disease, riots, wars, assassinations, scandals, the exits and entrances of political leaders and parties, accidents, trials, inventions and the like. The money markets, compromising banks, currency dealers, speculators react to these phenomena in the financial centres of the globe. The foreign exchange market in London is estimated by the Central Bank Survey and the Bank of International Settlements to transact 32 per cent of global turnover and America only 18 per cent.[29] Anything that influences confidence is significant to the money markets.

No dealer anywhere in the world would predict with certainty the value of any currency at noon of the morrow. For that value will depend upon many unknown factors. The market is a spontaneous market and values depend upon the hour. The supposition that the Chancellor of the Exchequer or the Governor of the Bank of England knows the forward values of currencies is touching. But they have no idea of what will happen in the globe tomorrow. As Mr Blair has so often stressed: 'The euro project is . . . of course, an intensely political act.'[30] Such a view was echoed by the Governor of the Bank of England,[31] no doubt because he did not want the blame for its failure to fall on him.

The continuance of De Gaulle as President of France stifled every move towards a common currency because he believed the matter of the French currency was his concern only. When he resigned, Pierre Werner, the Prime Minister of Luxemburg, was appointed to chair a committee to consider monetary union, which the French termed 'the royal approach to political union'. The Council of Ministers recommended in March 1971 an introduction of a Community-controlled currency in two stages with a three-year starting period. The initial idea was to hold Community currencies within narrow bands of value. Within two months, however, of beginning this monetary experiment, the Germans were keen to leave and let the D-Mark float upwards freely on the open financial markets. The system broke up quickly. In 1972 the Bretton

---

[28] *Eurofacts*, 9 January 1998, p. 5.
[29] *Ibid.* 18 June 1999.
[30] *Hansard*, 23 February 1999, col 181.
[31] *Ibid* 2 July 1999.

Woods Agreement, after the US dollar had been unhinged the year before from gold, it became evident that the US could not finance war in Vietnam and the Great Society programme at home. In February 1972 another parity-fixing scheme, to be called *the snake in the tunnel*, was launched. It was so called because the EEC currencies entwined round a central parity and over a period resembled a snake contained in a tunnel shaped by permitted parity bands. Britain joined the Community in 1973 while the snake was still in the tunnel. Within six weeks of crawling inside, Britain abandoned the scheme. Six months later the Italian lira left the tunnel. In January 1974 France left 'the royal approach' and, when it re-joined eighteen months later, it remained inside the tunnel only a few months. Only Germany, Denmark and the Benelux countries remained inside. The second phase of the Werner Committee recommendations was forgotten.

In the mid-1970s bureaucratic progress in the Community slowed and seemed to stagnate. Efforts to create a Community currency were revived, largely by Roy Jenkins, the President of the Commission. It was, wrote Heath, a step towards a more ordered and stable monetary system. Yet, order and stability is better secured by a free money market, in which there are no sudden devaluations and no public costs. Replacing the market with its speculators by the State is a recipe for expensive disorder. A year later the Council approved the creation of the European Monetary System (EMS) and the European unit of account, called the ecu. It was intended that instead of creating a parallel currency, the EMS would concentrate on an exchange rate stabilisation through a scheme of exchange rate mechanism (ERM). This imposed a discipline on participating currencies to keep their currencies within 2.25 per cent on either side of an agreed value given to the *ecu*, the currency created under the ERM. The authorities whose currency was falling out of the bottom of the lower parity band had to purchase their own currencies with their foreign reserves until they could not afford to spend more. Then they had to rely on raising their overnight interest rates dramatically, in order to catch out the speculators, who were supposed to borrow short-term loans. Currency dealers needed to finance their sales of the currency under attack in the futures market with the hope of buying it at a cheaper rate once it had been forced to devalue, whilst those whose currency exceeded the upper parity had to buy with foreign currency by selling their own until it fell within the parity. This arrangement did not appear equally effective to the countries with weaker currencies. Italy was able to secure agreement to a wider band between parities of 6 per cent and credits were agreed for currencies to be employed when their currencies were under pressure on the foreign exchange market.

In 1988 a further European monetary initiative was launched by Jacques Delors, the next President of the Commission, who launched the plan for monetary union, known as European Monetary Union (EMU) with a single European currency and Central Bank. The plan towards greater monetary union would be in three stages: first, the members outside the ERM would join; in the second stage parity bands would be tightened and central banks would combine to create a system of control; and in the last stage a single currency would be created under the direction of the European Central Bank.

In its first decade of the existence of ERM from 1979, there were no less than ten adjustments to the parities. Britain joined the ERM in October 1990. The ERM was under strain with the Spanish peseta breaking its upper limit and France, followed by Britain, falling through the lower parity.In July 1992 the ERM was in disarray again. Sterling followed the US dollar downwards. In late August the British Chancellor of Exchequer announced that the ERM parity of the pound would be maintained by all necessary means; in other words, central banks would buy sterling and their demand would lift it from the floor. The lira came under pressure as speculators sold it knowing they could buy it back cheaper after it had been forced out of the ERM. Then the Finnish were followed by the Swedes and Norwegians, who had pegged their currencies to the ecu, despite an increase in the overnight interest rate to 24 per cent and then 75 per cent! Then the lira was devalued by 7 per cent on 13 September. The pressure against sterling immediately intensified. George Soros, the currency speculator, raised loans of $10 billion outside the overnight lending market to finance sales of sterling and Bank of England borrowed £10 billion worth of D-Mark. On 16 September British rates were raised to 12 per cent and then to 15 per cent, in a bid to catch out speculators who were financing their operations with overnight borrowing. Britain could not maintain the value of Sterling and on 16 September 1992 it left the ERM. As the pound was devalued by 11 per cent Soros realised a profit of almost a £1 billion by buying Sterling more cheaply after devaluation than he sold it on the future market while the ERM was in being.

The loss to the Bank of England was never disclosed. Norman Lamont, the Chancellor of the Exchequer, explains[32] the episode involved movement between reserve currencies held by the Bank of England. By buying sterling the Bank were attempting to hold up the value of sterling. When the pound, however, rejoined the free market after leaving the ERM, it did so at a value lower by 11 per cent, representing the difference between the central rate of the ERM – 2.95 DM – and the rate to which the pound fell on 17 September in New York, Tokyo and London – 2.63 DM.[33] The Bank suffered a devaluation of their reserves. In straight-forward terms the Bank suffered a loss. The Bank is an arm of the state and thus the taxpayer bore the loss attributable to the folly of fixed-currency experiments.

The pressure was then put on the peseta and lira again. Spain devalued five per cent, the Portuguese *escudo* followed, the lira was temporarily removed from the ERM. France was saved by special help from the Bundesbank, due under the 'sweetheart' arrangement existing between Germany and France. But a few months later Ireland was forced out. In July 1993 the pressures from the free market proved too strong to resist and the bands of the ERM had to be widened to plus or minus 15 per cent. In

---

[32] *In Office*, N. Lamont, p. 259.
[33] *The Times* 18 September 1992.

short, the ERM had been a sacred cow while it lived, despite its revaluation, devaluations, desertions, but after July 1993 it was merely a carcass. Delors recovered self-esteem by blaming the crisis on 'Anglo-Saxon' speculators. Heath shared that blinkered view. The truth of the matter is that in the free currency markets State money was doomed to fail, because it has not the flexibility required to live in a free market.

Connolly, gave his conclusion on the ERM:

The true story of the ERM has been one of duplicity, skulduggery, conflict; of economic harm done to every country in the caste interests of the elite; of the distortion of economic logic and the dilution of political accountability.[34]

However, in May 1993, the EU finance ministers concluded that there was nothing fundamentally wrong with the ERM; it had been destroyed, it was pretended, by the decisions of individual governments.

The ERM was only the second stage towards monetary union within the Community. The final stage toward monetary union was negotiated in the Maastricht Treaty. It approved EMU, under which a common EU currency would emerge. The official currency, the ecu, would be managed by the European Central Bank, which was so structured to minimise or exclude political control. Britain was able to negotiate the right to decide later about joining EMU.

EMU was not popular with many people of the EU. The Danish rejected the Treaty in June 1992. This was a serious blow because reforms to the Treaty of Rome had to be be approved by each member. In September there was a narrow majority in the French referendum. After amendment a second referendum in Denmark in May 1993 delivered a majority.

After the Maastricht Treaty the EU concentrated on the transition to the third stage of promoting convergence criteria. These limited the rate of inflation, Budget deficits, currency behaviour and long-term interest rates and government debt but the Treaty allowed for modification. In October 1997 Gordon Brown, the British Chancellor, told the House of Commons that the British Government's decision to join EMU depended on it being satisfied that his five criteria would show that it was in Britain's net interest to join EMU. These concerned compatability of business cycles, sufficient flexibility of operation, no damage to inward investment, financial services, growth or jobs.

The statement left the Commons and press in confusion. Indeed the policy of the British Government seems to depend on the speaker and the venue. Blair and Brown appear keen to recommend to the British people that Britain should join some time after the dissolution of the present Parliament. But the thorn in their side is Rupert Murdoch, who owned *The Sun* newspaper, which enjoys an estimated daily readership of 10 million. There is no question of a referendum on the possibility of joining the euro while that paper is so clearly against it. The Conservatives' policy is to put off a

---

[34] *The Rotten Heart of Europe*, B. Connolly, p. 378.

decision about joining for this and the next Parliament. The costs of conversion from the pound to the euro are considerable and will represent an incentive to businessmen to argue that the national interest of Britain consists in redeeming their interest.

The Maastricht Treaty laid down five criteria which members had to meet in order to qualify to join the euro, concerning rates of inflation, rates of interest, Budget deficits and government debt.

The Council of Ministers would have three reports to consider before making their decisions, one from the EU Commission, one from EMI, the forerunner of the European Central Bank (ECB) and one from the European Parliament. They were allowed flexibility of interpretation by article 109 j (i) of the Maastricht Treaty. What the Germans had won by insisting upon the five criteria, they lost under Article 109j (i).

In its *Monthly Report* for April 1998 the Bundesbank stated that of the eleven candidates for joining the euro only four might conceivably balance their Budgets for a decade to reach the 60 per cent ratio of debt with GDP. The decision to join was taken on 2 May 1998 by eleven nations and only Greece failed to meet the standard criteria, while Britain and Sweden preferred not to join. The first stage of the single currency was first traded on 4 January 1999 and three years later the euro will replace the currencies of the members, if it goes well meanwhile. In its first twelve months of operations the euro lost about thirteen per cent of its value against the major currencies of the world. France was allowed for the initial agreement to include a receipt of about 37.5 billion francs in respect of the future pensions of France Telécom as State income, Belgium sold property assets and counted the proceeds as current income and Italy used sums set aside as severance pay upon privatisation as income and removed subsidies paid to transport and local authorities from expenditure and Germany, despite protests from the Bundesbank, revalued its gold and credited the profit as current income. Certainly there was much more than flexibility of interpretation of the above-mentioned criteria. Mario Monti, Italy's EU Commissioner, was speaking for several candidates when he said compliance with the Budgetary requirements would allow Italy in but 'cured and dead'.[35]

In May 1998 there was an unseemly struggle over the appointment of the chief of the European Central Bank, which came into existence in Frankfurt a month later. As President Chirac explained succinctly, 'A Frenchman is needed . . . to defend French interests.'[36] France wanted to reduce the dominance of the Bundesbank. Eventually a compromise was found whereby Wim Duisberg, a Dutchman, who would resign after four years in favour of Jean-Claude Trichet, a Frenchman, who would then serve the full term required by the Treaty of Maastricht, which had attempted to keep politics out of the Bank! As Dr Tietmeyer, President of the Bundesbank, observed gravely, ' timely warning, and a lesson to be learned by all'.[37] Blair, then President of the EU,

---

[35] *Eurofacts*, 6 December 1996.
[36] *Ibid*, 3 July 1998.
[37] *Ibid*, 3 July 1998.

submitted to the French and showed a lack of integrity and strength by citing afterwards that Duisberg had made a 'voluntary' statement that he would not serve his full-term in view of his age and thus had preserved the 'sanctity' of the Maastricht Treaty.

The glaring admission from his criteria is the most important in a democracy. Namely does EMU increase the liberties and standard of life of the individual in Britain? Do they enjoy the benefits of trading freely in the largest market while being surrounded by the Common External Tariff, of keeping their eggs in as many baskets as possible, of having free access with the free currency markets of the world at no public cost?

The free markets are far larger and more extensive than the European limb. They move in response to the economic decisions of hundreds of million individual decisions. The money markets are democratic instruments. They are concerned with many more currencies than the ecu. When confronted by State-backed currencies, they operate like predators in Nature. They wait until one nation falls behind the pack and a small amount of speculation separates the ailing currency still more. They risk enormous resources to finance selling the currency in question. Certainly more nerve is required than for shelling peas, but the operation is essentially as simple. Often the speculators lose. They risk their own fortunes while central bankers play with State funds. Yet the operation is simple in concept. Dr Tietmeyer acknowledged the strength of the free markets when he stated: 'Neither the Bundesbank today or the European Central Bank tomorrow can steer the the exchange rate against the assessments of the market.'[38]

Despite their failures with the *snake in the tunnel* and the ERM, the EU plunges towards a common currency with a stubbornness that is alarming. Heath writing in the late 1990s stated that the euro could be as strong as the dollar.[39] The EU is spending and will continue to spend millions on lying propaganda about the common currency. They will highlight some slight advantage to travellers and tourists by stating that currency exchanges will disappear.

Money should be left to bankers and others in the large commercial centres, rather as the mind delegates digestion to the stomach and intestines. Left to themselves, bankers have created over centuries the world's largest currency market, estimated to be almost twice as large as New York and three times the size of Tokyo. The London market trades 41 per cent more than done *in total* by fourteen EU members.

Brown seeks to control the British economy. His five criteria are those of a protectionist, who fails to understand the intelligence of a developed economy. He prefers instead his ideas of State control and coercion. If the referendum on joining the euro comes British people should vote for their liberties by rejecting his judgment.

The first flaw of the British referendum on the euro will be that the people have not been told that every fixed currency[40] has failed. Since the Second World War the three

---

[38] *Ibid*, 19 July 1998.
[39] *The Course of My Lfe*, Sir E. Heath, p. 712.
[40] Fixed currency denotes a currency which is managed outside the free currency markets.

experiments have collapsed: the Bretton Woods scheme put together in 1944 failed in August 1971, after the US was forced to take the dollar off the gold standard; the EU's snake in the tunnel collapsed after a few weeks in 1972; and the ERM followed in the early 1990s. The reason of these failures is simple to understand. The failed currencies have been fixed by the State at certain values, rather like a growing tree that is tethered so tightly to a post that it cannot sway in the wind. Consequently, the tree develops no roots and is blown over in the first storm. Similarly, a currency which cannot respond to daily shocks is knocked out by a loss of confidence.The chances of the euro becoming a permanent currency are nil. It will fail first in the marginal countries of the EU, then in Britain and finally in its heart.

The second flaw is that the people have not been informed of the costs of previous fixed-exchange experiments. If the British people were offered two soap powders and told that one was new, untried, manufactured by European politicians, and likely to cost billions to use and billions more to clear up whereas the old proven brand still cost only a few pence, the people would probably stay with the latter. If, however, they were offered two powders without being told either the potential cost, or damage, the sellers would be bankrupted for their negligence and deception. But, when the seller is the Government, they can behave as they like with impunity. It was an irony that the minister who introduced an Act to prevent financial trickery by a host of regulations is now a leading Commissioner in Brussels, who can act almost without any constraint. Rumours of costs suffered on the collapse of the pound within the ERM were the natural consequence of these costs never being divulged. The lessons of that expensive experiment have not been learnt because Government suppressed the financial truth of what happened. Politicians playing with money should be exposed as poor gamblers, who have little understanding of the game they are attempting to play.

The third flaw is there has been no admission of who paid the bills. Money has been gambled and lost on the Bretton Woods currency scheme, the snake in the tunnel and the ERM and there has been no admission and no accountability. The financial backer of the Government is the taxpayer. Ever gambler should be told the extent of his losses, for that may help get his feet on the ground again. .This is a classic situation of a people being deceived by their government.

The fourth flaw is that no costs of support since its inception will be revealed. If the costs are not known how can the experiment be evaluated? The British people are invited to infer that the exchange value of the euro speaks for itself, but they have not been told the cost involved.

The fifth flaw is that British political leaders will not concede that the present free currency markets have never broken down during centuries of global trading. They maintain exchange rates between trading currencies twenty-four hours a day through-out the world. They are sensitive to every tremor in the actual, or economic or political world.

The sixth flaw is that it is justified not by reasoned argument, but by a crude appeal to national interest. The British people are told on many occasions that the national interest requires greater effort, greater privation and greater taxation. The idea that a nation can enjoy a national interest in peacetime at the expense of the individual within it is a preposterous notion. The Government has no idea about weighing the liberty of the individual against the cost of the EU.

The seventh flaw is that the backing from much of industry is disingenuous and, therefore, unreliable. There are honourable exceptions among industrialists. But those who support the euro should be seen as selfish and narrow-minded advocates. It is selfish because industry wants to eliminate their foreign exchange costs, while knowing the costs of running the euro and cleaning up when it has failed are borne, not by them, but by the taxpayer. It is narrow-minded for industry to take a free ride at the expense of the taxpayer, who is ultimately their final customer. They equate the national interest with the interest of an grotesque fiction called Britain plc. To compare a nation to a profit-making corporation is simplistic and fallacious. Yet large industries constitute the chosen battering ram of the Government. They have been induced to invest heavily in the conversion to the euro, so they will have an incentive to herd the people towards a positive vote.

The eighth flaw concerns the timing of the referendum. The Prime Minister is postponing it until after the next General Election for a reason that has little to do with the euro. He wants to be re-elected for a second term. That is the main principle of his first administration.

The euro is unlike the ERM in one important respect: there is no exit, in theory. But when Portugal, Italy and Spain become disenchanted, Britain will surely follow. The euro will break up and mercifully, the floating currency markets, which will replace it will last as long as man trades. The lesson about protectionism, or the political interference in trade and monetary affairs, has yet to be learnt. The euro will become an expensive but undeniable lesson that Britain might have learnt two centuries ago.

THE SINGLE MARKET

The great prize to Britain, which far outweighed the unlovely CAP, the fish fiasco and the phoney money system, was pretended by the supporters of the EU to be the single market in industrial and commercial goods. It was hailed as the grand achievement of the EU. It was to be a theatre of prosperity and a production of absolute fairness and equality. The level playing field would make unregulated merchants seem like a mass of squabbling savages. However, the level field means that every member of the EU should be subject to the same regulations.

The Treaty of Rome had allowed for the possibility that France would resist the lifting of her tariffs on industrial goods by providing that member tariffs would be gradually lifted within a period of between twelve and fifteen years. After it was signed they were some immediate years of economic prosperity and the movement to removing internal industrial tariffs gathered momentum. Yet France insisted that a common external tariff be erected around the EEC at the same pace. In fact internal tariffs between members were lifted by 1968. Germany and Holland maintained low tariffs and preferred to keep their own, rather than hide behind France's higher tariff.

The first decade after the treaty were years of prosperity among members and trade between them quadrupled. The average rate of growth in the EEC between 1950–73 was 5.4 per cent and the rate of unemployment was less than 2 per cent. But the growth rate fell to 2.1 per cent between 1973–96 and unemployment rose to 7 per cent, and after 1979 the rate fell to 1.7 per cent and the unemployment rate rose to 12 per cent. These figures suggest that the greater the control and regulation the greater the decline.

The single market in Europe represents the benefit to Germany. France recognised that Germany was more interested in creating a market for industrial goods. By securing the benefit of the CAP for French landed interests, France had effectively harnessed German industrial wealth by relying on her becoming a paymaster of the CAP. Ludwig Erhard, the German Economics Minister, explained the thinking of the French:

> France has considered . . . (the EU) solely from the point of view of protecting its economy and cares little for the true freedom of trade. The result will not be a market with free competition, but an economic burden for Europe.[41]

The move towards a single market was taken in the Single European Act 1986. The single market would create one of the largest consumer market in the world. It would create the level playing field, which replaced the moving train, without route or destination, which featured so often in the 1980s. It would create according to the official Cechini Report 1988, an annual growth rate of seven per cent and five million new jobs. The single market was officially unfurled on the EU on 1 January 1993.

The standardisation of manufacture, packaging, transport would have brought delight to Colbert's wildest dreams. He would have loved the concept of sitting down with bureaucrats to create a free-trade area. He would have thoroughly approved of France deriving advantage from the CAP. Perhaps his only regret would have been that the important matters were not discussed in French only.

The Commission's White Paper on the Single Market published in 1985 listed almost 300 reforms in three sectors: physical, fiscal and technical. The first category consisted of the removal of border controls, the second of alignments of indirect taxation and the third technical matters. The last category was the largest. It concerns creating uniform specifications, industrial standards over a range of industrial products and services down to the shapes of bananas and the diameter of peaches.

The performance of the single market has been disappointing. Europe has proved to be a poor rival to other economies. Europe's record on unemployment has been higher than elsewhere. Traders based in Britain have traditionally traded with world-wide partners. The US is the location of the largest export market of £46 billion per annum.

Arming bureaucrats with powers to enforce technical standards, codes of health and safety across the whole range of business in Britain – the majority never trade abroad

---

[41] Quoted in by F. Willis, *France, Germany and the New Europe 1945–67*, from *Le Monde* 20 March 1957.

– is like opening Pandora's box. It is a well established experience that officials love saying 'Non!' and imposing penalties. The idea of protectionists trying to expose 'hidden protectionism' is enough to make a cat collapse in laughter.

Protectionists betray their beliefs when they refer to a free-trade area. When the area is confined to the EU, the Pacific Rim, South East Asia, the United States, these areas are bounded by protectionism. These areas are contradictions in terms because free trade is global. Whilst boasting about the free-trade within the EU, single marketeers ignore the Common External Tariff erected by the EU against the world. Use of the phrase free trade within the EU displays a pitiful misunderstanding of one elementary principle of political economy. Free trade areas, even ones numbering almost 400 million people, are not even small replicas of free trade and should be renamed protectionist areas. Free trade does not need one regulation, one official, but only one law outlawing import controls in one nation. Free trade would then exist between one nation and mankind. While protectionism lurks throughout the world global free trade, involving every nation, remains an impossibility Global free trade cannot be delivered through State control or protectionism, for free trade depends upon the withdrawal of government from commerce. The issue of protectionism was thoroughly debated in Britain during the 1830s and 1840s. The issue of the so-called free-trade areas was debated thoroughly in the early 1900s under the issue of Tariff Reform which pretended to create a free-trade area within the British Empire. The idea was vehemently defeated in the General Election of 1906. The embracing of the protectionism by Britain represents returning to the exposed and defeated doctrines of the early nineteenth century.

To argue that a single nation is too weak to stand alone commercially is a pathetic notion. It might also be said that an individual is too weak to remain unattached to a gang or that an individual is too weak to think his or her thoughts. In reality the EU is weak at its core and enfeebled by amassing too many petty powers. A signal box becomes a nightmare when there are too many levers.

The EU's control of trade is akin to medieval protectionism, that is based on the underlying fallacy that nations trade with each other. Trade between democracies is conducted between individuals or private bodies. Politicians are not used to commercial trading and cannot be trusted to trade as much as paper clips. There are some strange facts about trade between British residents and those in Switzerland and Norway. In 1996 the Swiss brought from British partners 2.3 times and the Norwegians 1.7 times more than each resident of the EU.[42] The total trade between British residents and EU countries is grossly distorted by assuming goods shipped to continental ports are destined only for the EU. In 1996 48.8 per cent of British exports of visible and invisible exports went to EU members.[43]

It is enough for Eurocrats to recite that the EU contains a market of million to justify the attempt to control trade. Yet Britain enjoys a traditional world trading

---

[42] *Eurofacts*, 9 Jan 1998.
[43] *Ibid.*

174

market and invests more in the United States than Europe. What is a boon to British people is a matter of intense frustration in Brussels.

British Governments pretend that Britain gains from membership of the EU through investment from businesses resident abroad. Yet inward investment, excluding investment in real estate, represents only about one-seventieth of Gross Domestic Product. In the decade to 1995 almost half inward investment came from the United States and Commonwealth and 29 per cent from the other fourteen countries of the EU. Indeed 41 per cent of foreign direct investment belongs to investors in the United States.[44]

The belief that the single market represents the high point of European development is deranged. In truth it is a curse to the producers, although protection invariably is framed for their benefit – through endless regulation – and to consumers – through the Common External Tariff. The freedom of the individual to buy whatever he or she pleases is suspended by the Common External Tariff. The British consumer has been denied access to the free market of the world and traditional suppliers all over the globe have been repressed by quotas. The Commonwealth was held together by trade but the strongest link is sentimentality and language.

Checks on the freedom to trade are as ridiculous as restrictions on the freedom of speech. Both freedoms are birthrights and there is no justification in a democracy for restrictions on trade and speech.

Fraud and corruption in the EU permeates the EU from the Council of Ministers to the criminal. It is endemic in the complexity and dishonesty of Ministers, Commissioners and officials.[45] It is beyond political or financial calculation. Some rough idea of its financial scale is given by the fact that the auditors have refused to sign the accounts of the EU for the past five years and actual fraud is reckoned to amount to amount to 10 per cent of the total Budget: about £6 billion. But by definition fraud is incalculable in terms of liberty, political integrity, health or even money.

The dismissal of the Commission under President Santer brought to prominence Romano Prodi and Niel Kinnock. The former is shadowed by legal proceedings in Italy and the latter represents political naivety on stilts when he reveled plans to purge the Commission of fraud. How can this be pretended when the whole institution is sunk in protectionism and fraud? Even arming the court of auditors with machine guns could not have that effect.

The EU represents a second example of politicians acting together in a scheme which lies outside political administration. Politicians in the EU have no idea from where it came, what similar exercises in protectionism have ended in, no interest in the corruption caused by its operation, no accountability to anyone and no idea where it is going. It is one of the most grotesque political experiments of modern political history.

---

[44] *Ibid* 10 January 1997.
[45] See *Europe on the Fiddle*, N. Tutt.

The desire to unify the warring nations in Europe after the First World War was a natural response. Churchill at the Aldwych Club, London, in 1923, stated: 'The whole solution of European difficulties lies in a reconciliation between France and Germany.' He still saw the need after the Second World War for the same reconciliation. He deprecated becoming involved in 'the tangles and intricacies of rigid constitution making', but the means chosen to effect this impulse are deeply flawed and the proof is contained in the ample political discussion of British history over the last two centuries.

The EU has within its protectionist basis the seeds of its own destruction. Its agriculture policy fails to benefit agriculture as opposed to landowning, its fish policy has been a cover for piracy, its money is phoney, its free-trade area is a contradiction in terms, its Council of Ministers is politically dishonest, its Commission is undemocratic and its champions are powered more by emotion and propaganda than objective reason. It does not represent the interests of consumers throughout the EU. It will never achieve a fraction of what could be secured by free trade for the unity of mankind and the welfare of individuals within the EU, without financial, diplomatic or strategic costs.

The interests of the British people, so vividly illustrated during her experience of free trade, will never coincide with protectionism. Why the only leading nation with experience of free trade should grasp this hopeless branch of protectionism proves that liberties are never won for all time.

13

The Tradition of Poverty in Britain

Laws grind the poor, and rich men rule the law.
                                                    Oliver Goldsmith

The existence of mass poverty is the bottom question in a democratic society. Before embarking on ideas to combat poverty it is essential first to determine its causes. The real solution is then to eradicate them. The politics of mitigation of poverty of the unresolved causes degenerates into sentimental make-believe. When these efforts fail to have the desired effect, dishonesty becomes the political refuge.

British people value tradition highly, even one bound up with injustice. Nothing comes so easily as turning off the technology of the hour, to put on a fancy garment and antique title in order to enact some quaint ceremony, whose original significance has altogether vanished from human memory. Indeed, the love of tradition seems to vary inversely to the life embodied in it. The class system is not quaint or distinctive: merely the evidence that a few are rich and independent and the many without either.

Britain has endured mass poverty for six centuries, without break. Indeed it may be said that one of the longest traditions in British history is poverty, which prevents an able-bodied individual earning a livelihood sufficient to support themselves and family throughout their lives or live an independent life. Maybe the poverty is disguised by the ownership of cars, computers and colour televisions. But the fact that only a few enjoy independent livelihoods and are able to look after their natural responsibilities, is the evidence which will be argued is a condition of poverty. In former times of British history and in many parts of the world poverty is associated with starvation. But to imagine the absence of starvation amounts to an elimination of poverty is simplistic.

The actions of Ministers, debates in Parliament, deliberations of Royal Commissions and the concern of charities in over six centuries have failed to solve that unnecessary condition.The reason is that they have been concerned only with the distressing symptoms, instead of eradicating its cause.

The customary treatment of the history of poverty is to tabulate the failed attempts to relieve it and conclude that it is a condition so intractably woven into human society that it can only be moderated, rather than eradicated. Indeed the passage in the Bible about the existence of poverty is recited as though it were a necessary evil. Two factors, however, suggest that this is a weak and hopeless conclusion.

First, Nature draws attention to a problem by the manifestation of pain. Cholera swept the globe in the nineteenth and earlier centuries, until it was observed eventually that sewage was contaminating drinking water. AIDS broke out in the last decades of the twentieth century and the cause has been attributed to wild and irresponsible monkeys in Africa. That diagnosis seemed to fit the political correctness of the hour. But the disease continues, although its progress in the developed world has been checked, and that suggests that the cause has not been diagnosed.

Secondly, there was no record of the existence of able-bodied beggars in England until the end of the thirteenth century. This fact raises the question of what conditions pertained in earlier centuries and what changes thereafter caused this evidence of poverty to occur.

In Saxon England, at least in the central regions, during the ninth century the basic pattern of an agricultural society consisted in a number of villages separated from each other by large areas of waste and forest. Communities cultivated three large arable fields and each male inhabitant was allotted equal strips of land throughout the fields. They were also free to graze so many animals in attached meadows, to gather gleanings after harvest and to take material from the waste. Each village was self-sufficient in everything but iron and salt. At the head of many communities there was a thegn, who gave protection to the village, rather like a Scottish chieftain. As an individual, the thegn enjoyed no additional strips of land but he was entitled to dues paid by cultivators. Although the waste was often called the lord's waste, the thegn had no greater claim to it than anyone else. In Saxon England no freeman was landless. Land was described as bookland, that is land held by book or charter, or folkland, held under custom or common law. Bookland applied to land held by the Church or by royal grantees.

The ninth century appears to be the last in which individuals, apart from the slaves, in England were free of civil and economic slavery. To attribute the loss of freedom to growth of population is facile. English history reveals a number of factors which reduced the free individual to the wage slave of the twentieth century.

The earliest influence which distorted this state of independence of the individual [slavery apart] was the coming of feudalism in the tenth century. It introduced two profound changes. First, it altered the tenure of land by introducing a lord. After the Conquest in 1066 folkland became known as the king's land. The legal theory of landholding of the feudal state,

treats [cultivators] as derived from a private and exclusive ownership of the lord. The lord's ownership itself may be traced as a dependent tenure and traced ultimately to a grant of the king. Second, the idea that every man needed a lord was the hallmark of this dread discipline, but it seemed only a slight variation of the Saxon idea that a lordless man was an outlaw. But the Saxons believed that every freeman was entitled to the protection of a thegn, who was a very different person from a lord of a manor. Nature provides a mother for an infant but never a lord for an adult. Such are of human invention. In 1086 Domesday Book gives a detailed picture of England south of Cheshire and Yorkshire. In the eleventh century the population of England was estimated at 1,375,000.[1] [of whom about 25,000 were serfs].

Feudalism brought in an artificial hierarchy which gave rise to the unnatural system of most superior, superior and inferior. The lord of the manor had command over the services of villeins, who comprised the most numerous class of cultivators and lesser tenants, to work his strips of land. The changes in the tenure of land became apparent as the lords began to increase their holdings. Parts of the waste of unoccupied and uncultivated land were fenced off by lords. In 1236 the Statute of Merton required the lords to have regard to the sufficiency of waste remaining and in 1285 the Statute of Westminster II extended the provisions of the Statute of Merton to the commons of pasture for animals in the meadows, rights of gleaning after harvest and pasture of animals by those who were living outside the manor. In effect, these two statutes confirmed the vesting of the wastes and meadows in the lords of the manor.The medieval enclosures developed in two ways.

First, by direct enclosure of the waste. Secondly, by gradual encroachment on the waste and by the dexterity of lawyers, the lesser tenants began to accept that the lords were the origin of rights which had belonged to them in Saxon times. Allowing that Parliament traditionally moves to enact measures after a mischief has become manifest for some time, it is reasonable to assume that enclosure by stealth had been occurring for some time.

Although the status of the individual had changed in regard to his civil relationship with his lord and also in regard to his landholding, there was little evidence of unemployment or poverty up to the middle of the fourteenth century. Except for famine in 1315–16, life was relatively prosperous for the whole of society up to the Black Death of 1348, which was spread by the flees of black rats.The Plague carried away between 30 per cent and 50 per cent of the population in three outbreaks up to 1375.

The shortage of labour became intense and wages rose dramatically by 100 per cent and more. The largest lords and landowners sought immediate redress from Parliament which represented their interests as freeholders. It enacted in 1349 the Statute of Labourers, which attempted to restrict wages to pre-Plague levels. Despite harsh penalties on both those who asked for higher wages and those who paid them and on tenants who moved from their parishes, wages soared. The Statute was re-enacted several times in vain. These attempts provide evidence of Parliament's inability to control wages, markets and prices, which each depend on natural forces. Such matters

---

[1] *Domesday and Beyond*, F. Maitland.

arise naturally. Not only were wages high but prices of agricultural produce remained at their previous level because there was much competition between tenants who worked their holdings. But the freeholders and villeins, who continued to work their larger holdings, could not raise the price of their produce. The landlords were damaged and had to let their holdings, for they could not afford to farm them. They turned in vain for assistance to the rights to demand labour from their tenants, but their service had been mostly commuted into money payments.The lords looked instead to other servitudes due by villeins such as payments on the villein's death or on the marriage of his daughters, or after having had his grain ground at the lord's mill. There were other grievances. A villein could not plead in court against his lord, or sell or leave his farm without permission of the lord, for he had become bound to his lord and the soil. The demands for money payments were in part the cause of the Peasants Revolt (1381). The rising was inspired by the preaching of John Ball, a cleric, who reminded people that the labour of the poor enabled the rich to enjoy luxury, and by John Wyclif, the religious reformer.Wyclif sent forth a number of poor, itinerant priests. He believed that all things belonged to God and that only the righteous could hold anything of Him. His creed seemed a form of medieval communism. Later he abandoned his theory of 'dominion' and became a revolutionary in religion. Between 1377–80 three poll taxes of a shilling a head were imposed. These proved the last straws. Risings broke out in Essex, Kent, Yorkshire, Dorset, Somerset, Devon, Cornwall, Hertfordshire, Buckinghamshire, Hertfordshire and East Anglia. The peasants, under Wat Tyler, executed the Chancellor, the Treasurer and a Chief Justice before their demands were met.

As a result remaining labour dues were commuted and leases to villeins and serfs were extended. It was a golden age for the serfs and lesser tenants, whose labour was highly sought. They moved around seeking better conditions. Times were good at first, until the reality of landless labourers became apparent. William Langland, the fourteenth-century poet, referred to the condition of labour: 'Labourers that have no land to live on but their hands'. In that one line he depicted the fallen status of a free peasantry with holdings of land, who did not depend on wages. But vagrancy became a problem and was noted in London. A proclamation against it was issued in 1359. The House of Commons complained about the problem in 1376 and issued an Act in 1378, which distinguished between able-bodied and impotent beggars.

A last resort for landowners was sheep farming, which required less labour than arable or cattle farming. However, sheep farming required large areas of enclosed land. This, in turn motivated freeholders and tenants to consolidate their holdings of strips and convert from arable to pasture. The lord of a manor held about about 30–50 per cent of the manor. The enclosing for pasture of this acreage deprived the lesser tenants of work on the lord's land and caused a loss of the right to glean after harvest. The lords also began to enclose the waste. The boom in wool at the beginning of the fifteenth century provided the incentive for the first land enclosures under the Tudors in the first half of the sixteenth century. Parliament forbade destruction of towns in

1489, Sir Thomas More complained about the mischief; in 1516 an Act was enacted to prevent the pulling down of towns; a Government Commission of 1517–18 reported critically on enclosures; and many Acts followed during the first half of the sixteenth century. All in vain, as the weakening of the bonds of individual to feudal land tenure provided the means for the lord to defeat the ancient rights of the lesser tenants.

Then in 1539 a second blow was added to the landless when Henry VIII began dissolving monasteries, many of which possessed considerable landholdings. This policy dispossessed tenants and the recipients of monastic alms. By 1540 the king had taken the lands and property of 800 monasteries.

Throughout the sixteenth century statutes against beggars become more frequent, and despite punishments of whipping and branding the able-bodied beggars continued to grow. At length in 1601 all these statutes were consolidated into the Poor Law Act, which put the relief of the sick and infirm on the parish rates. This Act constitutes a legislative landmark in the melancholy tradition of poverty but could never be effective in dealing with it because it did not link beggary with the dispossession of the weakest from land enclosures. The Poor Law Act embodies the sentimental compassion which has been the traditional response to the poverty of able-bodied individuals who have been the heirs of those who unjustly threw them out of their holdings. Moreover, the local charity extended to these unfortunate beggars came not from the pockets of the landowners but from the pockets of the ratepayer. This injustice has never been reversed and it can never be compensated.

It has been estimated that freeholders at this time owned about 20 per cent of the land, leaseholders about 13 per cent and customary tenants about 61 per cent, but the pattern over the country had local variations.[2] By customary tenant is meant mostly copyholders, who had legal rights against the lord, tenants at will, and those who held subject to the customs of the manor and without copy. The vast majority of customary tenants were peasants, assisted by their families. They formed the mass of society. The forerunner of the customary tenant was the villein strip farmers, who had disappeared by 1600.

The enclosures under the Tudors were encouraged by the conversion to sheep farming and augmented by the Dissolution of the Monasteries which began in the mid-1530s.

Under the Stuart reign enclosures continued but lacked their earlier economic imperative.They comprised a consolidation and continuance of what had happened in the previous century. They were, according to Tawney, 'smeared with the trail of finance'.[3]

A third large and last wave of enclosures began after the Restoration in 1660 and continued throughout the eighteenth and first half of the nineteenth centuries. The Restoration brought peace after a disturbing interlude of civil war and the protests

[2] *The Agrarian Problem in the Sixteenth Century*, R. Tawney, p. 25.
[3] *Ibid* p. 391.

became less shrill. New forms of agriculture came into being. Roots were now grown as a crop vegetables, new grasses were bred, soil drainage introduced and these together with a new rotation inspired a belief that agriculture must be conducted on a large scale, almost as a matter of public policy or, indeed, the national interest, whatever is meant by such an expression. Pamphlets in favour of enclosures replaced those against in the fifteenth and sixteenth centuries. Arthur Young, the writer and agriculturalist, likened the open-field cultivators to 'Goths and Vandals'.

Enclosures in the eighteenth century were promulgated by Arthur Young and 'improving landlords' like Thomas Coke and Turnip Townshend. While pursuing his crusade during the later decades of the eighteenth century to enclose waste land, Young had the humanity to admit that 'By nineteen out of twenty Enclosure Bills the poor are injured and most grossly'.[4] The general opinion was that enclosures increased national wealth and ignored the fact that the landowner alone was enriched. Cobbett paints this portrait of the farmer made prosperous through enclosure:

> The English farmer has, of late years, become a totally different character. A fox-hunting horse; polished boots; a spanking trot to market; a 'get out of the way or by G-d I'll ride over you' to every poor devil upon the road; wine at his dinner; a servant [sometimes in livery] to wait at his table; a painted lady for a wife; sons aping the young squires and lords; a house crammed up with sofas, pianos and all sorts of fooleries.[5]

Loss of fuel, whether wood or turf, grazing rights and gleanings were disregarded by enclosers, who argued that labourers would be better employed after enclosure and could buy theses articles in shops. The Game Law of Charles II provided that only those with freehold estates of £100 per annum or a leasehold worth £150 could shoot game. In 1770 an Act introduced penalties of imprisonment for up to six months for killing game at night. An Act of 1800 stiffened penalties for imprisonment to two years with hard labour and whipping. In 1816 the penalty for night poaching was increased to seven years of transportation, which punishment must have been most pleasing to the Rev Thomas Malthus, who believed England was over-populated by the poor. Between the years 1827–30 convictions under the Game Laws, 8502 in number equalled one in seven of criminal convictions. In 1828 Brougham fulminated:

> There is not a worse-constituted tribunal on earth not even that of the Turkish Caadi, than that at which the summary convictions on the Game Laws take place.

Resisting a game-keeper in an act of self-defence with arms constituted a capital crime. A report of the trial of eighteen poachers at the spring Assizes in Bedford was

---

[4] *British History in the Nineteenth Century*, G. Trevelyan, p. 146.
[5] *Ibid* p. 147.

reported in *The Times*.[6] Potter Macqueen, the local Member of Parliament, met the prisoners and found that they were of good character but desperate for work to feed themselves or their families. Poaching had long been considered an appropriate use of Nature's wild. Landowners employed spring guns which exploded like land-mines, until banned in 1825.The Game Laws were buttressed by the Malicious Trespass Act 1820, which granted immunity for damage done by 'persons engaged in hunting, and qualified persons in pursuit of game', which included rabbit, long hunted by country people.

There have been national and local protests at the enclosure of land. In the fifteenth century John Rous, a priest in Warwick, complained of sixty enclosures in Warwickshire and the destruction of villages. In the early sixteenth century Sir Thomas More drew attention in his book, *Utopia*, to enclosures, and William Tyndale and Hugh Latimer, among other priests, protested against them in their sermons.The enclosures and the particular practice of charging extortionate sums on the admission of heirs to copyhold tenancies caused the rising in the Northern Pilgrimage of Grace in 1536 and risings in the West Country in 1549. In the late sixteenth century William Harrison made the most rigorous exposure of the injustice wrought by enclosures. In the seventeenth century there were many pamphlets against enclosures. Jerrard Winstanley led a movement called the Diggers in the mid seventeenth century and spoke simply and directly on the evil of enclosures. Edward Sexby, on behalf of the soldiers, replied to Ireton in the Putney debates in 1647 in words, which could have even been uttered on behalf of troops returning from wars since:

> We have engaged in this kingdom and ventured our lives, and it was all for this: to recover our birthrights and privileges as Englishmen: and by the arguments urged there are none. There are many thousands of us soldiers that have ventured our lives, we have had little property in the Kingdom, yet we have had a birthright ... I wonder we were so deceived. If we had not a right to the kingdom, we are mere mercenaries soldiers. I think the poor and meaner of this kingdom ... have been the means of the preservation of this kingdom.[7]

There had been riots in 1795 after poor harvests and winters of hunger and the danger of more was avoided by magistrates at Speenhamland in Berkshire.They linked the Poor Law relief to the price of bread. Nevertheless riots broke out in East Anglia during 1816. More serious riots broke out in 1830 throughout southern England. In December Brougham, now Lord Chancellor, warned that 'the sword of justice shall be unleashed to smite, if necessary, with a firm and vigorous hand'.

Oliver Goldsmith wrote a poem, *The Deserted Village* in 1770, after being closely involved in the matter of enclosures for several years. He described the typical village

---

[6] 18 December 1830.
[7] *Clarke Papers*, Firth (ed.) pp. 330–3.

with 'its sports beneath the spreading tree and pastimes circled in the shade' and of its lifelessness after enclosure.

A time there was, ere England's griefs began,
When every rood of ground maintained its man;
For him light labour spread her wholesome store,
Just gave what life required, but gave no more:
His best companions, innocence and health;
And his best riches, ignorance of wealth.

George Crabbe, the poet from Aldeburgh, encapsulated the landless condition of the the rural community in a longer poem, entitled *Rapine and Wrong and Fear: The Rural Poor*, which he wrote in 1783. A few lines speak with force about the tragedy:

Where Plenty smiles, alas! she smiles for few,
And those who taste not, yet behold her store,
Are as slaves that dig the golden ore,
The wealth around them makes them doubly poor.

The only survey to compare with the 'Domesday Book' was the Government paper, entitled *Inquiry of 1874–5*, which was presented in abstract as a House of Commons paper, *Summary of Returns of Owners of Land in England and Wales*. It showed that 9836 owners shared the spoils of 33 million acres, but 703,289 owned less than an acre. The Hon. George Brodrick estimates, in his book *English Land and English Landlords*, that 4000 owned 19 million acres. By eliminating double-counting he estimates that 150,000 owned the remainder of estates above one acre. Geary concludes that 2000 own half the land in England.[8] What had previously been the common birthright of individuals in England had passed into private property, making most of society landless. When the totals are apportioned to rural counties, the realities which they reveal become even more startling:

Norfolk: 1348 owned three-quarters, 16,552 owned less than a quarter and 412,820 nothing.
Essex: 1471 owned three-quarters, 14,823 owned on average less than one third of an acre and 446,656 nothing.
Hertfordshire: 430 owned three-quarters, 9556 on average less than a third of an acre and 180,047 nothing.
Surrey: 556 owned three-quarters and 325,000 nothing.

---

[8] *Land Tenure and Unemployment*, F. Geary, p. 135.

The misery of the depopulation of rural areas was reflected by the over-crowding in the slums of industrial centres. The slums and urban poverty gave rise to the employment of children aged from four or five years in mines, factories and as chimney sweeps. There was an Act of 1788 to limit the ages of boys below eight years being employed as sweeps. But no method of enforcement was provided and the Act was ignored. Attempts by parents to increase or resist reductions of their miserable wages, which reflected the simple fact that they had only their labour to sell in competition with their fellows, were declared illegal by the Combination Laws of 1799 and 1800 and the Acts outlawed agreements among employers to fix wages. In practice, however, employers were free to do as they pleased. These Acts were implemented with such partiality by magistrates that workmen were forced to work on the conditions set for them.

The Combination Laws were furthered strengthened by an Act of 1825 which set up Special Commissions to tour the counties in which there had been risings among country people. Offences concerned damage to machinery and buildings, rick firings and insolent disobedience of local officials. Details of the most distressing scenes outside courts were reported in *The Times*. The anguish of one trial was reported as follows:

> Such total prostration of the mental faculties by fear, and such a terrible exhibition of anguish and despair, I have never before witnessed in a Court of Justice. Immediately on the conclusion of this sentence a number of women, who were seated behind the prisoners, set up a dreadful shriek of lamentation . . . The whole proceeding of this day in court were of the most afflicting and distressing nature. But the laceration of feelings did not end with the proceedings in court. The car for the removal of the prisoners was at the back entrance to the court-house and was surrounded by crowds of mothers, wives, sisters and children, anxiously waiting for a glance at their condemned relatives. The weeping and wailing of the different parties, as they pressed the hands of the convicts as they stepped into the car, was truly heartrending. We never saw so distressing a spectacle before . . .[9]

Proceedings were harsh and swift and attempts to plead dire poverty were brushed aside. Several rioters were hanged.

Carlile was sentenced in 1830 to three years' imprisonment, after he himself had delivered his defence in a speech of four and a half hours and after the jury acquitted him on another charge of bringing the Crown into contempt. In 1831 Cobbett was prosecuted for sedition in respect of articles in the *Weekly Political Register*. His defence was devastating when he showed that Brougham, as President of the Society for the Diffusion of Useful Knowledge,[10] had asked for permission to reprint his *Letter*

---

[9] *The Village Labourer*, J. & B. Hammond, pp. 298–9.
[10] Founded in 1826. Dwindled in 1830s.

to the Luddites as a means to turn labourers from rioting. Cobbett issued a subpoena against Brougham, the Lord Chancellor, who appeared as a witness. Cobbett then moved from defence to attack and brought to court Grey, Melbourne and Palmerston and two other Ministers to explain the pardoning of a rioter, whose 'confession' was the main evidence against Cobbett. At this point Cobbett produced a statement signed by 103 present at the meeting, who denied Cobbett had said the things alleged. Then he contrasted the pardon of the informant with the miserable fate of those transported. Many sentences were pardoned but over 450 were shipped to Australia.

Another cruel pressure which the poor had to bear was the Corn Laws imposed after the Napoleonic Wars to prevent imports below 80 shillings a quarter. During the war the price of wheat rose 43 shillings per quarter in 1812. But after a good harvest in 1813 prices fell sharply. The Corn Laws had the effect of putting the staple diet beyond the means of the poorest members of society. During the Napoleonic trade embargo they were intended to encourage native agriculture but after 1815 they were imposed to swell the receipts of the landowners and inflicted hardship on the poor. An economic slump after the conclusion of war in 1815 was a further hurt. It occurred as the Army and Navy shed two-thirds of their number – 100,000 in 1815.

In 1819 Parliament intervened to prescribe rules for children employed in the textile mills and factories, about forty years after the practice had begun. Children under nine were barred from working in textile production, and the hours worked by those between nine and sixteen were limited to thirteen and half per day and night work was abolished. In the rest of industry and in chimney sweeping conditions remained unaltered. In the same year the House of Commons also debated the question of chimney sweeps and concluded that the miseries were exaggerated, necessary and less than evils which would result from interference. Many of the children had no parents and were taken into workhouses or had been sold by parents too poor to keep them at home. Their sufferings, which were revealed by a number of witnesses to Parliamentary Committees, represent one of the most horrifying episodes of English history. Their situation was but another dreadful detail in the wretched status which the weakest members of the nation suffered as a result of the enclosures. Cobbett ridiculed the greatest of Britain in the Commons. In times past, Cobbett boasted, the navy was said to be the glory of the nation, then manufactures, then the land, then the Bank of England but in 1833 the greatness and prosperity was due to 300,000 children in Lancashire. For it was said that if these workers worked just two hours less a day the country would be ruined and open our trade to the rest of the world!

The story of William Temple, as he told it to the Committee of Artisans and Machinery of the Commons, reveals the unjust severity of the Combination Laws. After service in the army in Corunna, he became a weaver in Lancashire. He and twenty others gave notice that they intended to quit their employment unless their wages were made equal to what other employers were paying. When the employer, Smith, refused they left his employ. Smith prevented their re-employment by giving their names to other employers. Temple consulted a lawyer and raised funds for an action against Smith. He was gaoled under the Combination Laws for conspiracy to raise wages. Smith prosecuted in both Lancashire where Temple had left his employ and in Cheshire where he had raised funds, so that two demands for bail of £200 had to be met. He was not able to raise the bail and as a consequence spent three months in gaol until the money could be raised. As the trial was still three months off, he issued a broadsheet appealing for funds against 'the savage grasp of an overbearing and hard-hearted employer'. Temple was taken into custody for libel on instructions of the clerk. Bail was less stringent: a mere £100. At the conspiracy trial Temple was given a sentence of twelve months for leaving his employ and for asking for help to defend himself. On release after sixteen (sic) months he could not find work for a year. Another defendant received the same sentence for calling a meeting and another three months for asking a stranger in the street, 'I wish you would come forward for these men, otherwise they will fall through.' Magistrates employed spies to infiltrate work places. Women in employment suffered similar treatment when they expressed dissatisfaction with their wages. When simple people turned to religion the magistrates were keen to pounce on sedition and conspiracy. When a curate addressed the congregation and said the deceased, who had been hanged for arson, was actually murdered, the Derbyshire magistrates asked for a warrant, describing the curate as 'of the lowest order of clergyman, uneducated, of vulgar habits, and low connections'. In fact, he had often been a magistrate himself.

The dark period which followed the French Revolution and persisted for the first two decades of the nineteenth century was ended by an amelioration of legislation. Peel repealed the Combination Laws in 1824–5 and trade unions were recognised in 1827, the man-traps and spring-guns designed to enforce the dreadful Game Laws were declared illegal, the 'bloody code' of death penalties under the Game Laws was eased in the 1820s because juries would not convict. In 1832 Lord Chancellor Brougham ended prosecutions of seditious libel, and the House of Commons brought in the first Reform Act. In 1833 slavery was abolished throughout the Empire, and factory legislation was extended beyond workers in the cotton industry by the Factory Acts 1833, 1844 and 1850. In 1846 the Corn Laws were repealed.

No principle or reasoned argument appears to have been argued to justify the enclosure of land and no claim that it was just. In 1607 the House of Lords published its conclusion that gentlemen must have their desire to enclose and the surplus population should be transferred to wars or colonies. Various enclosers argued the merit of replacing wealth where there had been poverty. The eighteenth century saw the introduction of new crops and grasses, novel rotations which required large-scale farming. But it is an argument devoid of justice or humanity to allow small-holdings to be eliminated in the name of improvement. Landowners depended more on lawyers, whose fees put their skills out of reach of small holders. They often required small holders to prove good legal title. They erased Nature's birthrights in Saxon England by supposing that an original grant of land from a lord had been lost.

As the last wave of enclosures were taking place in the late eighteenth century the powerful interests were seduced by the empty elegance of Adam Smith when he spoke about natural liberty and Malthus, who both encouraged the richer folk to concentrate on their own self-interest and ignore the condition of the poor. Smith's 'obvious and simple system of natural liberty' was claimed to be the mainspring of the capitalist system and that was a plausible idea, which was popular with the richer interests. But the concept of a society built of self-interest had been demolished a century earlier. In 1664 Locke had written about the question whether self-interest was the foundation of natural law and decided emphatically that it was not. He introduced justice as of greater importance than self-interest:

> What reason is left for the fulfilment of promises, what protection for the interests, what sense of community and common purpose between men, when equity and justice are the same as self-interest? What can social life amongst men consist in, if not fraud, violence, hatred, robbery, murder, and so forth, when every man not only is allowed, but is obliged to grab what he can, by any means, from his neighbour, while his neighbour, for his part, is obliged to hang onto it at all costs?[11]

In 1766 Turgot filled out Locke's argument and introduced a system of capitalism based on foundations of justice. The important distinction between the thinking of Turgot and Smith goes to the basis of their arguments. Turgot believed that co-operation with Nature necessitated the introduction of justice between men. Smith stated that the invisible hand would determine the affairs of men but he failed to add that, without justice, the rich would be few and the poor many. Since Smith was writing for the powerful interests, it was more acceptable to them if he did not mention the need of justice. Turgot did not support the poor or the rich: he concentrated on the natural rights of the individual.

Malthus completed the burial of the economic rights of the poor with his inhuman doctrines. First, that wages were fixed by Nature and that humans could not alter that natural fact. Second, the rate of increase of population constantly outstripped the resources needed to sustain it. Thus, money expended on Poor Law encouraged the birth of more poor. These two men were not just heartless and wanting in humanity, but both were superficial in their thinking.

At the end of the eighteenth century Thomas Spence, a radical, wrote against the injustice of private property in land, which had the effect of depriving the landless from a leading species of public property. He argued that a parish should receive the rent of land within it for common purposes. In 1792 he came to London and was active in the Corresponding Societies. He was imprisoned in 1794 and again in 1801 when he described himself as 'unfeed' Advocate of the disinherited seed of Adam'. Plainly, he

---

[11] *Political Writings*, J Locke, Penguin edn, p 182.

he did not fit the society as described by Jane Austen and others and so had to be put away as an undisciplined ruffian. He believed in the dangerous idea that democracy should be human and follow Nature.

The orthodoxy of nineteenth-century thought was interrupted by one important voice of dissent on the private ownership of land. A young writer, Herbert Spencer, employed by *The Economist*, wrote about the ownership of land in his book, *Social Statics* (1850). He questioned the right of ownership in the the most uncompromising terms and showed that the right derived from battle or trickery:

> Either men have a right to make the soil private property, or they have not. There is no medium. We must choose one of the two positions. There can be no half opinions. In the nature of things the fact must be one way or the other.

He decided the question unambiguously in the negative. The private ownership of land was, he insisted, against natural equity. Later he became a celebrated writer and natural philosopher and little was heard of his work. But interest in it revived during the 1880s. It was withdrawn from circulation and the author became ensnared in correspondence in *The Times*, in which he unsuccessfully attempted to preface his robust and youthful writing with several 'ifs' and 'maybes' and to pass it off as youthful idealism.The young man who had championed reason and justice became an old, celebrated man put to rest by the desire of social conformity, even though it involved cowardice.

Enclosure has probably been effected by stealth and theft throughout the last six centuries; from the thirteenth century small parts of the waste under the Statutes of Merton and of Westminster; in the fifteenth and sixteenth centuries under an alleged custom of the manor, according to which a lord or tenant could enclose, provided he abandoned his rights on common land and obtaining in advance the sanction of the court; in the seventeenth century the means became local agreement, which was confirmed by and obtained in the court of Chancery; and in the eighteenth and the first half of the nineteenth century more than 7 million acres were enclosed by Acts of Parliament. The term Enclosure Act in Tudor and Stuart times had signified measures to resist enclosures but after 1660 it became a means to authorise them.[12]

It must be remembered that throughout this time Parliament, as yet little affected by the Reform Acts, answered to the landowner as faithfully as a mirror reflects the image in front of it. The private Acts, which replaced the Chancery or court of Exchequer decrees in the mid eighteenth century, were replaced in in 1836 by the General Enclosure Act, after many Bills had failed to pass Parliament since 1795. This Act required the consent of two-thirds of the interests affected before allowing enclosure without any need to apply to the Parliament. The overwhelming reason for the General Enclosure Act was to save the expense and inconvenience born by the

---

[12] *Stealing Our Land*, K. Jupp cased edn, p. 27 pb edn, p. 38.

enclosers. Enclosures in the metropolitan area of London were forbidden from 1845. The last enclosures of the nineteenth century were completed by 1873. Enclosures in the mid nineteenth century ensured that the reformed Parliament presided over a nation in which a few were landed and the mass of society became landless, nay, even worse: trespassers in the land of their birth.

When the procedure of enclosure, if conducted by legal means, involved a private Act of Parliament, parliamentary agents were required to prepare the Bill. It was estimated that between 1786-99 the annual fees of these agents, handling 707 cases of enclosure, amounted to £120,000.[13] After a General Act was introduced, compensation was provided for the parliamentary officials.[14]

The enclosure of land had occurred throughout the world by similar means, which amounted to suppression of the weak by the strong, who, because they were first-comers or the strongest, have been allowed to disinherit the greater number. In the west of America it was accomplished between about 1850 and about 1880. The injustice of land enclosure was exposed by Henry George,[15] who concentrated on the injustice of converting the value from a public fund into a private possession. When he died in 1897 he had become a best-selling author, whose world-wide fame was reckoned as second, among Americans, only to Mark Twain. Yet within two decades powerful interests had erased his memory from history.

It is tempting to imagine that the horrors of dark and unjust periods are a matter only of history, to be glimpsed from drawings. It is a simple notion that beer, television, sport and lotteries wipe out the past. But in the life of an individual an unjust act in childhood may affect an entire life. Similarly, in the life of a nation the enclosures of land continue to affect the economic liberty of the mass of its people a century after the last enclosure. The enclosures removed the status of freemen and replaced with wage slavery.

The enclosures hit the weakest members of society hard indeed. In destroying the livelihood of the weakest folk in the country, they unhinged the livelihood of everyone with only their labour to sell, wherever they happened to be. The liberties of Britain are to be measured by the security of those at the margin of society. The enclosures were one of the original causes of the creation of wage slavery, whereby the individual is forced to compete against others for the lowest wage acceptable to the unemployed.

The enclosures were a wrong against Nature. The only authority for the enclosures was given by unreformed Parliaments, for the enclosures were almost complete before the passage of the second Reform Act. Few examples in British history can more clearly distinguish between the law of Nature and the law of Parliament. For Nature grants a birthright to every person born on earth to air, sunshine, water and land and Parliament has sanctioned the private appropriation of land and other natural resources.

---

[13] *Ibid* p. 71 fn 1.
[14] *Ibid* p. 99.
[15] See *The Man Who Said No!*, M. Hill.

Those who pretend that the highest sovereignty in Britain belongs to Parliament cannot comprehend the grand dimension of political thought revealed by the light of Nature. In Britain political sovereignty is inherent in the people who can employ the machinery of Parliament to restore the birthrights created by Nature. If the rule of law includes the ability of Parliament to set aside Nature, it becomes a concept of great danger. The history of Parliament shows that in relation to economic liberty it has been a constitutional machine which has worked unjustly for centuries. Whilst it can create crimes by the score, it cannot create birthrights. The law in violation of Nature's bequest to all human beings is no law known to justice or humanity.

Unless people claim their fundamental rights from Nature, they will not achieve complete freedom. Parliament cannot outdo Nature or achieve even a small approximation of her endowment. How right was the statement that 'Parliament can do anything, except make man a woman.' It has attempted to do that and the consequence has been to set a foundation for wage slavery.

Enclosure of land committed two principal violations of Nature. First, it divided mankind into landed and landless, which division reflected the contrast of the few, who happened to be rich and the mass of society, who are poor. Secondly, it deprived society of the value of land, which had been created not by the landowner, but by every member of society.

In every society when mass poverty exists or where an able-bodied individual cannot look after himself or family, it is certain that the land of the nation has been enclosed. Poverty is often the base of racial or class suppression. The nation that eradicates the causes of general poverty will render to itself a state of society not seen in modern history and to mankind an example which should never be erased from human memory. The great weakness of the British Empire was that it spread the system of injustice that existed at home.

14

An Example of Mitigation – The Welfare State

Parliament has been dominated to this this day by political forces which lack the courage and character to identify the causes of poverty and eradicate them. Instead they are bound to mitigate the ill while leaving its causes to continue. Such a posture must rank as political quackery. It is futile for students to study this melancholy history without making a diagnosis of the condition.

The welfare state is erected on three foundations of falsehood. First, that politicians are caring or compassionate. If they were either they would eradicate the cause of the suffering of the mass of the people. Second, that the poor are relieved at the expense of the rich. The welfare state is financed from taxation which falls not as Parliament deliberate but as a dead burden on the whole of society. As it is collected though the pricing system, it falls most disproportionately on the poorest. Third, that the causes of poverty can be swept under the carpet. That can only continue as long as the people are content to live in a state of ignorance of political thought.

Up to the sixteenth century pauperism was considered an individual condition of sin. The concept of sin and failure has always been employed to make men and women feel insecure and unworthy. The first rather crude attempts to suppress beggary date from the fourteenth century. Labour became scarce after the Black Death in 1348–9, which carried away between a third and a half of England's population. Labour enjoyed higher remuneration over the next half century. Impotent beggars were distinguished in 1338 from able-bodied and ordered to return to their places of origin or residence, and it was decreed in 1392 that an appropriation of funds to church or cathedral be reserved for the poor. This policy of treating beggars as communal litter was advanced in 1495, when disabled beggars were ordered to return to their home parish, where they could beg and vagabonds among them could be put in stocks for three days and nights with only bread and water. In 1537 a technological refinement was introduced; vagabonds could be branded with a hot iron.

Poor aid came from private sources, guilds, hospitals, municipalities and, chiefly, from the Church, who set up a poor fund financed from tithes. The fund did not always remain available for the poor; often it was appropriated by absentee clerics.

The introduction of measures for mitigating poverty was often made by towns and Parliament approved and adopted these experiments in their enactments. In 1533–4 a number of Acts were passed in an attempt to fix prices of food, for as one of the Acts stated, the hungry 'be so discouraged with misery and poverty that they fall daily to theft, robbery, and other inconvenience, or pitifully die for hunger and cold'. Justices were empowered in 1531 to license both 'deserving' and 'undeserving poor'. The deserving poor were limited to the disabled and they were allowed to beg in their own parish. Other persons caught begging were to be tied naked to a cart and whipped through the streets of a town bleeding. Then he was dispatched to his birthplace or to a place in which he had resided for a period of three years; 'there put himself to labour like as a true man oweth to do'. Each parish was made responsible in 1536 for relieving its 'poor creatures' and setting to work its 'sturdy vagabonds and valiant beggars', in such a way that they would not have to beg.

It also provided for a poor fund to be financed by voluntary donations. The donations, under such permissive legislation, do not seem to have sprung as spontaneously and as generously as the situation demanded and, in 1547, the voluntary mechanism was described more precisely and local officials were required for the first time to provide cottages for the impotent, maimed and aged. In Whitsun week after the service the parson was bidden to 'quietly' call upon his congregation to appoint collectors, who would 'gently ask and demand' parishioners what weekly sum they intended to give for the poor. If they refused to contribute and resisted the exhortations of the parson, then they could be summoned to explain themselves to the bishop. Even this direct attack on the recusant's conscience evidently failed to open his purse, for, in 1563, the bishop is empowered to bind him to appear before the sessions. The Act of 1547 also increased the punishments for sturdy beggars; enslavement for periods from two years to life and offenders to be branded with a 'V' across the chest. By the same measure the mayors of towns and churchwardens were instructed to compile lists of those able to contribute.

In 1572 the punishment of vagabonds and the relief of poverty was the aim of a more comprehensive act. Its preamble declared that:

[T]his realm of England and Wales be presently with rogues, vagabonds and sturdy beggars exceedingly pestered, by means whereof happeneth horrible murders, thefts, and other great outrages, to the high displeasure of Almighty God and to the great annoyance of the common weal.

Other statutes of this time refer include in this number gypsies, known then as egyptians. If anyone over fourteen, man or woman, be caught begging or herding with the gypsies they were to be detained for appearance at the sessions. Conviction rendered the beggar liable 'to be grievously whipped and burnt through the gristle of the right ear with a hot iron of the compass of an inch about'. A third conviction would attract the penalty of death and forfeiture of property.

These rather crude methods of deterring beggars proved of little effect in the second half of the sixteenth century. Despite the passage of many statutes the army of beggars had been rising. Thus, in 1576 comprehensive measures were adopted to oblige justices of the peace to construct houses of correction provisioned with stocks of wool, hemp flax and iron, so that the poor, who refused to work under the direction of the overseer, and the obstinate beggar or convicted rogue, who could not be returned whence he had come, could be put to work. Bridewell, a former palace in London, which had been converted into a house of correction in 1553, served as an example. The justices were also empowered to levy compulsory rates. The preamble of an enactment in 1597 listed as public enemies

all persons calling themselves scholars going about begging; all seafaring men pretending losses of their ships and goods on the sea; all idle persons going about begging or using any subtle craft or unlawful games and plays, or feigning to have knowledge in physiognomy, palmistry, and other like crafty science, or pretending that they tell destinies, fortunes, or such other fantastical imaginations; all fencers, bearwards, common players, and minstrels; all jugglers, tinkers, peddlers, and petty chapmen; all wandering persons and common labourers, able in body, and refusing to work for wages commonly given; all persons that wander abroad begging pretending losses by fire or otherwise; and all persons pretending to be Egyptians.

All of these description were to taken as 'rogues, vagabonds and sturdy beggars' and liable to public whipping and return to place of birth or former abode. The sick, wounded and disabled soldiers and mariners were shortly afterwards removed from the list and accorded, along with the impotent poor, a claim on parish funds. The remainder were to be punished as dissolute rogues.

The purpose of the legislation passed at the close of the sixteenth century had been to distinguish the impotent and needy from the sturdy and valiant, who were capable of earning their living, and to punish the latter if they resorted to begging. The former were covered to an extent by the measures of 1572 and 1576. A man, however able-bodied and sturdy, who is starving, will steal in order to exist. The sanction of morality or the dread of whipping or death may dissuade an upright individual with a full stomach, but neither will overbear the natural instinct to preserve life from starvation.

In 1601 the earlier measures to relieve poverty and to repress begging, dating back to the Black Death, were repealed and replaced by a Poor Law which was to endure in its essentials into the present century.

After three generations in which the attempt to stamp out vagrancy by police measures of hideous brutality [wrote Tawney] the momentous admission was made that its cause was economic distress, not merely personal idleness and that the whip had no terrors for the man who must either tramp or starve.[1]

That change of attitude, however, was not reflected in an attempt to reveal the causes of the economic distress. The British have preferred to believe that biblical passage which states: 'The poor will always be with us.' But it cannot be pretended that an ill can exist without a cause.

In 1601 the authorities embarked upon an endeavour of mitigating general poverty or in other words, to exterminate weeds by trimming their stems. Though the removal of the cause of poverty as a social disease might have been as effected as simply and decisively, say as cholera, the Government preferred to get involved in detail of unending complexity and progressive failure. From this date begins the tradition of welfare failure in Britain. There is a link between the next four centuries. It is hopeless blindness, which has been tempered with sentimental political thinking and cant.

The parish was established as the responsible authority for poor relief. The provision for the needy poor of work and for the able poor and housing for the disabled poor fell to the parish overseers, whose expenditure was covered by a compulsory poor rate. The 1601 Act specified three forms of institutional relief: for the impotent poor the almshouse, for the able-bodied poor a workhouse and for the idle a residential house of correction. The distinctions held good as long as the poor constituted a small number but as poverty entrapped a more significant proportion, so it became a common term and so the impotent were herded along with the able-bodied and the idle into the workhouse.

The Poor Law was administered centrally by the Privy Council, but during the Civil War (1640–7) the Council was divested of this power and the Poor Law fell to be administered locally by parishes. Some parishes were richer or more generous than others and their relative programmes became known to those in search of their assistance and the best payers acted, like the welfare state after the Second World War, as a magnet for those prepared to travel.

During the seventeenth century towns expanded with trade. The drift into urban communities was discernible in every part of the country but the pull of London was strongest. In 1662 the Settlement Act addressed the problem by allowing justices of the peace to remove a settler living in a tenement of less than £10 yearly value within forty days of his arrival, before he became chargeable to a parish, and return him to the parish from which he had come. Writing in 1688, Roger North, a lawyer and writer, attacked the Settlement Act:

Surely it is a great imprisonment, if not slavery, to a poor family to be under such restraint by law that they must always live in one place . . . [They] are imprisoned in their towns and chained down to their wants, so they are deprived of means to

---

[1] *Religion and the Rise of Capitalism*, R.H. Tawney, p. 262.

mend their condition, but if any chance to move for experiment (arises) they are then sent back and tossed from pillar to post in carts, till they return to their old settled misery again.[2]

The measure was passed essentially to allow metropolitan areas to return paupers congregating in the towns back to their rural origins and so prevent them becoming chargeable on urban poor relief. The Act was no aid to parishes inundated with immigrants, particularly the Irish, who came from lands without parishes. Like a host of impractical regulations which depend on fixity of abode, it fails because it is as much the tendency of man to move as it his instinct to settle.

In 1722–3 the Workhouse or General Act allowed parishes to hire or to purchase or erect buildings to be used as a poor house or workhouse and applied the workhouse test; that relief could be refused to an able-bodied applicant who declined to enter a workhouse.

The harvest of 1795 was bad and the price of grain rose, as much on account of the failure as also on account of the Napoleonic Wars. The justices at Speenhamland decided that a poor man in work whose living standard, measured according to the price of bread and the size of his family, fell below a prescribed standard would be granted a subsidy from the poor rate. The scheme or variants of it was adopted in other parishes to mitigate the shortage of food. In 1796 overseers were empowered to give relief outside workhouses and poor houses to the able-bodied poor and, so, the workhouse test was abandoned.

Malthus admitted the benign intentions of those who wished to mitigate poverty but he opposed the Poor Law on the ground that it would encourage the poor to enlarge their families and increase the burden of the poor rate without increasing the supply of food. Malthus had maintained that the rate of human reproduction exceeded the rate of increase of food production. Comparison need only be made between vegetable and human reproduction to see the fallacy in his theory. He joined many others who have put forward specious political argument which are pleasing to the richest classes.

David Ricardo, a British economist, reiterated the myth of a wages fund and propounded the idea that moneys spent on the Poor Law reduced the amount of the fund which could be devoted to wages. Neither substantiated their arguments, but they were widely believed and the demand for the reform of the Poor Law was strengthened. It was believed widely, and one might say instinctively, that there must be alternatives methods of combating poverty.

Alexis de Tocqueville visited England, 'that Eden of modern civilisation' as he called it, and was astonished that in such a rich country bustling with industry, full of well-fed cattle and traversed by serviceable roads about a sixth of the population – an exaggeration – was existing on poor relief. He compared the situation with that

---

[2] *The English Poor*, T. Mackay, p. 123.

in Portugal, which, though primitive and largely uncultivated, had no pauper population.

[He was] deeply convinced that any permanent, regular, administrative system whose aim will be to provide for the needs of the poor, will breed more miseries than it can cure, will deprave the population which it wants to help and comfort, will in time reduce the rich to being no more than the tenant-farmers of the poor, will dry up the sources of saving, will stop the accumulation of capital, will retard the development of trade, will benumb human industry and activity, will culminate by bringing about a violent revolution in the State, when the number of those who receive alms will have become as large as those who give it, and the indigent, no longer being able to take from the impoverished rich the means of providing for his needs, will find the it easier to plunder them of all their property at one stroke than to ask their help.[3]

De Tocqueville was writing when the Swing Riots of 1830 were still fresh in people's memories. They had broken out in rural districts at first as a protest against the mechanised threshing machines and developed into general protests signified by the firing of ricks and barns. The riots were exaggerated in the news press and Parliament, for the fear of revolution on the French model had lingered. Bills containing reforms of the Poor Law were presented and but the will to introduce them were blunted by the fact that the Poor Laws were supporting nearly two million dependants. The Poor Law system had undergone a number of changes since 1601, but it still remained in its essentials unchanged. It was still controlled and administered through the officers of some 15,000 parishes, whose treatment of the poor depended on local resources, the attitudes of the officers and the political composition of the parish. During the last two decades of the eighteenth century the cost of the Poor Law rose sharply. In 1785 from a total of just under £2 million in 1785, it had doubled by 1803 and by 1817 it reached £6 million. Some of the rise was accounted for by the increasing resort to rates in aid of wages, but more seems attributable to the increasing numbers of poor and the greater readiness of parishes to provide relief.

But the Napoleonic Wars also contributed directly to these increases by causing prices to rise through disruption of trade and mounting taxation and by extending the Poor Law to cover payments to the families of militiamen at the front. When peace was followed by a good harvests after 1820, which reduced prices to a half of their wartime levels, the expenditure on the poor dipped. Whatever the arithmetic, as established by painstaking research, may now show of total expenditure, the general perception was that the Poor Law was requiring a heavy rate. The ending of the war had reduced the fears of revolutionary insurrection and, accordingly, it was less pressing to buy off unrest. Nonetheless it has been estimated that up to 20 per cent of

---

[3] *Tocqueville and Beaumont on Social Reform, Drescher* (ed.) (1968) pp. 24–5.

the population were paupers. Malthus had made people think about the effects of the Poor Law. A number of parliamentary committees embarked on a series of enquiries during the 1820s. These culminated in the appointment of a royal commission in 1832 to review the operation of the Poor Law.

The Commissioners completed a 200-page report, accompanied by fifteen volumes of testimonies, within two years. The Poor Law Amendment Act 1834 introduced the principal recommendations of the Commissioners. First relief, granted to the able-bodied outside workhouses, called 'out-door relief', was curtailed. Thus relief was available only for the inmates of workhouses and for the impotent poor who were entitled to receive assistance in their homes. The Commissioners had endeavoured to establish the principle of 'less eligibility', which would place the pauper in receipt of relief at a lower standard of living than the poorest labourer, who was contributing to their relief through the poor rate. Thus out-door relief provided for the impotent would be fixed below the lowest wage and the relief obtainable in a workhouse would be fixed at an appreciably lower rate. Second, responsibility for the administration of the Poor Law was taken out of the hands of parishes and their officers and vested in twenty-one Poor Law districts to be supervised by a deputy-commissioner appointed by the central board of three commissioners.

The 1834 Act steadied the expenditure committed to the poor. The poor rates fell from their peak in the 1820s of £7 million to £4.5 million per annum and over the next two decades did not exceed £6 million. The workhouse and financial reliefs were suitable for discouraging idleness and criminality in a village or small rural town, along with the stocks and the ducking pond, but they were out of place in large towns and industrial centres. The retention of these absurd institutions throughout the nineteenth century marks the impotence of a society who did not want to examine the causes of poverty. At a time when industry was rising from village craft to scientific levels and was being developed by the rise of international trade, the idea of removing the causes of poverty, instead of designing petty regulations to conceal beggary and poverty, did not seize a hold.

The widening of the franchise by successive Acts had given a political identity to the poorer classes; votes could be won by appealing to the poor, political programmes had to include their interests and the Poor Law, acceptable perhaps hitherto, was not the form of relief which a democrat would wish upon himself. The London Congregational Union published in 1883 an inquiry, *The Bitter Cry of Outcast London*, into the housing of the poor in central London. It depicted conditions so primitive and inhabitants so poor that appeals were made to the Government to remedy ills which private agencies could not reform.

Lord Salisbury, a future Tory Prime Minister, offered to subsidise the rent of the poor. This may seem a surprising and almost generous offer from an aristocrat, a Cecil, but it is explained by a fear that the attack on private property in land mounted by Henry George was becoming so popular that, when coupled with the evidence detailed in *The Bitter Cry*, the whole institution of the private ownership of land value would come under attack. Henry George, an American political thinker, visited England after the British publication of his book, *Progress and Poverty*, in 1881. His concept of the natural provision for the collection of land value through taxation attracted lively support from the newly formed Fabian Society. Though many supporters, most notably Bernard Shaw, devoted their energies to building socialist programmes, the idea was taken up by Campbell-Bannerman's Liberal administration. It provided an explanation of both the cause and the remedy of conditions described in *The Bitter Cry* – the private ownership not of land but of land value. Such was the nature of the attack on poverty and landlordism which prompted Salisbury to make an offer which would otherwise have seemed out of character.

In 1886 a meeting of unemployed men assembled in Trafalgar Square. The meeting was inflamed by an attack on private property, wealth and privilege. Many of the audience set off on a rampage down Pall Mall up to Hyde Park. A number of windows were smashed, carriages were invaded and some shops were looted. What distinguished the riot from ones earlier in the century was that it had been directed against property owners in the heart of their domain. Though the physical damage was comparatively slight, the portents were alarming.

The dockers, obeying a call from their trade union, came out on strike in 1889. They were an unskilled body competing for daily hire and to make a strike hold in the docks was both an achievement and a sure sign of cohesion in such an industry. In 1892 three Members of Parliament were returned as representatives of the Independent Labour Party and in the 1906 election their number increased to twenty-nine and twenty-four unaffiliated members represented 'working people'. A new force with roots on the shop floor was aspiring for political office.

The Boer War, which broke out in 1899, recruited large numbers of volunteers. Many were in such poor condition they were rejected.

> What [questioned Asquith] is the use of talking of Empire if here, at its very centre, there is always to be found a mass of people, stunted in education, a prey to intemperance, huddled and congested beyond the possibility of realising in any true sense either social or domestic life.[4]

The report of the Inspector-General of Recruiting initiated a public debate on the health of children and cast such doubt on the unregulated system that demands for state intervention were inevitable.

During the winter of 1892–3 when unemployment stood at over 750,000 local authorities found employment for 26,875. More significant than the number was the fact that the state had acted to relieve unemployment. In 1904 local authorities interviewed 46,000 soldiers returning from the Boer War. They offered poor relief to 11,000 and work was invented for the remainder. In the following year local authorities

---

[4] *The Evolution of National Insurance*, B.B. Gilbert (1966) p. 77.

were empowered to relieve unemployment by outdoor relief and by setting up labour exchanges. The pressure on central government to intervene grew.

The poor limped into the twentieth century to be bought off by the creation of the welfare state. That the Poor Law lasted from 1601 to 1914 does not speak of its excellence in any degree. But it marks the superficial starched-collar morality of Victorian Britain. Society preferred the dazzling imperialism of Disraeli to that of reforming injustice at home.

A Royal Commission was appointed in 1905. The majority recommended that the Poor Law be transferred from the guardians to public assistance committees run by local authorities and that these committees be given wider social responsibilities. Nevertheless they believed that poverty was still a matter of individual and moral weakness. Beatrice Webb wrote the minority report which attributed poverty to economic arrangements. She also favoured local administration but she recommended such administration should be undertaken by a number of specialised departments. She sketched the outline of the welfare State. The Poor Law administration was dissolved 1929.

That the modern welfare state owes its rise to this tradition of ignorant weakness is a sad reflection on politics. For were the British minded to address themselves to the causes of poverty they would wonder that their forbears ever continued a system of failure so long. That the solution to the problem was so simple and effective would only heighten their sense of incredulity.

THE FIRST STEPS TOWARDS THE WELFARE STATE

The Liberal administrations, which held power from the landside election of 1906, with an overall majority of 132 seats, up till after the First World War, introduced pensions, national health insurance and unemployment insurance. They took the first steps to the extensive mitigation of poverty which came to be called the welfare state.

The first intervention of this type taken by the Liberal Government – the feeding of school children – was not of their devising. The Bill was taken over from a private Labour member, not from conviction, but more because they could not been seen to oppose it. It was enacted in 1906 to allow local authorities to supply school meals and to provide that a parent who did not pay for them would not lose his civil and constitutional privileges. In fact, those local authorities which provided meals found it impossible to recover more than a fraction of the cost from parents. The measure was opposed by Dicey because he could not accept that parental duties should be assumed by the State and the parent be permitted not to reimburse the costs. Children had become the offspring of a nation and and its taxpayers their parents. In 1908 the Childrens Act made it an offence to neglect the medical treatment of children. Thus in cases when a child's health was neglected by its parents, the State was charged to do so. The responsibility was passed to local education authorities, who were obliged to introduce school medical treatment.

The second step taken by the Liberal Government, headed by Asquith after Campbell-Bannerman's death, was the introduction of an old age pension in 1908. In

1878 the Revd Blackley had proposed the first plan for national pensions: that a youth under twenty-one should pay £10 into an annuity fund which would cover him for sickness at eight shillings a week and for retirement over seventy at four shillings. Various schemes for contributory pensions were proposed and rejected during the 1890s. In 1899 the Labour movement demanded no-contributory pensions for those over sixty. But the stumbling block was cash. Asquith professed throughout the early part of 1907 to favour a State pension but pleaded lack of funds. In July 1907 the Liberal administration lost two by-elections to Labour and pensions were put at the top of the agenda. Those over seventy and eligible for the pension, estimated at 572,000, received five shillings per week. A number of conditions had to be met by the recipient; it had to be shown that he or she was not a lunatic; had not been in prison for the previous ten years; and was not receiving poor relief, and had been a British subject and resident in the UK for twenty years, and received a income of less that £31 per annum. The pension prevented the aged seeking outdoor relief under the Poor Law, though it did not effect the number of those over seventy receiving relief inside a workhouse. There was little provision for pensions for the manual labourer for he rarely survived to pensionable age. The public health measures increased longevity. It was the first measure designed to retain support drifting away to Labour and of course the entitlement to pensions could be extended considerably and increased in amount.

As soon as the Old Age Pension Act was enacted Lloyd George, Chancellor of the Exchequer, and Churchill, President of the Board of Trade, turned to Germany where Bismark had introduced extensive schemes of social policy. During a visit in August 1908 Lloyd George was surprised by the scale of social insurance in Germany and began planning a more ambitious scheme than an extension of the Pension Act. Lloyd George had been planning the National Insurance Act 1911 with Churchill. It became the major piece of welfare legislation enacted by the Liberal Government in response to the influences already described. This Act was the forerunner of endless major welfare measures. It was long and complicated; to create rights for some and to exclude others, to interfere in private provision, and to set guidelines for bureaucracies are not simple matters to enact.

The first part of the Act provided insurance to cover those earning less than £160 per annum after the age of sixteen and manual workers if they earned in excess of two shillings a day. The Act obliged employers to deduct four pennies per week from eligible employees and to contribute themselves the sum of three pennies and the State was required to pay into the appointed fund the comparatively modest amount of two pennies; sufficient, however, for Lloyd George to take credit for a political triumph and to proclaim that the employee had reaped nine pennies for four pennies. He did not acknowledge that prices would increase to accommodate both the taxation of employers and to cover the contribution of the State. In reality the people would pay in increased prices the 9d and receive back that sum less charges of the State. Those compulsorily insured were covered for sickness after four days off work at ten shillings per week for twenty-six weeks, for medical attention, for disability at the rate of five shillings per week indefinitely, a maternity benefit of thirty shillings payable to the mother and a sanatorial benefit to the insured and his family suffering tuberculosis. The costs of these benefits were assessed at 5s 4d and the balance of 3s 6d being absorbed in the first sixteen years to fund the older element who would be admitted without a reserve being created for them. The insured would choose a doctor named on the local panel.

It was estimated that 39 million people in Britain lived off incomes below £160 per annum at around the turn of the century. Health service was available to some, who lived in large towns, at the voluntary hospitals but to most at Poor Law infirmaries, which, though often as good as the voluntary hospitals, were tainted by the Poor Law stigma. There were dispensaries in some places, operated by doctors, friendly societies, medical clubs and there were doctors, contracted by friendly societies or working on their own account. In addition there were health clubs, benefit societies of many descriptions designed to spread the cost, rather like schemes of insurance. Often these services overlapped and in some districts none existed. The aim of the friendly societies and the health clubs was to keep members out of the Poor Law and the paupers' grave. The insurance companies, of whom the Prudential and the Pearl were the largest, issued death or funeral policies only and by 1910 they had sold almost 30 million policies, the great majority of which lapsed. They employed 70,000 door-to-door collectors, who made weekly collections, of which almost 50 per cent were accounted for by commissions and expenses. They did not sell sickness or unemployment insurance because there had never been a profit in that business.

The insurance companies were a strong lobby and the insurance companies persuaded Lloyd George to exclude any idea of including death benefits or widows pensions from his bill. He had to pilot his bill through the lobbying of the insurance companies, the friendly societies and the doctors and when accommodation was reached with one discord was set off with another.

The second part of 1911 Act introduced insurance against unemployment. A few attempts to provide assistance to the unemployed had been tried. In the early 1900s various attempts were made by the Salvation Army and the East End boroughs of London to put unemployed men to work on agricultural land, but they were fanciful, expensive and ineffective. In 1905 the London boroughs interviewed 46,000 unemployed men, sent 11,000 for poor relief and employed the remainder on civil work around London. It was successful and the Government passed the Unemployed Workmen Act 1905 in order to extend the scheme all over the country. But employment improved markedly and the Act was not brought into use.

Notwithstanding these attempts Churchill called unemployment 'the untrodden field of politics'. As President of the Board of Trade with responsibility for this measure, he proposed to bring the 'magic of averages' into play. He recruited William Beveridge who was committed to labour exchanges. They were introduced in 1910 and by 1913 there were 430 exchanges, each placing around 2000 unemployed a year. The unemployment insurance provisions, passed without demur in Parliament, covered

2.25 million employed in the construction, shipbuilding, vehicle manufacture, iron-founding, mechanical engineering and saw-milling industries, which experienced the highest incidence of unemployment. There was little reliable statistical information about unemployment and, therefore, the Treasury, who underwrote the unemployment fund, insisted that a pilot scheme was introduced. Employees and employers in these industries paid 2s 5p a week and the Government 1s 6p, or about a third of the total. Benefits became payable in 1913 but the next year the First World War ended unemployment. The unemployment fund went into surplus.

These first steps towards a welfare state were taken blindly with no regard to the causes of the problem of poverty.

BETWEEN THE WARS

During the First World War the state directed the economy and civilian life to a degree it had not done before. Government was not minded to relinquish its extensive powers when the purpose, for which they had been acquired, came to an end. Speaking to the leaders of the Labour Party in 1917 Lloyd George uttered, not the traditional spirit of Liberalism, but the new credo of socialism, which has dominated political thought to this day.

> The present war . . . presents an opportunity for reconstruction of industrial and economic conditions of this country such as has never been presented in the life of, probably, the world. The whole state of society is more or less molten and you can stamp upon that molten mass almost anything so long as you do it with firmness and determination.[5]

A Ministry of Reconstruction was dreamt up and particular emphasis was put on State housing. Lloyd George coined another ready phrase to launch his housing illusion; what was required, he stated, 'to make a country fit for heroes to live in'. The Housing and Town Planning Act 1919 obliged local authorities to supply housing and provided public subsidies for the purpose. Within two years the housing programme ran out of funds and was abandoned after 213,000 homes had been completed. In 1923 the Government offered a subsidy for houses built privately and in the following year one for private accommodation built to rent. Up to the Second World War local authorities built 1.1 million houses, the subsidies were paid on 400,000 private houses, while the private sector built about 2.5 million. In 1930 grants were introduced for local authorities undertaking slum clearance.

Lloyd George extended unemployment insurance to cover all those earning less than £250 per annum. In 1921 the insurance fund, which had built up a surplus during the First World War, went into deficit after the extension of the cover. The 'magic of averages' could be trusted when unemployment was temporary and slight but not

---

[5] *Evolution of the Welfare State*, D. Fraser p. 166.

during a recession, like that which set in during the 1920s and culminated in the Great Depression. As the account slipped into deficit a number of expedients were seized upon: unemployment relief limited under the 1911 Act by the number of premiums already paid became an uncovenanted benefit; and, as Beveridge observed magisterially, 'the principle of insurance' had been replaced 'by the practice of largesse'. In 1927 Parliament accepted that unemployment relief should be paid according to need, provided only that the applicant was contributing something to the fund and was genuinely seeking work.'

In order to relieve pressure on the fund the Labour Government provided in 1930 that uncovenanted relief should be financed from the general revenue. In a year it had cost £19 million and was a factor which brought on the financial crisis of 1931. The bankers insisted on a reduction of 10 per cent in unemployment relief and the Labour Government resigned rather than oblige. The Coalition Government, which came to power in 1931, made the cut, limited the payment of covenanted relief to twenty-six weeks and transferred responsibility of uncovenanted relief to Public Assistance Committees. These Committees, operated by local authorities, applied the means test to those claiming for longer than twenty-six weeks under the insurance fund and to those who were not covered by insurance. The means test involved inquiry into the financial means of whole families. The findings of these committees as to eligibility and as to the amounts of relief were so varied that the system became as unpopular as the Poor Law, which to a large extent it had replaced. The incidence of unemployment was heaviest in Scotland, northern England and Wales, whereas with the south east England, where much of the wealth was concentrated, it was slight. To remove the local discretions and to relieve the poorest regions unemployment relief was transferred to a national Unemployment Assistance Board, which was empowered to adopt its own scales of relief and form of means test. After two years spent adjusting scales of relief the Board took over relief of all able-bodied males, leaving only the care of the sick and children to the local Public Assistance Committees. It did so at a time when unemployment was falling as the impending war generated employment.

POST-SECOND WAR

In the spring of 1941, a few months after the Battle of Britain, a committee under Beveridge was formed to report on social insurance. The committee swiftly shrank to just Beveridge himself. Out of this seemingly unimportant brief and by means of a report, Beveridge conjured a coup of publicity. He offered a Britain wearied by war the prospect of peace in which 'the five giant evils', as he called them, of poverty, would be banished; he offered the creation of a New Jerusalem.

'A revolutionary moment in the world's history is a time for revolutions, not for patching', began the report.[6] It was based on a social survey conducted between the wars in major cities. This showed, apparently, that 75 per cent of poverty was

---

[6] Cmnd 6404 p. 6.

attributable to loss of earnings and that the balance was caused by failure of those in work to match personal expenditure to income. Beveridge sought, therefore, to provide that social security would ensure a certain level of income. But he went far beyond seeking a solution depending on insurance. Social security, he stated:

> should be accompanied by a determination to use the powers of the State to whatever extent may prove necessary to ensure for all, not indeed absolute continuity of work, but a reasonable chance of productive employment.The plan for social security is put forward as part of a general programme of social policy. It is part of an attack upon five giant evils: upon the physical Want with which it is directly concerned, upon Disease causes that Want and brings more troubles in its train, upon Ignorance which no democracy can afford among its citizens, upon Squalor which arises through haphazard distribution of industry and population and upon Idleness, which destroys wealth and corrupts men, whether they are well fed or not.[7]

Beveridge advocated child allowances of eight shillings per child after the first and a health service. The latter proposal was put forward as a duty which the State owed to the sick. Somewhat naively he added two 'logical corollaries' to the payment of high disability payments: 'that determined efforts should be made by the State to reduce the number of causes for which benefit is needed . . . that the individual should recognise the duty to be well and to co-operate in all stages which may lead to diagnosis of disease in early stages when it can be prevented'.[8]

Beveridge costed the plan at £86 million and predicted that by 1965 the cost would have risen slightly. Keynes read the unpublished report and told Beveridge that his report 'leave[s] me in a wild state of excitement. I think it is a vast constructive reform of real importance and am relieved that it is so financially possible'.[9] Keynes agreed to support the report provided the cost was kept below £100 million for the first five years. However, Beveridge had never bothered himself much about the cost; the New Jerusalem was so desirable that the cost would be found. In 1944 a White Paper presented a more modest plan, which the Treasury costed at £240 million. The actual cost of Health Service doubled within two years of its introduction to surpass £100 million.

The Beveridge Report was published in November 1942, though its contents had been extensively leaked. It was hailed at home, abroad by British troops and throughout the English-speaking world. It sold over 600,000 copies. Beveridge noted with satisfaction, 'The public boom in the Report was overwhelming. I became at a blow one of the best-known characters in the country.'[10] The Archbishop of

---

[7] *Ibid* p. 170.
[8] *Ibid* p. 158.
[9] *Power and Influence*, W. Beveridge p. 309.
[10] *Ibid*; 319.

Canterbury, William Temple, announced 'that it was the first time anyone had set out to embody the whole spirit of the Christian ethic in an Act of Parliament'.[11] A pious but misconceived plaudit.

Only Churchill and the Conservative members of the Cabinet declined to greet the report with enthusiasm. They were still caught up in the drama of the war, whose outcome was still unsettled, and, though provision had been made for reconstruction after the war, no plans had been formulated. The Chancellor of the Exchequer costed the open-ended report and saw that it would grow to immense proportions. Churchill and several ministers feared that war aid from the United States would dry up if the Government embraced a programme of welfare which had no bearing on the war. Churchill had witnessed the failure of reconstruction after the First World War; it had excited aspirations and only left debt. Churchill instructed ministers to refrain from committing themselves to the proposals in debate on the Report. The War Office countermanded its decision to circulate the report to troops. The rejection of the report by Churchill cost him the 1945 General Election and put Labour into power to fight Beveridge's war against 'the five giants'.

The plan made an assumption which was intended to underpin the economic fabric of society: the maintenance of full employment. When Beveridge saw the Government's resolve to bury his report on social security he embarked on a second under the title *Full Employment in a Free Society*. This report assumed that the proposals about child allowances and the health service had been adopted. He identified the cause of unemployment between the wars as 'chronic insufficiency of demand'. What a grotesque notion! Unemployment was also attributable to a lesser extent by a 'misdirection of demand' and a lack of organisation in the labour market which caused insufficient or excessive mobility of labour; these causes could be counteracted by planned location of industry.

The insufficiency of demand must be made good by the State.

> Acceptance of this new responsibility . . . marks the line we must cross, in order to pass from the old Britain of unemployment and jealousy and fear to the new Britain of opportunity and service for all.[12]

The precedent for crossing this line had been provided by the role which the state had played during the War.

> The experience of war is relevant to peace; that unemployment disappears and that all men have value when the State sets up unlimited demand for a compelling purpose. By the spectacular achievement of its planned economy war shows how great is the waste of unemployment. Finally war experience confirms the

---

[11] *Beveridge and His Plan*, J. Beveridge p. 135.
[12] *Full Employment in a Free Society*, W. Beveridge p. 29.

possibility of securing full employment by socialisation of demand without the socialisation of production.[13]

Demand would be maintained by state expenditure on the

re-equipping industry so as to make it more efficient, while maintaining the health and strength of the working population, so as to make them more efficient is better to employ people on digging holes and filling them up than not to employ them at all; those who are taken into useless employment will, by what they earn and spend, give employment to others.[14]

The reasons why demand cannot be left wholly in private, individual hands, it was contended, are that it would not be wisely directed, having regard to the quality and location of labour, that it would not promote consumption which was most socially desirable nor would it produce communal goods such as schools and hospitals.

The maintenance of full employment would involve the State in price control, import control, public investment in industry, control of marketing of primary products, control of transport, international trading agreements and the creation of public monopolies. It would also demand industrial discipline. 'Bargaining for wages must be responsible, looking not to snatching short sectional advantages, but to the permanent good of the community.'[15]

Beveridge concluded his second report with the assertion that British people, having acquiesced in the creation of so powerful a State, would remain free, and not only free but employed: a contradiction in terms.

The two important implementations of the Beveridge Report were the National Insurance Act 1946 and the National Health Act 1948. The welfare state appears to have brought education, health and social security to millions who otherwise could not have afforded these services. The reason why able-bodied people could not afford these essentials of life was not due to their ignorance or impotence but simply because competition for work had rendered such expenditure unnecessary for survival. Earnings had been reduced by competition among wage earners to a bare minimum. State expenditure is filtered through light-weight politicians, who reckon expenditure on welfare is a boon.

In weighing the benefits of the welfare state the burden of taxation required to finance this experiment falls heaviest on the mass of society. That burden has devastated the marginal livelihood even further. The land enclosures was one blade of the scissors and unjust taxation is the other blade which has wrought a state of wage slavery in a land enjoying civil liberty. It seems to have liberated poverty if the

---

[13] *Ibid* p. 29.
[14] *Ibid* p. 147.
[15] *Ibid* p. 23.

politician's blandishments about expenditure are believed. But as soon as the system is considered it becomes clear that the cost of sweeping the problem of poverty under the carpet is that the welfare state perpetuates the very condition which it attempts to relieve. It represents a political lie of incalculable dimension.

The growth of the welfare state in the twentieth century has unloosed in equal measure political lying and sentimentality. The lie is that poverty has been relieved by the State. The reason why the poverty of the mass has not been overcome is simple. Its cause has not been eradicated. If a stone is not removed from a shoe it will cause continuing pain, injure the foot, derange the skeletal structure and thereby interfere with the nervous system until the health of the whole body and mind is impaired. Trying to mitigate the ill of poverty without removing its cause amounts to failing to eject the stone in the shoe of the nation.

In May 1844 Cobden warned the House of Commons:

We often hear a great deal about charity, but what have we to do with charity? Yes, I say, what have we to do with charity in this House? The people ask for justice and not charity.We are bound to deal out justice; how can charity be dealt out to an entire nation? Where the nation were the recipients, it is difficult to imagine, who would be the donors.[16]

---

[16] !5: 5; 1843. Hansard LXIX Col 400.

15

A Just Distribution of Wealth

In a democracy the distribution of wealth ranks in importance with other leading liberties. The essence of democracy is the individual living in society in which he is political master with full possession of birthrights. Such an icon portrays the stature of man as able to look after himself or herself. It is as powerful as the man drawn by Leonardo da Vinci standing outstretched in a circle, representing Man in the Universe.

But Parliament has been dominated by a general belief that the individual is too weak and too poor to command the services available in a society. It has become a political convention of our constitution that it is never questioned why in a democratic society a few are rich and many of them idle and the mass are poor and mostly industrious.

At the beginning of the twentieth century the economic situation of the individual was clear. The mass were unable to look after themselves or their families, except at survival levels which did not admit schooling, health care, retirement or care of sick relatives. When an able-bodied individual cannot provide for such essentials for his or her family from the remuneration of work, something is profoundly wrong in society.

Earnings were restricted to a minimum required for survival by the competition of unemployed individuals looking for jobs. In a society in which the overwhelming majority are employed, the unemployed individual performs a crucial role. They need a job so badly that they are not worried about demanding sufficient pay to recompense for health, education, holiday, retirement, or absence from work. Therefore, he competes for earnings at a level which do not include these 'luxuries'. Such is the power of the unemployed individual that no one competing against him for a job can demand sufficient earnings to meet these natural expenses of life. No matter how industrious or skilful an individual may be, his or her earnings will be related to the minimum set for the job in question by the unemployed individual.

So stark were these economic strictures that young men in rural parts, even after the Second World War, allowed their teeth to be extracted in order to replace them with dentures as a device to avoid the expenses of dentistry and ignored symptoms of illness because they disliked the arrogance and expense of doctors. Likewise, youths in eighteenth-century France amputated their trigger figure in order to render themselves ineligible for military service.

Politicians fail to diagnose why this situation of mass poverty existed, because they lacked the courage to offend vested interests, who profit from wage slavery. Instead, they resorted to mitigation of the ills of poverty by the State. By concentrating on the weak, Parliament has lost even the concept of the free man, who can look after himself and family.

The low level of earnings, set by unemployment, is the first element of the trap of wage slavery besetting the mass of society and limiting them to poverty.

The second element of the trap is that the price of land will rise to the most that the individual can afford. Everyone needs somewhere to live and work. While they are being paid the least that an unemployed individual will accept, they will have to pay for the land which they occupy at the rate of the most they can afford. This price is often confused with the price of the building. However, the building starts depreciating from the moment that it is built and exposed to the elements. Therefore, the value of housing is continually depreciating. The rising prices, which are generally described as the price of housing, reflect a decline in the value of buildings and the rise in the price of land. To escape this hardship of paying the most that can be afforded from the least acceptable wage mothers go out to work for a second income. Few women, except the poorest, worked outside their home in 1900 but by the end of the century most did. On the face of things each couple have two incomes but since 1900 the price of land has risen and most of the earnings of the wife go towards paying more for the land on which their dwelling stands.

The third element of the trap of wage slavery is the burden of taxation. It is generally forgotten that the welfare of the State has to be paid for through taxation. As this is a compulsory charge falling on the employed and unemployed alike, taxation did not enter into the computation of the minimum earnings which an unemployed individual would take for the job. Taxpayers are encouraged by politicians to believe that tax is graduated according to income. In fact, the people pay tax, not as a Finance Act declares, but through their own daily expenditure, for commercial prices include about 50 per cent taxation. The only person who evades taxation from the first day of life to beyond the grave is one who never parts with a penny. The fact that the mass of society with the lowest incomes pay the highest proportion in tax and the richest pay the least proportion is buried beneath a mass of lies and detailed argument.This is self-evident from the fact that the poorest spend their entire income on survival, whereas the rich person does not. The Reform Act changed little, for whether a Member represents Old Sarum or a thriving city, he or she cannot pretend the interests of the taxpayer is represented in Parliament. The House of Commons is filled with Members who believe State expenditure is good and that the Chancellor of the Exchequer is brilliant.

These three elements – unjust distribution of wealth, an unjust system of land ownership and the taxation of labour – reduce the individual to a condition of wage slavery. This slavery is a vile, pernicious influence which consists not of irons and shackles but of slavery of thinking like an individual without the power of an independent mind. It is much more difficult to cast aside thinking born of fear and insecurity connected with loss of a job and the possibility of a loss of a home. The first step is to remove the sources of fear.When an individual cannot look after himself or herself or family or work their way out of poverty, he is being deprived of his manhood and she of her womanhood.

The provision of school meals in 1906, pensions, insurance against illness and unemployment were the beginnings of the welfare state. Later it included housing, education, medicine and social security. After a century of increasing State expenditure, the social pattern is essentially unchanged – the mass cannot provide for their family's basic needs and this privilege is only within the means of a few rich.

The distribution of wealth is unaltered. The same forces operate in the same way they have operated since the formation of society. The level of earnings are governed not by Parliament, but by natural laws. When unemployment is high earnings will fall and when it is absent earnings will rise.

The need to obtain employment is assumed without question. The idea that an individual needs an employer is redolent of the feudal insistence that every man needed a lord. Yet there are many who would prefer to work for themselves and enjoy an independent livelihood rather than a subsistence wage. The desires of man are diverse and inexhaustible and form a sure foundation for the livelihoods of those who could satisfy them by a diversity of skills. But the consumers of the skills are in the same position as the suppliers – they are too poor to afford each other.

The system of capitalism is a mechanism, rather than an ideology. It is built of self-interest. When Parliament fails to liberate the restraints on natural liberty which prevent the individual looking after himself or herself it comes to resemble an assembly, often parochial and sometimes dictatorial.The capitalist system will work hand-in-hand with a framework of justice, which liberates the ability of the individual to look himself or herself and limits government to the least extent.

Slavery is not always accompanied by chains, locks, dungeons, but some forms of slavery are more subtle and control minds as effectively as irons controlled bodies.The mass of the British people have been made landless and driven from independent livelihood into a condition, in which they compete for employment and remuneration against each other. When there is a pool of unemployed, earnings drop to levels which the unemployed will accept to obtain work. This profound change of status has come about as a result of reducing the mass of society to the hand-to-mouth of wage slavery.

The rottenness at the heart of political thought in Britain, as elsewhere, is that injustice of this scale, affecting the great mass of society, is tolerated as a fact of existence. Yet it is both inhuman and unnecessary. In considering a just distribution of wealth, the argument in this chapter will attempt to discover the natural birthright of man.

Locke stated that one of the purposes of society was to preserve the property of the individual.[1] Turgot believed that the distribution of wealth depended on the distinction

---

[1] *Second Treatise on Government*, J. Locke Chs. v & ix.

between public and private property. Indeed he believed the matter of property was the bottom question of government. The importance of a clear understanding of the foundation of property was emphasised by Churchill in a speech which he delivered at Edinburgh in 1909:

> It is . . . of the first importance to the country – to any country – that there should be vigilant and persistent efforts to prevent abuses, to distribute the public burdens fairly among all classes, and to establish good laws governing the methods by which wealth may be acquired. The best way to make private property secure and respected is to bring the processes by which it is gained into harmony with the general interests of the public. When and where property is associated with the idea of reward for services rendered, with the idea of recompense for high gifts and special aptitudes or for faithful labour done, then property will be honoured. When it is associated with processes which are beneficial, or which at the worse are not actually injurious to the common wealth, then property will be unmolested; but when it is associated with ideas of wrong and of unfairness, with processes of restriction and monopoly, and other forms of injury to the community, then I think that you will find that property will be assailed and will be endangered.[2]

The precise definition of the property is an important key of political thought. The meaning ascribed to property by popular usage should be disregarded in political thought. Property [from *propietas* in Latin], or a right to something, arises in an individual or body of individuals who produce an object or a service. These may vary from a lump of steel to a curl spun by a hairdresser, a legal opinion or beautiful performance of music. Yet there can be no property in the natural gifts of air, sunshine, water and land. These are gifts to mankind in common and, as there is no human effort involved in their production, no property rights arise in them. But solar energy gathered and turned into heat or rainwater collected in a container or a berry plucked from a wild brush convert gifts of Nature into private property. However, a berry on a bush growing in an orchard or on cultivated ground is private property by virtue of the labour expended on its cultivation.

The maker of a thing or producer of a service have a natural property in their product. Indeed, the root of property is often proved by showing title derived from the original maker. Title can be disposed by him by contract, gift or will. The title to a book is conveyed from author to the buyer anywhere in the world.

Those who pollute the natural gifts of Nature, such as fresh air and water, should be treated severely. Pollution is a violation of Nature and should not be tolerated as a necessary evil, merely because the polluter represents a large vested interest or because the revenue of government profits greatly from products which cause

---

[2] *The Times* 17 July 1909.

pollution. If the full cost of a product reflected the cost of removing the pollution caused by its use, then consumers would not be able to afford it and inventors would be encouraged to introduced alternative products which do not pollute. For example, the cost of the combustion engine should include the cost of removing the heavy pollution of urban air and treating breathing ailments; food produced with nitrogen fertilisers and pesticides should reflect the cost of these poisons. Drugs which gather in water systems should be outlawed. The manufacturers of pollution should face imprisonment if convicted and the consumers should be charged the costs of production and pollution.

English law developed concepts to deal with those situations when property is lost or is conveyed by 'falling off the back of a lorry'. A person walking down the street may spot a cut diamond earring, lying apparently abandoned on the pavement. He may sell it to a jeweller and the original owner may later see it for sale in his shop window. Her lawyers will say that she lost it and, therefore, never abandoned her possession. The jeweller will state that he paid money for the ring and his lawyers may endeavour to prove that he purchased in good faith from the man who found it. It would be difficult for a jeweller to sustain his protestation of good faith, when he purchased only one earring from a stranger outside his trade. Retailers are careful in making sure what is offered to them did not fall off a lorry. Likewise a woman may throw out a hat as a piece of rubbish and someone passing by may spot it awaiting collection. Is she able to appropriate it? A case held that articles left for rubbish collection belonged in law to the refuse collectors and could not be taken by a member of the public. Had the case decided the other way, chaos would have resulted with every rubbish being scattered and picked over. But these situations apart, it can be said that the hallmark of private property is that its title is derived from the maker.

Parliament may at one time declare railways, water companies or anything else are private and at another time public, but its distinctions are only of legal significance which is changeable according to political fashion. Parliament can even declare men to be women or the colour black to be white but Nature remains unchanged. Water companies and railways are by their nature activities which enhance communal life and constitute, whatever Parliament may determine, forms of public service. The accountant may believe railway companies should live by the ticket income paid by travellers. Politicians believe they should be subsidised. But ticket income is too little and subsidies are too great a public burden.

Public property also attaches only to things produced by human effort. Thus while there is no property in the sky, there can be property in a defined and controlled air space or in the orbit or situation of a satellite Although there cannot be property in public broadcasts uttered by a town crier, it can exist in a system of radio frequencies. Public property attaches to things everyone had created and, therefore, had the same right to use. Thus a public building is built at the expense of taxpayers, which definition includes every member of society. It could be argued that charges could be levied on roads, bridges, parks, street parking, libraries or museums. It is most efficient for local government to determine these sorts of charges in the light of local conditions and opinion.

Apart from things created at public expense, the hallmark of public property is that it has been created not by an individual but by a whole society. The presence of a whole society from babe in the pram to monarch on the throne creates the demand for the use of land or the seabed; for that value reflects the demand for its use. Provided the population is not declining the value of land across a society would be generally maintained, although there are regional fluctuations unrelated to the birth-rate. In Britain during 1999, for example, it was advertised that council houses in Newcastle were being offered for sale at fifty pence, because their value reflected a large move of population from northern to southern England, where the cost of dwellings soared, it was reported, to the sum of £100,000 for an average house.

The value of land is highest in the centre of cities where demand for its use is greatest and public services most concentrated. Railways, roads, bridges, underground railways and buses abound, different areas are devoted in London to different specialists. Other centres in Britain have the same pull and this is reflected in the value of land there. It will be less than in London because the demand there is most intense. The capital lies on the air route between the United States and Europe is linked to a tunnel. Within London different areas are more or less valuable according to the demand for their use. Within the same streets the angle of sunshine, the proximity of an Underground or bus stop will determine different values for the same size of area. The value will reflect demand for the use of land – use within existing planning permission.

The creation of the value of land by a whole society inhabiting the land was observed clearly by Churchill:

Fancy comparing these healthy processes [productive efforts] with the enrichment which comes to the landlord who happens to own a plot of land on the outskirts or at the centre of one of our great cities, who watches the busy population around him making the city larger, richer, more convenient, more famous every day, and all the while sits still and does nothing! Roads are made, streets are made, railway services are improved, electric light turns night into day, electric trams glide swiftly to and fro, water is brought from reservoirs a hundred miles off in the mountains – and all the while the landlord sits still. Every one of those improvements is effected by the labour and at the cost of other people. Many of the most important are effected at the cost of the municipality and of the ratepayers. To not one of those improvements does the land monopolist, as a land monopolist, contribute, and yet by every one of them the value of his land is sensibly enhanced.[3]

It is a rare for a politician to acknowledge the part the presence of society plays in its enrichment. Yet it is a natural fact which is beyond the power of Parliament to alter.

---

[3] *Ibid.*

No individual or body created the value of land by themselves, for it arises only from the moment when the same piece of land is demanded by at least two people. Suppose an individual lay out sumptuous buildings in the Sahara and advertises his facilities throughout the world. If his advertising is successful, thousands may come to enjoy his facilities. He will say after a few years of operating that he has created the value of land where none previously existed. Previously it was desert where the occasional camel wandered and was valueless, as no one wanted to live there. As an entrepreneur he could sense an opportunity and when he constructed buildings he acquired private property in them. He advertised and spent billions. But that expenditure did not create land value. Until other people actually wanted to go there, the empty desert had no value. He saw the potential and his reward is as hotelier or entrepreneur, rather than landowner. For the only basis for his claim to own the land on which he operates is that he got there first, which is no basis of justice.

An island was created in New York harbour by piling rubble on the seabed. The surface was valuable in that location, but an individual or body of individuals cannot claim to have created the base on which the rubble was piled. A surface suspended over sea or over roads can be considered as both private and public property. The structure attaching to the surface to earth can be a private structure, only if built at private expense, but the surface is public property as it constitutes a new surface of land. In Holland dry land was created by excluding the sea behind dykes and in places marshlands have been drained but in these cases the dykes and the drains are constructed by labour and are, therefore, private property but the land remains a gift to man and its value, being of human creation, constitutes public property. When marshes are drained and reclaimed private property attaches only to the drainage during its wasting life.

In other words, if someone gain quiet possession of land, it is just and reasonable that the individual or private body compensates society for restricting them from the area which is occupied.

Every sensible public improvement increases the value of land. A new bridge, railway, school, hospital road, police and fire station or railway can enhance that value. But when public expenditure attempts to secure political advantage, it fails often to secure a public benefit.

In Britain there is a legal fiction that land is tenanted from the Crown. The fiction survives from feudal times when William I became possessed of everything which he had conquered. His estate in the land held of him was virtually destroyed when his leading tenants rid themselves of supplying fighting forces under knight services in the twelfth century and later not paying money under scutage in the fourteenth century. The surviving charges on land were abolished in 1660, when the freehold estate came into being. During the Napoleonic War at the end of the eighteenth century a property tax was introduced but after Napoleon's defeat it was repealed. Henceforth, landowners were held free of any claim from a higher authority. But so fond of tradition are the British that the fiction has been preserved that even freeholders hold their estate from the Crown. The reality is that the source of a freehold title to land is that Parliament does not impose charges upon land. English law has concentrated on the possession of land rather than ownership. Lawyers take pains to convey 'quiet possession' of land. That much is necessary to prevent the community invading the privacy of a garden or building.

To restore harmony between the two aspects of property, there could be a resettlement of possession of land. That would allow the position to return to Saxon England when every family shared land equally. But such a measure would be tedious to arrange and would be attempting to go backwards to an earlier period of history to an agricultural state, at a time when the overwhelming majority of the population live and work in cities. Equality which arose naturally cannot be re-imposed by control to return to fields departed long ago.

The land could be nationalised and the present landowners compensated for the loss of land which they have learnt over centuries to call their own property. That would represent an expense which no people could discharge. The National Debt is far too large without further increase. When the slave-owners were dispossessed by a change in law in the eighteenth century there was no question of the State, even when administered by a small body of powerful interests, compensating slave-owners. At a stroke their chattels became human beings, whose value could no longer by gauged in money terms. The enclosures were accomplished by violating Nature and it is not within the power of Parliament to brush aside Nature and its reactions. Just as a criminal, who has been living off his fruits of crime, has no just claim for compensation if he abandons his ways, so the landowner has none for forfeiting his freehold estate. Indeed, society has a natural and at least a moral claim for compensation from landowners for the revenue which has been unjustly appropriated for centuries. But society's claim in law would be barred by the rule of law, which cannot allow a present injustice previously allowed to be remedied from an earlier time.

The hallmark of Nature is simplicity. The just remedy to bring to an end wage slavery of the last 700 years and to reverse the injustice of that slavery is to convert the value of land into public property by taxing it on its annual rental value: it should be collected as public revenue. Thus possession of land would be enjoyed privately on condition that the rest of society are reimbursed by the value which they create. Such a proposition accords with the thinking of Locke. Writing to a Member of Parliament in 1692, he stated:

> Taxes, however contrived, and out whose Hand soever immediately taken, do, in a Country, where the great Fund is Land, do for the most part terminate on land ... It is in vain, in a Country whose great Fund is Land to lay the publick charge of the Government on anything else, there at last it will terminate.[4]

---

[4] *Collected Works of John Locke*, 12th ed, [1824] vol iv, p. 55.

It may appear at first glance that land was the great fund of Britain in the seventeenth century and that it replaced in the following centuries by capital and technology. Maybe land is less important in everyday thinking but every advance in wealth and technology has been accompanied by a steady increase in the value of land. It is, indeed, still a great fund of Britain, as it is a fund of public property in every society. Locke stressed the point that taxation levied on land is paid by the owner and no-one else. The tax, unlike most taxes raised in Britain, cannot be shifted onto prices.

The basis of the collection of the value of land by society has to be founded in justice and Nature. A landowner may claim ownership as a matter of tradition back beyond human memory. That claim is sufficient in common law to create an easement or right to possession of vacant land, but it cannot be applied to the private ownership of land value created by an entire country with a population of 57 million souls. Alternatively, a landowner may base himself in contract law. Most purchased land in good faith. That would be sufficient to convey goods made by man. But it is not sufficient to convey an element not made by man.

If a tax were imposed on the value of land, that move would mark the fact that it ceased to be private property and, therefore, any mortgage arrears outstanding in respect of land, but not of buildings, would cease to be an enforceable debt. For the evident reason that an individual could not be reasonably obliged to pay private and public charges on the same piece of land. Were that reform introduced overnight it would destroy much security in the financial world, but it would follow a public debate spread over years, in which the holders of this form of security would have ample notice to adjust their security.

This move would put every individual on the same foundation of democracy by according him a share in the public revenue and by granting him or her access to the use of land on the same basis as everyone else. In the place of the unemployed individual controlling the level of earnings at the margin of society would arise a free individual, capable of earning his full income and paying his way in life. It would restore the freedom briefly glimpsed in Saxon England and remove the shadow of servitude, which feudalism cast upon society from the tenth century.

The distribution of wealth would be transformed by unloosing productive energies, which during wage slavery remain untapped. Millions of people accept wage slavery in order to survive in jobs they do not want, do not enjoy and to which they are not suited. As the mass of society are paid a minimum they tend to work at least exertion. Furthermore, there is a growing number of individuals working for the State enforcing tedious regulations, collecting complex taxes or handing out social security.

The mother of production is the unsatisfied desires which a population have to enjoy a more comfortable and satisfying life. Slaves have to be driven by authority to accomplish as much as their reluctance will allow. If free individuals keep their full production after paying the value of the land they use, they need no direction. They will comprehend, as Adam Smith did not, that in a just society their self-interest will be sufficient to guide them.

The value of land represents public property and buildings or improvements erected at private expense represent private property. The value of land was measured succinctly by Mason Gaffney, an American economist, as the value which remains after a good fire. But Parliament has confused the two species of property. Consequently taxation falls like a ton of bricks on almost every form of private property and is not levied on the public property created by society. What is inherently private property Parliament determines to be public and what is evidently public property it deems private.

The collection of public property would achieve four principal results. First, it would make land available to the individual on a basis that would be the same for everyone. This has not been the position in England for the last millennium, when able-bodied beggars were all but unknown. Second, government could be reduced dramatically. Instead of paying for government to provide services, taxpayers would be able to pay for these themselves directly. In Cabinet there would be empty chairs as various ministries would become redundant. Third, he or she could earn as much as they could on any piece of land in the country without the expectation of a tap on the shoulder from the unemployed individual in search of his job or the tax man in search of private property. This would lift earnings from the floor set by the unemployed to the level of their productive work. To meet the basic needs of every individual is more than can ever be produced anywhere on earth because the moment one desire is satisfied, another thousand take its place. Fourth, an enormous advantage would rebound to society. At present every communal improvement like a road; railway line, bridge, airport, hospital, fire or police station, or school, impoverishes society since it must be paid out of taxation or through incurring debt. But the value of these benefits is collected by default by private landowners as a bonus for their investment in a gift of nature. If the financial benefit returned to society the individual could be freed of taxation and debt. An improvement would improve community and individuals living within it, because the increased value of land due to the improvement would be collected.

Instead of reaping peace and prosperity, the British people have reaped the fruits of injustice in the distribution of wealth, which flow from disharmony between Parliament and Nature. This chaotic disharmony causes wage slavery, which has been the inhuman condition of millions in Britain for most of the last millennium.

This confusion is created by Parliament disregarding Nature and perpetuated by deranged politics, which have become gradually worse over the last millennium. The distribution of wealth is an extremely important matter, which underlies the daily labours of the adult population and the prosperity of their dependents. By ignoring Nature Parliament has been reduced to a shadow of itself. It legislates furiously, it regulates unnecessarily, it debates tediously, its thinking in economic matters is often both sentimental and corrupt. Pretending that democracy can be attainted without a clear division between public and private property is like pretending that there can be music without sound and silence.

Conclusion

This book opened with the argument that political sovereignty lies with the British people. It was argued that their sovereignty is exercisable through a culture of political thought, and that it could reach its highest power by developing in conformity with Nature: for then justice, humanity and prosperity would flower. It was argued also that education in schools lacks principles of political thought. Without such an education young people enter society unprepared for adulthood. But if such instruction were ever mounted by government young people, who were previously starving, would be poisoned by lies and propaganda.

A young person needs to learn the principles of a just and natural society, the birthrights of the individual, the essential duties and the limitations of government, the basic principles of justice to protect these rights against other individuals and the State. Just as a doctor needs to keep in his mind the picture of a healthy individual when diagnosing and treating a disease, so the elector needs to compare human government with a just and natural model of society.

In the second part of the book the history of a few leading civil liberties shows that these liberties were not handed on a plate to the British people by authority. They were fought for and some brave individuals paid a heavy price, so that posterity might enjoy the degree of civil freedom, which is their birthright.

The role of the police in a democracy depends to a large extent on the level of political thought. If the people were minded to develop a democracy on foundations of justice and Nature, policing would be a simpler matter.

Judges hold a strange position in public life; impregnable in the constitution but most can be dislodged by a tap on the shoulder. They follow a tradition which has avoided corruption. This achievement has been easier to follow because the British people have a high degree of justice in the civil realm. Had they been acting as public servants in a nation flooded with corruption, they would have been prey to that culture. Their power in criminal law has been balanced by the presence of a trial jury, who bring only their innate feeling of justice. The jury has often refused to allow law to be employed as an instrument of State.

The judiciary is a grand asset of Britain and to imagine that it might have an enlarged role in promoting justice is not an unreasonable speculation. For the objectivity, reason and training of a judge provide a more solid foundation of liberty than political parties, whose judgment is self-interested and, often, corrupt in aim and weak in justification. In civil liberty the judiciary are supported by the clear understanding of the people of the principles of civil justice. To suggest judicial involvement to determine public and private property in the present state of political culture is simplistic. It would repeat in the most gross form the error of bringing the judiciary into areas of public controversy, which have been described above. But if the people were to follow the advice of Locke that society exists to enhance the liberty and the property of the individual and develop as clear an idea of property as they already have of civil liberty, then a new situation would arise in the understanding of justice. If the people understood the profound distinction between private and public property, the excessive domination of Parliament and government would diminish and their power would become more focused. The judiciary would become a counter-weight to Parliament and government. Indeed the liberty of the people of Britain in modern history has, with the two exceptions of Napoleon and Hitler, been attacked more by its own authorities, than by an external enemy. The need for the judicial review of government is one of the best protections of the individual, but it extends at present more to his person than his property.

Freedom of speech is the leading freedom in Britain. It was won over three centuries by struggle against authority. That struggle achieved for the individual what was bequeathed to him or her by Nature as a birthright. Yet freedom of speech needs to be linked with freedom of thinking beyond the narrow scope of political correctness. Neglect of so important an aspect of history is to risk losing it. The persecution of Rushdie, the novelist, was in reality an attack on the British freedom of speech. He responded with the courage of other remarkable figures who have fought for this noble freedom.

The right to believe anything in religion or spirituality is also a natural right. The Creator of the Universe does not seem to mind what an individual believes and does not appear to have favoured any particular religion or sect. It is remarkable how they try to distinguish themselves by hats, customs, rituals, beliefs and even gods and claim exclusivity. Sincere prayers and meditations are the essence of religion or spirituality and proclaim the fact that Man is a spiritual being.

Public order is a prerequisite for a society at peace, but change through protest is as natural as the eruption of a volcano. Public order is much more than an absence of disorder. Where there is widespread poverty peace degenerates into a sullen impotence. Public order in every society depends more upon the conduct of the people than upon authority.

The third part of the book is concerned with public and private property. Indeed, the battle for democratic freedom is only half-won. The human being with only civil liberty is part free and part slave. In the evolution of man the full realisation of democracy is the natural state. Considering man as a creative human being, it is essential that he develops both dimensions of his natural liberty.

The two largest experiments in British political life outside political administration during the twentieth century are chosen to represent expensive failure. They cover the creation of the welfare state in the first half of the twentieth century and of the European Union in the second. The welfare state has become a vast growth attempting to mitigate of poverty, while its causes are ignored. If those causes were eradicated there would be no need for action by the State in education, health, housing or social security. The welfare state will never accomplish what fundamental reform would achieve without cost or political action. The EU was born out of fear and an adamantine refusal to accept that people, given the freedom to trade, can effect much more without State regulation. Such a realisation was the cause behind the cry of merchants of the seventeenth century – laissez-faire. Neither the welfare state nor the EU is presented to the people in an open democratic way by government. Rather both experiments are explained with political disingenuity to highlight supposed benefits and to conceal the costs in both financial and social terms. The two men who were most associated with these two experiments were both men without any sort of vision. Beveridge had no insight into the causes of poverty, but he set out to conquer ills resulting from it. Monnet was a busy bureaucrat and had no grand idea of the unity of Europe, nor any natural means of achieving it. How much simpler might history have been if they had been locked up as dangerous men and left to play with matches, instead of nations.

To argue that the individual in Britain is in part free and in part slave is likely to be dismissed either as fantasy or exaggeration. But it is intended to stand as a reasonable and serious argument. Wage slavery has been described in this book as a condition in which the individual cannot provide for himself or herself throughout adulthood and retirement from his work, because earnings are related, not to what an independent individual can produce, but to what an unemployed person will accept as earnings. How few parents are able to look after the education and health of their families. If Nature extends the ability of reproduction, it implies that the parent is able to care for the child.

When compared with birthrights, as revealed by Locke, this condition can reasonably be called wage slavery. That an individual should compete for a job against an unemployed person in a free country is ridiculous. Yet competition in products and services is healthy. That an able-bodied individual should ever worry about being unemployed is unnecessary, that an individual should be paid the minimum necessary for survival rather than his full production is laughable, that an individual should pay another for land, which none created nor made valuable, is plainly untenable. Yet society is held in this straight-jacket of injustice and the individual is condemned to wage slavery.

The work required to be done is as challenging as any political activity in the past. The British people have yet to establish a culture of political thought, to look beyond politicians and Parliament, to eradicate poverty, to drastically diminish government and to allow prosperity for the entire society to arise, as a consequence of the efforts of free individuals. They need to root out injustice regarding the distribution of wealth with the same determination as they freed themselves from civil injustice. The heart of the injustice is that able-bodied individuals cannot command sufficient earnings from their work to look after themselves and their families. That disability in a democratic nation denotes something is seriously unjust. It is a speculative notion that Nature would sanction human birth on a planet without providing for the protection of human life. If the able-bodied individual cannot discharge his responsibilities then it is axiomatic that government cannot either. In the same way that if a nation cannot remove injustice, no international body has any hope of doing so. If they had the power to tax the rich for the welfare of the poor, then they might be able to do. But the dread truth is that taxation, even when Parliament intends it to fall on the rich, falls on the prices of goods and services consumed by the mass of society who happen to be poor.[1]

In terms of the liberty of property Britain stands as it stood in relation to civil liberty in 1500, when government considered it unthinkable that a person could speak or write freely, choose a religion, or protest. Historians in a few centuries time will ask themselves why the British people, with their remarkable record of fighting for civil liberty, did not use their liberty of free speech and their democratic Parliament to eradicate injustice in its principal manifestations.

But justice and liberty, her offspring, are not won won by half-hearted attempts. The fight to put the objective interest of the individual before particular vested interests will be long and hard. The fact that something so simple and fundamental as free speech took so long to achieve, does not suggest that public property created by the whole society can be won from private hands without a considerable struggle. The fight for civil liberties became easier after the power of government over political activity, civil justice, censorship, conscience and slavery had been overcome. But the fight for economic liberties will be a much harder and, possibly longer, road. Standing between the birthrights of individuals in Britain are multitudinous vested interests of the richest and most powerful in society. Given a general political inertia, these interests continue almost inviolate, although there is no basis in justice or reason why wage slavery need persist. There is no inevitability for government to proceed from one century to another in a hugger-mugger fashion. preserving a state of injustice in relation to the distribution of wealth.

Injustice may be guarded by powerful vested interest but its patent weakness is that it has no reasonable arguments to defend itself. Five centuries ago it was considered wild and seditious to suggest that the individual might be free. Today it is considered equally dangerous that the individual should be free to look after himself and his responsibilities, instead of having to look after government.

When the British eradicate wage slavery, they will ask themselves why it took so long to achieve what Nature intended for them at the dawn of human existence. It will be as though they had suddenly awoken to the realisation that in summer it is not necessary to wear an overcoat. But after a time, they will tend to take justice and liberty for granted and lose it again by listening to crackpot ideas bandied about by political adventurers. For, as Pascal remarked: 'The problem of mankind is that it consists of human beings.'

---

[1] See *The Tyranny of Taxation*, M. Hill. [To be published in 2001]

Up to this point reference has been made to able-bodied individuals deliberately. The prosperity of society depends on liberating their labours. The disabled can be looked after by the able-bodied, if the latter are given the freedom to look after themselves and their families. In a just society charity can thrive, but in an unjust society that tendency becomes sentimentality, for charity cannot overcome injustice.

It may appear that politicians and Parliament have been criticised but that has not been the purpose. Politics in a democracy is ever the responsibility of people, and it is fruitless to blame the ills of society on those who represent them. Parliament is a machine for achieving whatever result the people wish. When it tolerates injustice, Parliament degenerates into a cockpit of disingenuous manoeuvring. The British people have to reject the policies assembled by political parties and put their will behind reforms which will return the essential birthrights to the whole people. Politicians will find it much easier to administer a state of an alert people, who insist on justice.

The British people have to raise their political culture to the level required of a just and democratic society. To muddle along with injustice is to haul invention and technology behind horse and cart. The change to a higher political culture is a step beyond Parliament and government.

The partnership between the people and politicians, necessary to develop democracy requires the people to will the ends of society and the politician to devise the means. To hope for deliverance by political parties or from their leader is an idle hope. The British people have to rise themselves to a challenge which they have not attempted before: to rise above pettiness, pantomime, politics and selfishness and consider the welfare of the whole of society. There are those who do not want a revolution of political thought and value their interests above the the welfare of their less fortunate fellows. They are powerful in some respects, and weak in others. They are rich but they are relatively few and they lack argument to justify suppressing birthrights of others. The fight for the full realisation of democracy will be a noble cause and the end is a noble one.

The vast majority of people living in Britain suffer the daily reality of wage slavery with its fruits of poverty and anxiety. They are not rich, powerful or the most articulate. But it is impossible to imagine a nation, even one as docile as Britain, will not reform the condition of wage slavery.

Two men have spoken eloquently about government and wisdom. Lao-tzu, the founder of Taoism, advised in the sixth century BC governors of Chinese provinces to govern as lightly 'as one cooks a small fish.' Turgot wrote to a friend on 12 December 1769:[2] Since the world began government has been essentially of two kinds: 'brigandocracy' and 'rascalocracy' and that will continue until the reign of enlightenment.[3]

---

[2] *Lettres de Turgot á la Duchesse d'Enville*, Professor Ruwett (ed.) [1976]
[3] Enlightenment meaning wisdom.

A great artist occasionally, and less occasionally a genius like Shakespeare or Mozart, abandons the progress of a work for a while, in order to reveal the brilliance of his artistry. Nature is a jewel which shines in the heart of man with its own light. If wisdom prevailed in government, society would become a thing of beauty by being just, democratic and prosperous. It would represent the flowering of an ideal born long, long ago in ancient Greece.

Index